CYBERCULTURE

This comprehensive A–Z guide provides a wide-ranging and up-to-date overview of the fast-changing and increasingly important world of cyberculture. Its clear and accessible entries cover aspects ranging from the technical to the theoretical, and from movies to the everyday, including:

- Artificial intelligence
- Cyberfeminism
- Cyberpunk
- Electronic government
- Games
- Hacktivists
- HTML
- *The Matrix*
- Netiquette
- Piracy.

Fully cross-referenced, easy to use and with suggestions for further reading, this is an essential resource for anyone interested in cyberculture.

David Bell is Professor of Cultural Studies at Staffordshire University, UK. **Brian D. Loader** is Director of CIRA at the University of Teesside, UK and editor of the international journal, *Information, Communication & Society*. **Nicholas Pleace** is a Senior Research Fellow at the University of York, UK. **Douglas Schuler** teaches at The Evergreen State College, USA, and is co-founder of the Seattle Community Network.

You may also be interested in the following Routledge Student Reference titles:

Cultural Theory: The Key Concepts
Edited by Andrew Edgar and Peter Sedgwick

Cultural Theory: The Key Thinkers
Andrew Edgar and Peter Sedgwick

*Communication, Cultural and Media Studies:
The Key Concepts (3rd edition)*
John Hartley

Fifty Key Contemporary Thinkers
John Lechte

Internet: The Basics
Jason Whittaker

*The Routledge Companion to Feminism and
Postfeminism*
Edited by Sarah Gamble

The Routledge Companion to Postmodernism
Edited by Stuart Sim

Popular Music: The Key Concepts
Roy Shuker

Post-Colonial Studies: The Key Concepts
Bill Ashcroft, Gareth Griffiths and Helen Tiffin

Semiotics: The Basics
Daniel Chandler

Television Studies: The Key Concepts
Neil Casey, Bernadette Casey, Justin Lewis,
Ben Calvert and Liam French

CYBERCULTURE

The Key Concepts

David Bell, Brian D. Loader,
Nicholas Pleace and Douglas Schuler

Routledge
Taylor & Francis Group

LONDON AND NEW YORK

First published 2004
by Routledge
11 New Fetter Lane, London EC4P 4EE

Simultaneously published in the USA and Canada
by Routledge
29 West 35th Street, New York, NY 10001

Routledge is an imprint of the Taylor & Francis Group

© 2004 David Bell, Brian D. Loader, Nicholas Pleace and Douglas Schuler

Typeset in Bembo by Taylor & Francis Books Ltd
Printed and bound in Great Britain by
TJ International Ltd, Padstow, Cornwall

British Library Cataloguing in Publication Data
A catalogue record for this book is available from the British Library

Library of Congress Cataloging-in-Publication Data
Cyberculture: the key concepts / David Bell ... [et al.].
p.cm.
1. Information technology–social aspects–Encyclopedias. 2. Computers and
civilization–Encyclopedias. 3. Internet–Encyclopedias.
I. Bell, David (David John), 1965-
T14.5.C95 2004
303.48′34–dc22
2003017827

ISBN 0–415–24753–5 (hbk)
ISBN 0–415–24754–3 (pbk)

CONTENTS

LIST OF CONCEPTS

Communications Decency Act (CDA)
Community
Community informatics (CI)
Community memory
Community networks
Community technology centers
Computer
Computer conferencing *see* Email
Computer-Generated Imagery (CGI)
Computer Mediated Communication (CMC)
Computer Mediated Social Support *see* Virtual social support
Computer Professionals for Social Responsibility (CPSR)
Computer Supported Community Work
Computer Supported Cooperative Work (CSCW)
Connectivity *see* Access
Console *see* Games
Convergence
Cookie
Copyleft
Corporate dominance
Corporeality *see* Body
Cross-dressing *see* Cyberfeminism
Cross-ownership
Cryptography *see* Encryption
CTCNET *see* Community technology centers
Cues filtered out
Cultural imperialism
Culture jamming
Cybercafés *see* Internet café
Cybercrime
Cyberfeminism
Cyberlibertarianism
Cyberorganizing
Cyberpet
Cyberpunk
Cyberspace
Cyborg
Database
Definition television *see* Digital television
Denial of Service (DOS) or Distributed Denial of Service (DDOS)
Digerati
Digital art

Gamer
Games
Geek
Gender
Gibson, William *see* Cyberpunk, *Johnny Mnemonic, Neuromancer*
Global Information Infrastructure Commission (GIIC)
Globalization
GNU Project
Graphical User Interface (GUI) *see* Interface
Hacker
Hacking
Hactivist
Halloween Documents
Health *see* Virtual social support
High Definition Television *see* Digital television
Hikikomori
Hits
Homepage
HTML (Hypertext Markup Language)
HTTP (Hypertext Transfer Protocol)
Human/computer interface *see* Interface
Hypercasualization
ICQ (I Seek You)
Identity
Indymedia (Independent media centers)
Information
Information and communications technology (ICT)
Information society
Information superhighway *see* Digital divide
Information technology *see* Information and communications technology
Information warfare
Instant messaging (IM)
Interactive television *see* Digital television
Interface
Internet
Internet banking *see* e-Commerce
Internet café
Internet Relay Chat (IRC)
Internet2 ®
IRL (In Real Life)
ISP (Internet Service Provider)
Jacking in

Java
Javascript
Johnny Mnemonic (movie)
Killer app
Knowledge society *see* Information society
Lara Croft
Liberalization *see* Information economy
LINUX
Listserv *see* Usenet
Lurking
Manga
Many-to-many communication *see* Computer mediated communication
Mario *see* Games
The Matrix (movie)
Memory
MOO
Mosaic *see* World Wide Web
MP3
MUD
Multimedia *see* Convergence
Municipal Information Infrastructure (MII)
National information infrastructure
National Public Telecomputing Network (NPTN)
Nerd *see* Geek
The Net (movie)
Netiquette
Netizen
Netwar *see* Information warfare
Network organizations
Network society *see* Information society
Neuromancer (book)
New cultural politics
New social movements
Newbie
Newsgroups *see* Usenet
Nick
Office of the e-Envoy
'On demand'
Online
Open source
Operating system *see* Interface
Otaku

Packet sniffing
Phreak
Piracy
Platform
Pokemon *see* Games
Pornography
Portal
Privacy
Prosthetics
Public access *see* Access
Public broadcasting
Public Electronic Network (PEN)
Public policy networks
Public sphere
Road warriors
Robot ('Bot')
Robot exclusion standard
Search engine
Self-help *see* Virtual social support
Semiotics
Server *see* World Wide Web
Sexism *see* Cyberfeminism, Games, Gender, Pornography
Silicon Valley
Simulation
Smileys
SMS (Short Message Service)
Social capital
Social informatics
Social shaping of technology
Software agents *see* Agents
Spam
Spider *see* Robot
Stephenson, Neal *see* Cyberpunk
Strange Days (movie)
Subcultures
Surfing
Technological determinism *see* Social shaping of technology
Telebanking
Telecenter *see* Community technology centers
Teleconferencing *see* New network organizations
Telecottage *see* Community technology centers
Telepresence *see* Virtual communities

INTRODUCTION

This book is intended to be of use to a wide range of readers who are looking for an informative and accessible guide to the terminology, concepts and debates surrounding the rapid development of the Internet and the World Wide Web. There has been, and continues to be, an explosion of interest around the world in the potentially transforming qualities of these new forms of media. The fusion of digital technology with television, computers and telephones bodes the transition from a broadcast medium to one characterized by multiple producers, consumers and distributors which act to re-configure previous communications boundaries. The advent of new 'virtual communities' where new forms of human interaction are developing heralds in turn the emergence of new cultural discourses by which such behaviour can be conducted, understood and disseminated. The implications of these emerging cybercultures as a means of gaining new insights, representations and communications about our place in the world are only just beginning to be considered.

In our view, cyberculture represents a contested and evolving discourse. Its discussants include activists, politicians, computer geeks, social scientists, science fiction writers, digital artists, etc., all of whom are involved in the creation of new concepts and ideas. Many of the terms and concepts they are developing and which are considered in this book are becoming commonplace. Some may be transient. Others are entering national vocabularies. Yet cyberculture's creative energies and exciting opportunities for mutual development can only be shared if its participants continue to increase in number and make their own contributions.

The book is structured to provide an A–Z guide to the main terms and concepts associated with the new media, such as the Internet, digital TV, smart cards, CD-ROMS and other emerging information and communications technologies (ICTs). Entries range from short, mainly factual expositions, to longer pieces dealing with the histories and debates arising from a particular concept. Within each entry linkages to other concepts will often be found to enable the reader to foster a more holistic understanding of the field of cybercultures.

This book makes no claim to provide a completely exhaustive list of every aspect of cyberculture. Rather, like all attempts to produce a comprehensive source of references, it is based upon the selections of the authors. If this particular choice is found to be popular they may be subject to future additions and revisions. Furthermore, each entry should be read as an interpretation rather than a dictionary definition. Our purpose is to inform and stimulate further exploration. Consequently each concept is augmented by a guide to further reading and sources. If this small book enables more people to gain an accessible insight into the debates and issues surrounding the impact of the new media upon their lives and hopefully encourages them to participate in what is a new and fascinating field of investigation, then the authors will feel very satisfied with their work.

David Bell
Brian. D. Loader
Nicholas Pleace
Douglas Schuler
January 2004

CYBERCULTURE
THE KEY CONCEPTS

ABBREVIATION

A central feature of many forms of **computer mediated communication** (CMC) and related use of **ICT**s, such as **text messaging** on mobile (cellular) telephones. Used both to increase typing speed and to increase the information being conveyed (useful on the small screen of a mobile/cell phone), abbreviation is often the norm among groups such as young people when using various forms of CMC.

See also: **Chat room**, **Computer mediated communication**, **Cues filtered out**, **Email**, **Internet Relay Chat**

ACCESS

The primary economic and social roles afforded to computer networks in the emerging **information society** makes access to these new **information and communications technologies** (ICTs) a prerequisite for commercial competitive advantage, social development and life chances. Increasingly large amounts of **information** are accessible via computer networks such as the **Internet**, and use of **electronic mail (email)** enables millions of people to communicate across the globe at any time of the day. Access to such channels of communication can be vital for a wide range of individual and communal opportunities, including employment prospects, educational achievement, health status, leisure experiences, political participation and business opportunities.

As Bill Dutton (1999) reminds us, access is also important as a way of understanding the information society and knowledge economy which are too frequently misperceived as ICTs *creating* new information or knowledge. Instead, what is distinctive about the new media and any social and economic forms it may facilitate is the manner in which it significantly changes people's access to knowledge, information or expertise.

The Internet and ICTs are at present accessible to only a very limited proportion of the world's population. The diffusion of the communication networks is not uniform between countries or even within societies. Indeed, it is estimated that not even half of the people on the planet have ever made a telephone call. This uneven access to the new media is believed to be giving rise to a **digital divide** between the *information-rich* and the *information-poor*. For some privileged groups life-chance opportunities may be significantly enhanced by access to the Internet through greater **bandwidth** and high-speed connectivity. For the majority of less well off, access may be non-existent or at best limited to slow telecommunications links. As the rate of development of ICTs becomes faster and the competitive advantage to the information-rich increases, it is possible that the digital divide will act to reinforce and even extend existing social and material inequalities between people.

See also: **Digital divide**

Further sources: Haywood (1995), Loader (1998), Dutton (1999)

ACCESSIBILITY *see* Usability

ADBUSTERS *see* Culture jamming

AGENT

An application that can organize and undertake tasks in an independent or quasi-independent way. The term is quite commonly used to describe software that takes 'decisions' within the parameters set by those who authored it. An 'agent' can also refer to an alternative human–computer **interface**. Rather than giving instructions to the computer through an operating system, a user can interact with an agent, which can be represented as a 'person' or a character. One quite early experiment was the 'Chatterbot' written at Carnegie Mellon University in the mid-1990s. In this case, a **MUD** called TINYMUD, which allowed several people to chat with one another in real time, was the basis for an experiment using an agent. Those using TINYMUD were unaware that one of the participants in their chatting sessions was an application designed to mimic human responses. In these and other similar experiments, individuals could be fooled into believing the agent was another person, at least for short periods.

The usefulness of such experiments is in the information that they can generate about creating a non-threatening and easy-to-use human–computer interface. Educational applications, for example, can allow children to interact with an agent as if it were a teacher, asking questions in ordinary language and receiving an easily understandable response. An agent can also be given a 'personality' and other characteristics that a child, or whomever the target user was, would find reassuring and attractive. There is also a possibility that they may eventually replace the traditional operating system, users interacting with computers through a person-to-(synthetic)-'person' interface. A range of functions have been developed, are planned or envisaged, with variations including information agents, intentional agents, software agents, softbots, knowbots and infobots.

See also: **Artificial intelligence**, **Robot**

Further sources: The University of Maryland, Baltimore County (UMBC) Agent Web: http://agents.umbc.edu/; Microsoft Agent Homepage: http://www.microsoft.com/msagent/

A.I. (MOVIE)

Directed by Stephen Spielberg, *A.I.* (2001) meditates on issues of love, family and what it means to be human. Set in a dystopian future, it tells the tale of David (Haley Joel Osment), a Mecha (robot) surrogate boy designed for human adoption. David is programmed with an Imprinting Protocol that makes him love his adoptive parents: but can humans love robots? David is adopted by a human family whose biological (Orga) son, Martin, is dead but cryogenically frozen. Later in the film, Martin is revived, and David is dumped by his 'mother'. Along with other abandoned Mechas, David gets caught and taken to the Flesh Fair, where Mechas are tortured in a 'celebration of life'. Here he meets a Loverbot, Gigolo Joe (Jude Law), and together they escape. David is on a quest to find the Blue Fairy from *Pinocchio*, convinced she can make him human. They head off to 'the end of the world' – Manhattan, now flooded as a result of global warming. There they meet David's maker, Professor Hobby (William Hurt). David discovers a production line of Davids, realises his status as non-human, and jumps into the ocean. On the seafloor he finds the Blue Fairy – a submerged fairground ride. He becomes trapped there, and the seas freeze. Two thousand years later, David is exhumed by extraterrestrial archaeologists, who read his memories. They clone David's adoptive mother – so that they can learn about humans. But she can only live again for one day. The two share a perfect day, before she leaves him again – but during that day their love is restored. Like many sci-fi films, therefore, *A.I.* ponders the human–machine divide, using Spielberg's usual motif of familial love. As in *Blade Runner*, a future society in which Mechas and Orgas live side-by-side introduces issues of the relative status and worth of different forms of life.

See also: **Artificial intelligence**, *Blade Runner*, **Cyberpunk**

A-LIFE (ARTIFICIAL LIFE)

Artificial Life (or A-Life) research centres on the possibilities for replicating biological processes, behaviours and life-forms in digital environments. Just as artificial intelligence research explores programming that can duplicate human thought processes, A-Life focuses on processes like replication, evolution and adaptation. Some forms of computer **virus** can be considered as primitive A-Life forms, as writers like Mark Ludwig (1996a) or N. Katherine Hayles (1999) rightly suggest. Other programs use the principles of natural selection to evolve virtual life-forms. Even smart toys or **cyberpets** can be considered in this way – as first steps in combining robotics, AI programming and A-Life systems to produce post-biological life-forms. But it is in cyberspace where we are currently witnessing the fastest growth in A-Life forms – we can think of cyberspace as a new habitat, and like all habitats it is presently being colonized by different life-forms, most notably viruses. Of course, thinking about post-biological A-Life forms as though they are alive raises questions about what being 'alive' means, and whether our definition of life needs expanding beyond carbon-based biological forms. This expansion is seen by some critics as a positive thing, while others worry about future implications once new life-forms evolve.

See also: **Artificial intelligence**, **Cyberpunk**, **Virus**

Further sources: Hayles (1999), Ludwig (1996a)

ANIME *see* **Manga**

APPLETS *see* **Java**

ARPA (ADVANCED RESEARCH PROJECTS AGENCY)

US Department of Defense agency (later, 'DARPA', when Defense was added to the agency name) responsible for initial sponsorship of the ARPANET, which evolved to become the Internet.

ARTIFICIAL INTELLIGENCE (AI)

The development of AI as an academic research field is concerned with addressing some fundamental cybercultural questions: Can computers think? What is thinking? What separates humans from machines? The term was coined in 1956, and the past fifty years have seen an explosion in activity. AI research focuses on the building of 'intelligent machines' and the writing of computer programs that in some way mimic or replicate human thought and behaviour processes. Among the most prominent uses of AI is in game-playing, especially for games requiring strategic thinking. The chess computer Deep Blue, which beat Chess Grand Master Gary Kasparov in 1997, is among the best-known AI devices. Other AI capabilities include mathematical problem-solving, language use, translation and reasoning, web crawling (using 'know-bots'), medical diagnosis and conversation. A simple conversational program called ELIZA was even devised to provide ersatz psychotherapeutic advice. Another AI, Julia, presents itself as a (human) player in **MUDs** (see Turkle 1997). When combined with research into robotics, AI can also involve work on locomotion and spatial perception, and then 'higher-level' processes such as learning and autonomy. Other human traits, such as emotion and empathy, have also been replicated (or impersonated) by AIs, leading to a further blurring of the human–machine distinction. The extent to which computers can pass as humans is the question behind the Turing Test, which asks whether a person can tell whether they are communicating with another human or with a machine. A similar test is depicted in the movie *Blade Runner*: the Voigt–Kampff Test, which looks for signs of empathy. Other sci-fi movies which explore the implications of AI include *2001*, *The Matrix* and *A.I.*

See also: *A.I.*, *Blade Runner*, *The Matrix*

Further sources: Turkle (1997), Weizenbaum (1976)

ASYNCHRONOUS COMMUNICATION *see* **Internet**

AVATAR

A graphic representation of a user within a graphical environment that is populated by other users. Avatars are used in graphical **MUDs** and have been employed in early experimental graphical chat systems like Microsoft's VChat. Rather than simply 'talking', as would be the case if using **IRC** or **ICQ**, users can wave to each other, smile, frown and, in the case of VChat, flirt by making their avatar perform pre-set sequences of animation. The extent to which this added another dimension to **CMC** was debatable at first, as such online environments were slow and the level of graphical detail quite limited. However, as processing power continues to increase and broadband access to networks like the Internet becomes the norm, these environments may grow increasingly sophisticated. A variety of online games use avatars, particularly online role playing games, but these representations may often be referred to by the players using the less technical term of 'character'.

See also: **Games**

BANDWIDTH

Bandwidth is an indication of the amount of information a telecommunication channel can carry (analogous to a measure of the bits-per-second rate of a digital channel). Typically the larger the bandwidth the greater the amount of traffic and speed of communication. Broadband telecommunication media, such as coaxial cable or optical fibre, can cope with the large volumes of data required for multimedia applications and media **convergence**. Currently however, **access** to broadband is unevenly distributed between urban and rural areas and between and within different countries. The roll-out of broadband is thus regarded as another major factor contributing to a **digital divide**.

See also: **Access**, **Convergence**, **Digital divide**

BIG SKY TELEGRAPH (BST)

The Big Sky Telegraph was launched in 1988 by Frank Odasz of Western Montana University in Dillon, Montana, a rural community of 4,000 inhabitants. The BST's first role was electronically linking more than forty one- and two-room schoolhouses and twelve rural libraries across Montana, using microcomputers and modems. Linking these schoolrooms provided a low-cost way for teachers to share information such as subject curricula, to ask questions and discuss concerns with other teachers, and to preview educational software before purchasing it. Big Sky Telegraph provided 600 K–12 lesson plans serving as a 'telecurricular clearinghouse' for K–12 projects running on networks all over the world. The system also offered online courses on how to use network and bulletin board services. Odasz used the telegraph as a metaphor for all aspects of BST, reflecting the communication technology of the last century that was influential in the rural American West.

See also: **Community informatics**, **Community networks**, **Distance education**

BLADE RUNNER (MOVIE)

One of the most influential sci-fi movies, Ridley Scott's *Blade Runner* (1982; Director's Cut 1992) virtually defined the 'tech-noir' *mise-en-scène* of the genre, with its depiction of post–holocaust Los Angeles in 2019. The film's central character, Deckard (Harrison Ford) is a 'blade runner' – a police officer tasked with tracking down and 'retiring' (killing) genetic **cyborgs** or replicants. These have been engineered by the Tyrell Corporation to perform menial labour in hostile environments. The replicants are designed to develop emotions, but carry a limited life-span of four years. Four renegade replicants are on the loose, led by Roy Batty (Rutger Hauer); they are in search of their creator, Tyrell. Central to the movie's plot is the Voigt–Kampff Test, a kind of Turing Test designed to sort replicants from humans, based on emotional and empathic response. Deckard hounds the replicants through the city, killing them as he finds them. He also meets Tyrell and his assistant, Rachel (Sean Young). Rachel, it transpires, is also a replicant – but has **prosthetic** memories implanted, so that she thinks she is human (until Deckard proves otherwise). Eventually, Batty meets Tyrell, beats him at chess (a reference to **AI** chess players), and ultimately kills him, before setting off to pursue Deckard – whose life he saves, before Batty himself 'dies', his life-span coming to an abrupt end. The film has two endings – in the 1982 version, Deckard returns for Rachel, and the pair head off to a wilderness. In the Director's Cut (1992), the audience sees a suggestion that Deckard, too, may be a replicant – although this is a matter of considerable debate (Bukatman 1997). The film's core theme, then, is the question of what makes us human, and what marks others as non-human – a trope familiar to the sci-fi genre (Kernan 1991).

See also: **Artificial intelligence, Cyborg, Cyberpunk, Memory, Prosthetics**

Further sources: Bukatman (1997), Kernan (1991)

BLOGGING

Short for web logging, blogging is a recent and fast-expanding form of web-based writing and publishing. Blogs are a form of personal homepage, used to record in a chronological, diary-like form day-to-day life experiences, reviews (particularly of other websites) and personal opinions of the writer. It is estimated that there are around half a million blogs currently on the web. Downloadable software can be used to set up a blog, with sites such as blogger.com making this freely available. The software has its origins at the National Center for Supercomputing Applications at the University of Illinois, where it was designed as a page of up-datable web links to carry up-to-date news items about computing developments. The term 'weblog' was first used in 1997 on a site called Robot Wisdom (robotwisdom.com) that carried links to personally- selected websites of interest. Blogs have since proliferated and diversified, and can cover virtually any topic deemed interesting by the site's creator. While blogs can be intensely personal to the point of self-indulgence, they are also seen as a new outlet for creative writing unconstrained by the conventional world of writing and publishing (although with their own emerging conventions). They also facilitate two-way communication, as bloggers interact with one another and their readers in a 'subculture' in some ways similar to earlier self-publishing and fanzine scenes.

BLUETOOTH *see* **Wireless**

BODY

There is widespread interest in questions relating to the human body across the humanities and social sciences, including in cyberculture studies. There are a number of different threads that can be followed in order to understand the centrality of the body to cyberculture. The first concerns the issue of embodiment versus disembodiment. One of the key motifs in cyberculture, inherited from cyberpunk, concerns the fantasy of experiencing disembodiment in cyberspace – of 'leaving the meat behind'. In this context, the biological body (we might shorten this to 'bio-body') is dead weight, and the ideal is to escape from its confines and exist as pure data or uploaded consciousness. This powerful image translates in cyberculture to a fascination with immersion – with providing virtual experiences and environments that encourage disembodiment (or at least a simulation of disembodiment) to occur. In the image of the stereotypical computer geek, moreover, disembodiment is represented as an active forgetting of the body and its needs; the pallid, undernourished, insomniac obsessive who spends too much of his or her life online is moving towards a form of disembodiment, here expressed as the repression or disavowal of the body. Against this loathed fleshy bio-body is set the dream of the imaginary data-body or the bodiless data-mind, the **jacked-in** self existing on screen. A good overview of these debates is provided by Deborah Lupton (2000).

Critics have signalled the impossibility and the undesirability of this dream of disembodiment. In 'What do cyborgs eat?', for example, Margaret Morse (1994) reminds us of the reality of hunger, as well as sleep and waste disposal, as embodied acts that cyberspace cannot free us from. In wishing the body away, moreover, we forget that much of what happens to us in cyberspace is experienced via the body, while the dream of leaving the meat behind reinstates the problematic mind–body split that much contemporary theory has attempted to unpick and unpack. However, for advocates, the freeing of the body from its biological bases permits new freedoms in cyberspace, including the freedom to experiment with aspects of personal identity, most notably **gender**. Whether this produces new constellations of bodies, or merely replicates real-life body norms and stereotypes, is a matter of considerable debate (Bassett 1997).

A second strand in debates about the body in cyberculture centres on the interface between the bio-body and other kinds of technological enhancements or **prosthetics** – interventions that produce new hybrids of body and machine. Most significant here are the **cyborg** and the post-human. In these two related forms of techno-body, the melding of cybertechnology with the flesh can be seen to produce productive but also troubling outcomes. The post-human body is able to overcome the limitations of the bio-body by the use of prosthetic enhancements, leading some commentators to herald it as the next step in human evolution, or the first step in post-human post-evolution (Stelarc 2000). Here, then, we can see a parallel perspective on the 'meat' – that it is a burden, holding us back from realizing fully the potential that cyberspace offers. Discussions of **artificial life (A-Life)** and **artificial intelligence** likewise carry traces of this split between worn-out bio-bodies and exciting new forms more suited to life in cyberspace. In some versions of the cyborg we witness similar ideas; however, cyborg theory tends to stress the ambiguities of this body–machine hybridization. In all these different manifestations, therefore, we can see that the coming together of the human body and cyberspace produces a range of theoretical and experiential outcomes, producing new forms of body and new ways of thinking about the body.

See also: **Cyborg, Jacking in, Prosthetics**

Further sources: Bell (2001), Lupton (2000), Morse (1994)

BOT *see* **Robot**

BROADBAND *see* **Bandwidth**

BROWSER *see* **World Wide Web**

BUG

Often confused with **virus** – as in the case of the misnamed Love Bug – a bug is a programming error or glitch. Software development involves countless stages of debugging, with errors being traced and rectified in the endless lines of code. Sometimes, however, bugs only come to light a considerable time after software has been in use. The most notable example of a bug was the Millennium or Y2K Bug, around which there was considerable panic in the run up to the start of the year 2000 – also tapping into other forms of apocalyptic or millennial panic. Due to the logic that computers are constantly evolving and improving, programmers developing software felt it would be unnecessary to include the full four-digit year in any line of code referring to the date – assuming that, by the time the millennium ended, the programs they had written would be superseded. As the year 2000 approached, however, the bug was identified as something that could cause massive systems failure, as computers crashed when the dateline changed from 99 to 00 – since the date 00 was nonsensical in terms of the program's operating logic. The UK government coordinated a huge compliance programme to minimize the disruption, which was anticipated in epidemic proportions. TV coverage of Millennium Eve celebrations included bulletins on Y2K incidents, which turned out to be small-scale and largely harmless. Nevertheless, like viruses and virus warnings, the Y2K bug revealed our anxieties about and ignorance of computers.

BULLETIN BOARD SYSTEM (BBS)

A computer system that allows users of an electronic network to leave messages that can be read by many other users.

CARNIVORE

Carnivore is the US Federal Bureau of Investigation's (FBI's) latest approach to reading large quantities of **email**. The system now goes by the more innocuous name of DCS – for Digital Collection System. Carnivore is a diagnostic tool developed by the FBI to surgically intercept and collect the communications which are the subject of a lawful (court) order while ignoring those communications which they are not authorized to intercept (FBI 2001) The system is motivated on the premise that organized crime groups and drug trafficking organizations rely heavily upon telecommunications to plan and execute their criminal activities (FBI 2001). The system's technical underpinnings are similar to other sniffing programs, and it is presumably named for its ability to find the 'meat' buried among terabytes of non-meaty (and legally forbidden to access) information. **Privacy** advocates have voiced concerns that Carnivore over-collects information and that the source code is unavailable for inspection.

See also: **Cybercrime, Encryption, Privacy**

Further sources: http://www.fbi.gov/hq/ab/carnivore/carnivore2.htm (accessed April 11, 2001)

CERT COORDINATION CENTER

CERT is a centre of Internet security expertise located at the Software Engineering Institute (funded by the US government) at Carnegie Mellon University in Pittsburgh, Pennsylvania. CERT routinely develops *alerts* that are intended to help administrators and users anticipate, defer and recover from malicious software attacks such as viruses or **denials of service**.

See also: **Cybercrime**, **Denial of service**, **Hacker**, **Information warfare**

Further sources: http://www.cert.org

CHANNEL *see* **World Wide Web**

CHAT ROOM

Used to describe a synchronous computer mediated communication forum in which individuals exchange typed comments with other participants (everyone else in the 'room'). Chat rooms, popularized by online services such as America Online (AOL), are typically identified by the subject matter or topic of the room, although conversations often range widely. Participants are identified by their screen names (**Nicks**). Some chat rooms offer small graphical worlds, allowing participants to choose an **avatar**, a graphical self-representation, and to display action or emotion. Most chat rooms, however, are currently text-based 'rooms' or 'channels' run via **Internet Relay Chat** (IRC) software, meaning that participants can only communicate with one another using written language. To compensate for the lack of context usually provided by non-verbal communication (such as tone of voice or gesture), participants often include emoticons in their messages. Although many don't fall into this category, chat rooms are associated with banal chit-chat or sexually-oriented discussion, and are dominated by teenagers. There have also been concerns about these environments being used by paedophiles who are stalking children who go there. However, this early form of **computer mediated communication** has helped to create many online relationships, and some chat rooms can rightfully be called **virtual communities**.

See also: **Internet, Virtual communities**

CHATTERBOX

An application that emulates a human presence in the way in which it interacts with a user. Some experiments have been carried out in which such applications take part in **computer mediated communication** with users and in the development of human-like software for teaching purposes.

See also: **Agent, Artificial intelligence**

CIVIC NETWORKING *see* Community networking

CLEVELAND FREE-NET (CFN)

Initiated by Tom Grundner at Case Western Reserve University in 1986, the CFN was the world's first **Free-Net** and served as a model for hundreds of other free community-oriented networking systems around the world. The Cleveland Free-Net provided a number of services such as free email and discussion forums in the late 1980s that would become almost routine a decade later. The CFN, like many community networks, was organized as a group of *buildings* in an electronic *city*. The *Administration Building* contained the purpose, technology, contents, policy and other administrative information, the *Post Office* was responsible for sending, receiving or filtering electronic mail, and the *Public Square* brought together several communication services including *The Cafe*, where users could chat, vote or participate in a number of forums. Other CFN buildings included the *Courthouse* and *Government Center*, the *Arts Center*, the *Science and Technology Center*, the *Medical Arts Building* and the *Schoolhouse*. Despite the fact that many people still used the system routinely, the plug was pulled on the Cleveland Free-Net on 1 September 1999 by the university administration, who claimed that the system was not year-2000 compliant.

See also: **Free-Net**, **Community informatics**, **Community networks**, **Community technology centers**

Further sources: Hauben (1995)

CLIPPER CHIP *see* Encryption

COMMUNICATIONS DECENCY ACT (CDA)

Passed in the USA in 1995 and signed into law in February 1996, CDA was one of the first government attempts to restrict communication on the Internet (specifically 'any comment, request, suggestion, proposal, image, or other communication which is obscene, lewd, lascivious, filthy, or indecent'). Offenders could be fined up to $100,000 or imprisoned for up to two years, or both. The American Civil Liberties Union, EPIC and others sued the government, stating the act was unconstitutional. In a decision issued on 26 June 1997, the US Supreme Court held that the Communications Decency Act violated the First Amendment's guarantee of freedom of speech. The Court's opinion, written by Justice John Paul Stevens, stated that 'the CDA places an unacceptably heavy burden on protected speech'. After the CDA was struck down, then-president Clinton resolved to 'help ensure that our children don't end up in the red light districts of cyberspace' through a combination of additional technology and ratings systems. Needless to say, the increasing ubiquity of the Internet and non-universality of cultural norms will see to it that the issue of how to deal with verbiage, images and other content in cyberspace that is objectionable to some people won't be going away soon.

See also: **Cybercrime**, **Encryption**, **Pornography**, **Privacy**

COMMUNITY

Although imprecise and contested, the term generally assumes one or more of three meanings. A community can comprise (1) people who live in a geographical area, (2) people who are 'like-minded' to some degree, forming a *community of interest* which shares goals, values, principles or other interests, or (3) a 'sense of community' exists when people have a sense of belonging to a greater social unity. Howard

Rheingold (1993) and others have raised the issue of community in cyberspace and much resulting discussion has taken place in relation to the validity or authenticity of this contention. Commercial websites have recently launched into the pursuit of community on their websites as part of their business strategy. With this approach, customers become community members who help support corporate goals in many ways. This approach has exacerbated the controversy regarding community in cyberspace and has raised questions as to whether cyberspace is subject to **corporate dominance** as with other media forms.

See also: **Community informatics**, **Community networks**, **Social capital**, **Virtual community**

Further sources: Bagdikian (1992), Rheingold (1993)

COMMUNITY INFORMATICS (CI)

CI is a multidisciplinary field of study devoted to understanding the potential of new **ICTs** for influencing the social, cultural and economic development of community structures and relationships. The origins of CI in the UK and Canada were associated with local economic development initiatives in declining industrialized regions. Consequently such initiatives have been regarded as an important means to combat the **digital divide** separating those who have **access** to the new communications media and those who are increasingly excluded.

In the north-east of England, approaches have been used to raise awareness of the potential benefits of new ICTs to improve employment opportunities, combat educational underachievement, enhance social support networks and improve people's quality of life. A variety of community-based projects have provided IT training and access to ICTs through **community technology centers** and electronic networks. The fundamental emphasis in all these CI initiatives is the adoption of a grassroots approach whereby community members are responsible for the design and direction of the project themselves. This is achieved by working in partnership with stakeholders (for example, local government, education institutions, local media, business interests and the like) rather than being directed by them from above.

A key factor shaping the success of CI programmes is their ability to overcome the technological phobias and fears often associated with social factors such as class, race, gender, age, disability, nationality and other social characteristics. A variety of innovative projects and schemes attempt to stimulate people's interest in ICTs by focusing less upon the technology and instead upon existing social relationships between people and their everyday interests. These include the efforts to help popularize folk music from Cape Breton and other towns in the Maritime provinces of north-eastern Canada (Gurstein 2000) through the imaginative use of the Internet; the development of popular online quizzes between communities in the UK and elsewhere (www.communitychallenge.org); and the development of numerous community group websites concerned with hobbies, interests and self-help.

See also: **Community networks**, **Community technology centers**, **Digital city**, **Digital divide**, **Social capital**

Further sources: Gurstein (2000), Keeble *et al.* (2001), www.cira.org.uk, Day and Schuler (2004)

COMMUNITY MEMORY

Community Memory, of Berkeley, California, created by Efrem Lipkin, Lee Felsenstein and Ken Colstad, was the world's first community network. Initially begun in the mid-1970s as a follow-up to experiments conducted in 1972 and 1973 on unmediated two-way access to a message database through public computer terminals, the Community Memory effort was intended to develop and distribute a technology supporting the free exchange of information to communities all over the world. The Community Memory brochure reflected this idea, making the point that 'strong, free, non hierarchical channels of communication – whether by computer and modem, pen and ink, telephone, or face-to-face – are the front line of reclaiming and revitalizing our communities'. Community Memory was influenced by several important ideas prominent at the time. The founders themselves shared the north Californian counter-culture values of the 1960s which celebrated free speech and the anti-war movement. They also had much in common with the Appropriate Technology Movement which championed ecological, low-cost, decentralized and convivial technology. The hacker counter-culture of **Silicon**

Valley and which called for 'computer liberation' made a further contribution to the Community Memory ideal.

Their commitment to reducing the barriers to information technology was demonstrated by the simplicity of the system training programs, and the insistence that all Community Memory terminals be located in public places. Terminals could be found in libraries and in launderettes but could not be reached via modem or from the Internet. Community Memory adopted a creative approach to funding. They offered coin-operated terminals through which forums were free to be read, but required 25 cents to post an opinion and a dollar to start a new forum. It was, however, the computer's potential for communication and community organizing which excited the Community Memory group most. As an alternative medium for community publishing the electronic system could help preserve the political, social and cultural memory of the local community. All this could be achieved, moreover, through the playful activities associated with a hippie counterculture. Although Community Memory ceased to operate in July 1994, when the last public kiosk was dismantled, its visions and ethos continued to serve in discussions around later **community network** initiatives.

See also: **Community informatics**, **Community networks**

COMMUNITY NETWORKS

These were developed in the USA as public computer-based systems that are intended to help support a geographical community by supporting, augmenting and extending already existing social networks. Similar in spirit and motivation to public libraries, community networks generally provide free or low-cost web space, email and other services, with no advertising; are run by and for the community; foster equal access to **ICTs**; stimulate **social capital**; and are focused on particular geographical locations rather than communities of interest or virtual communities (Schuler 1996). Community network organizations often engage in training and other services and sometimes are involved in policy work as well. Community networks is often used as a generic term which covers several generations of initiatives from **community memory**, through **Free-Nets** to more recent web-based examples such as the Boulder Community Network (BCN).

See also: **Community Informatics, Community memory, Free-Net**

Further sources: Kubicek and Wagner (2002), Schuler (1996), http://www.scn.org/ncn/

COMMUNITY TECHNOLOGY CENTERS

A physical location in a geographic community that provides **access** to computers and the Internet for education, training, or other types of social amelioration. A variety of alternative names have emerged to describe community technology centers such as Information Community Service Centres (ICSCs), Telecenters, Telecottages, **cyber-cafés** or **electronic village halls**. The distinction between them is usually fairly arbitrary, having more to do with the country of origin or rural/urban location than with any significant functional differences. Community technology centers, for example, is the term more commonly used in North America, whereas electronic village hall is more typical as a European description. The term telecottage is more familiar in rural areas while telecenters and cybercafés are usually to be found urban locations.

Such facilities are important components of many **community informatics** and **community networking** initiatives. As such, their title, function and operation will often reflect the diverse needs and characteristics of particular localities and populations. Indeed, their success may well depend upon their 'fit' with the social, economic and cultural profile of the communities within which they are embedded. This has led to a vast array of community technology centers being established around the world reflecting the differential needs and aspirations of their users. Typically, however, community technology centers will provide one or more of the following features: provision of **information and communications technologies** (ICTs) to enable local people to gain access to the rest of the world within or beyond their national boundaries through the Internet and the World Wide Web; *education and training* in computer literacy and by the use of ICTs; provision of an *information service* enabling local people to have access to municipal information, library catalogues and other national and international databases; provision of technical advice and support for local business, and civic organizational development; provision of facilities for teleworking in a social setting to facilitate workplace fellowship; and provision of facilities (meeting rooms, online access, council venues) to support the *political and cultural life* of the community. In the early 1990s a coalition of community technology centers was established in the United States called CTCNet. The coalition shares resources, promotes discussion among its members and sponsors an annual conference.

See also: **Community informatics, Community networking, Electronic village halls**

COMPUTER

An electronic device designed to store and process data by following programmed instructions. Mathematical ideas about computing had been developing for many decades, evidenced for example by Charles Babbage's nineteenth-century concept of the 'Analytical Engine', before practical machines were built. The story of modern computing is a North American – and particularly a Californian – story. However, the first programmable computer, which was called *Colossus*, technically a large electronic valve programmable logic calculator, was actually British. This machine, and ten others like it, were constructed by a team led by Dr Tommy Flowers in North London to help in the deciphering of the German Enigma code in 1943.

The first American machines were also essentially electronic calculators designed to solve complex mathematical problems. In 1945, the mathematician John Von Neuman wrote a series of papers which established what eventually became known as the 'Von Neuman Architecture' that formed the basis for the practical development of machines such as the UNIVAC (Universal Automatic Computer) by the engineers J. Presper Eckert and John Mauchly in 1951. Computing started to become big business in the United States when IBM (International Business Machines) began to introduce computers to replace the electronic mechanized punch-card systems that many businesses relied upon for their record keeping. These first large systems essentially automated existing processes, using the same punch-card technology as the earlier record-keeping systems. Jobs were submitted in batches, and computer time, which was very expensive, was carefully controlled. The computers produced weekly or monthly printouts that were then disseminated to the relevant departments in a business or government organization. It was to the reports from the computer, rather than to the machine itself, that individuals referred. Large US corporations and the US Government were the first customers for these machines. When businesses and governments outside the US began to computerize, they looked to IBM.

The picture began to change in the late 1950s. Machines called minicomputers began to appear, designed as cheaper systems for lower-level computing. These machines were, however, capable enough and affordable enough to mean that individual departments in a large organization could get access to their own computer and do what they wanted, rather than ask for jobs to be run on a single large 'mainframe' that served the whole organization. These machines also disseminated computing power because they worked in a different way to the mainframes. Rather than working through batches of jobs in a way that was almost like a production line, these systems allowed time-sharing of their resources in a sufficiently sophisticated way to mean that they could have several operators at once, all of whom had an illusion that the machine was wholly at their disposal. This direct interaction with the computer generated new ideas about what the machines could do and the ways in which they could be used. One of the leading companies in the creation of the minicomputer was the Digital Equipment Corporation (DEC), which was founded in 1957 in Massachusetts.

Another radical change was soon to follow with the invention of the integrated circuit or chip. The first computers had to be large because they relied on full-sized circuits and hundreds or thousands of valves to conduct their operations. A number of individuals and companies in the US, particularly Jack Kilby at Texas Instruments, were involved in the development of integrated circuits, which first appeared in 1958. The chip had the potential not only to allow for the miniaturization of existing systems, but it could also be mass produced and provide circuitry that was much more robust and reliable than had hitherto been available. The US Government played a crucial role in funding the development of the integrated circuit, which it wanted both for the space programme and, rather less romantically, for its Minuteman nuclear missle programme.

Stewart Brand's famous statement that 'ready or not, computers are coming to the people', in *Rolling Stone* on 7 December 1972, linked the computer to West Coast counter-culture. Brand even drew comparisons between its 'liberating' effects and those of LSD. The idea of the 'personal' computer as a means of liberation started to emerge. These ideas were anti-corporation and anti-government, but they were closer to what might be termed a kind of frontier liberalism (complete or near-complete individual freedom) than they were to socialism and were, arguably, also characterized by being rather vague. Echoes of these sentiments are arguably still evident in areas of the computing and communications industry.

When the Personal Computer (PC) appeared, ideas about the computer as 'liberation' came to the fore. The PC was not 'invented' as such, but instead slowly came together through the development of microprocessors (effectively what had been regarded as a whole computer was now on one chip, thanks to Intel), better storage systems (particularly the floppy disk) and suitable software. Two pieces of software in particular, the more reliable and enhanced BASIC produced by an embryonic Microsoft, and the controllers for floppy disks and other systems that would become known as the BIOS (Basic Input/Output System) developed by Gary Kildall, would prove crucial to the development of the PC. The view of these systems as 'people's computers' was reinforced by the role played by hobbyists, who began to meet across the US and develop the potential of these machines. Exactly who built the first PC, and when, is a matter of some debate, but the first machine with mass appeal and a price tag of $400 (which was a lot of money for most people in 1975) was developed by H. Edward Roberts and called the Altair. Combining this system and those like it with BASIC and what became BIOS produced a computer that one could program.

With the arrival of the Apple II in 1977 and its spreadsheet Visicalc, the personal computer began to appear in the office. However, arguably the true turning point was in 1981 with the release of the IBM PC, a system IBM based around components from other companies over which it did not have control, and also using an operating system, MSDOS, over which it also did not have control. This lack of control over the technology of the IBM PC allowed companies like Compaq to rapidly build up large businesses by undercutting IBM with 'clone' machines, a process that began to force costs down across the market. This was combined with the arrival of capable word-processors, databases and spreadsheets, particularly Lotus 123, which led to a revolution in office computing. The old model of a big, remote, inflexible mainframe had been undermined by the more accessible minicomputer, but now one could have one's own PC on one's desk. In reality, mainframe and mainframe-like computers were to remain better than anything else at record keeping and manipulation for some time to come, before eventually being replaced by what we now call servers, which act as the cores of networks and as hosts for websites.

Even as the PC began to dominate the landscape, ideas about it as a means not only of economic but of social change began to fade. As standardization spread, software became a hugely profitable commodity and, where IBM had dominated, Microsoft now ruled the US and world markets. By the late 1980s, even the notion of a PC as liberating the user from having to use the centralized large computer at work was starting to be undermined. Work at the Rank Xerox PARC research centre in the 1970s had led to the development not only of the Graphical User Interface (GUI) system (which evolved into Apple's operating system and Microsoft's Windows) but also to the development of a workstation called the Alto and to Ethernet, in what was effectively the first LAN (Local Area Network) connecting personal workstations together. **UNIX**-based networked workstations produced by companies like Sun appeared in the mid-1980s. Although many advantages flowed from the ease with which files could be shared and with which individuals could work together on a network, the individual lost total control over their desktop computer. The PC was at first incapable of following this model, as its processor and software were inadequate. However, the advent of more network-friendly operating systems and faster Intel processors soon meant that many large companies and universities in the industrialized world had PC networks, rather than lots of 'stand-alone' computers. With the advent of the Internet, the notion of 'personal' computing in the sense of a self-contained box that can function on its own, will continue to be undermined in government and business environments, and to an increasing extent for home users. Again, it was US companies like Oracle and Sun that were at the forefront of seeing the computer as part of a network rather than as a stand-alone machine.

The counterculture associated with computing, with its hobbyists and kids starting up multi-million dollar businesses in their parents' garages, might be seen as something of a smokescreen concealing a reality of huge self-serving corporations driving what is now the world's largest single industry. Yet the ideas and images persist. Apple launched the Macintosh, with its GUI that was years ahead of that used by contemporary Intel and DOS machines, and its famous 1984 advertising campaign in which shackled individuals are 'freed' from an oppressive regime. Yet the 'oppression' that was being fought was the dominance of one standard and one company's software, not the structure of society. While companies like Apple and operating systems like **LINUX** might to some extent present themselves as radical alternatives, what this actually amounts to is an argument that computers can be better than are the current Intel- and Microsoft-based systems. In many instances it is corporations which have the same fundamental profit motive as Intel or Microsoft, but which are currently less successful, that are talking about 'revolutions' in computing. Meanwhile, many of the ideas about computers as tools that will allow social change have shifted to the Internet, although the extent to which this will create a new form of society, as opposed to an electronic marketplace dominated by corporations, remains uncertain.

The next stage in the evolution of computing may be centred on the use of small, portable devices that give their users access to a network or networks. Handheld and tablet PCs can be used in conjunction with various **wireless** technologies, such as Bluetooth, to provide their users with same functionality as a desktop PC in a portable device. A businessperson can already read their email and access their company's databases and software applications from anywhere using handheld devices, just as a doctor in a hospital can summon up a patient's record using a handheld device. Over time, these devices may become smaller, more powerful and be usable in almost any setting, rather than at the 'hotspots' to which high-**bandwidth** wireless devices are confined at present.

Outside business or public service delivery settings, handheld or highly portable network devices (the obvious example being G3 or third-generation 'mobile' or 'cellular' telephones) are currently seen by some companies as a new way in which to sell content to customers on the move. Services might range from tourist guides, maps or videos of one's favourite football team scoring a goal, through to full, mobile Internet access (as distinct from the initial, primitive, **WAP** Internet access offered by many mobile phones at the end of the 1990s).

The importance of the **convergence** of digital technologies, particularly in the home, may also begin to become apparent. The vision of corporations like Microsoft, with its Xbox games console, and Sony, with its evolutions of the Playstation, is one of an entertainment centre, offering games, entertainment (movies) and full network access, alongside the sorts of applications one might currently find on a home PC.

In some senses, the device we understand as being a 'computer' may not in the future be something that many people use in something like its current form. The machines many of us have on our desks at home or at work may be replaced by televisions and mobile devices that deliver content and applications to us **'on demand'** from remote networks.

A staggering increase in processing power has occurred since the first computers appeared. In 1964, Gordon Moore noted that the number of circuits that could be placed on a single integrated circuit had doubled every year. 'Moore's Law' predicted that by the mid-1970s a single chip could contain logic circuits that would have the same power as a mainframe computer from the 1950s. The law held true and has done so ever since. Desktop and portable machines are now many times more powerful than most mainframes used to be, and the sheer power that is now carelessly used to run a word-processor would have staggered those working in the industry in the 1950s. A large modern server like the IBM RS/6000, for example, can conduct 3.88 trillion calculations a second, which, according to IBM, would take someone with a calculator about 63,000 years to do.

See also: **Convergence**, **Information and communications technology**

Further sources: Ceruzzi (1998), Cringely (1996)

COMPUTER CONFERENCING *see* Email

COMPUTER-GENERATED IMAGERY (CGI)

The term CGI is industry shorthand for cinematic special effects created using computers. Increasing synergies between the film and computer industries are bringing new forms of simulation to movie theatres, with computer **games** deploying filmic vocabularies and special effects becoming central to the production and consumption of the Hollywood blockbuster. A film like *The Matrix* shows the extent of this interplay from one perspective, while the movie version of *Tomb Raider* shows it from another.

From the perspective of cyberculture, CGIs represent a digital medium that produces new simulations of reality. They thus belong to the expanding family of virtual environments now available as sites for entertainment. Moreover, their close association with science fiction cinema makes them commonplace tools for imagining and depicting our cybercultural futures, giving cinematic shape to worlds yet to come. In this context, CGIs do two kinds of work: they represent a sci-fi future to us, but they also show us the capabilities of today's technologies to manifest that future (Pierson 1999). Our viewing pleasure comes from enjoying the special effects as special effects, marvelling at the artistry and technology of their production (Cubitt 1999). CGIs thus produce their own form of cyberspace, which we enter in a collective consensual hallucination at the cinema.

See also: **Games**, **Lara Croft**, *The Matrix*, **Simulation**

Further sources: Cubitt (1999), Pierson (1999)

COMPUTER MEDIATED COMMUNICATION (CMC)

A generic term referring to various means of communication. The term is something of a misnomer, because what it actually refers to is communication between computer users who can exchange messages and data with one another through their connection to a network, such as the Internet.

There are two main types of CMC: *asynchronous communication* and *synchronous communication*. Asynchronous communication involves the exchange of text-based messages, which, although it can be very rapid, does not actually involve what would in orthodox terms be regarded as conversation. The nearest analogy would perhaps be with a mechanism that allowed near instantaneous exchange of letters or telegrams. The best examples of this form of CMC are **email** and the newsgroups or **bulletin board systems** that operate on networks like **Usenet**. Asynchronous communication allows both one-to-one and many-to-many exchanges to take place. When someone uses email to send a message to someone else, they are using CMC in a way that is not dissimilar to an exchange of letters. They can, however, also subscribe to an email list, in which there are many participants, all exchanging information with one another. The use of newsgroups always potentially involves many-to-many communication (although some newsgroups can be small and insular, anyone can potentially read and participate in them). Groups of individuals who may be physically distant from one another can potentially form online groups, some of which may be looser in structure than others. These groups can become lively forums for the exchange of views, discussion and sharing of information. They can range in focus from political subjects to hobbies and the sharing of experience. Some examples include online health discussion in newsgroups within which people with a shared health condition offer mutual support and exchange information.

Synchronous CMC differs from newsgroups or email in that it offers something approaching conversation between participants. It is perhaps best described as offering what might be called a 'typed conversation'. The main forms of synchronous CMC are **Internet Relay Chat (IRC)**, **ICQ** and **Multi-User Domains (MUDs)**. IRC allows both one-to-one and many-to-many exchanges, within virtual spaces called 'chat rooms' or 'channels' that can be frequented by two or more individuals who converse with one another through typed messages (see **chat rooms**). ICQ offers similar facilities, but is designed for one-to-one exchanges. MUDs are very similar in operation to IRC chat rooms or channels, but they offer a themed virtual environment, with its origins in primitive online text-based adventure games (MUD originally stood for 'Multi-User Dungeon'), which may involve participants simply pretending they are in a bar, or may still involve playing a text based Dungeons and Dragons style adventure game with one another. All of these many-to-many synchronous environments are quite widely used for cybersex, which involves the exchange of sexual messages between CMC participants.

A great deal was read into the various forms of CMC when the Internet and related networks started to be used by US academics and other middle-class professionals in the late 1980s and early 1990s. Some commentators, notably Howard Rheingold, advanced the idea that many-to-many CMC venues such as bulletin board systems and newsgroups constituted not only a new form of communication, but a potential revolution in social organization. Rheingold argued that 'communities of shared interest' would arise, using CMC, sometimes existing alongside, and sometimes replacing, traditional geographically based communities. Others, such as Sherry Turkle, took the view that CMC also changed communication and social identity in other ways, particularly with regard to the lack of visual, aural and other 'cues' offered by CMC (see **cues filtered out**). One could invent an identity, create a 'virtual self', that might differ from one's 'real self' in ethnicity, gender, sexuality and a host of other respects. The sociological idea of the **cyborg**, a part-real, part-virtual person, was associated with this sort of thinking. Many felt that the lack of cues for identification created possibilities for equity and fairness in exchanges through CMC that were not possible in face-to-face communication. This was because one's gender, ethnicity and anything that might mean one was not spoken to, or otherwise undermined or excluded from a conversation, was invisible.

At the time these sorts of ideas were being advanced, CMC was dominated by the sorts of professional people of which these academics and commentators were themselves examples. The widely discussed 'Mr Bungle' case, reported by Julian Dibbell, in which someone misbehaved in a MUD dominated by middle-class professional people by typing that they were committing acts of sexual violence against another participant, perhaps exemplifies the rather exclusive experience of CMC that many of these early commentators had.

The reality of CMC soon started to become apparent. Rather than resulting in new kinds of exchange in which new forms of equality and fairness based on the presentation of a 'virtual self' were possible, it began to be clear that CMC was going to be rather human after all. Participants in IRC 'shout' at each other using capital letters, some participants in various forms of CMC act as **trolls**, essentially looking to sow discontent in various many-to-many fora. Teenagers crash into CMC settings and insult everyone there until they get thrown out. Groups can be characterized by flaming, with participants insulting and threatening each other to levels that would not often occur in face-to-face exchanges. This is something that some commentators have associated with participants not being able to see or hear one another. Thus the absence of visual cues acting as 'barriers', that some early commentators on CMC saw as facilitating new forms of communication, also facilitated new levels of hostility in communication.

Other important issues also tended to be forgotten. To use CMC one needed to be able to type, something a person with bad arthritis of the hands might not be able to do. Unless one had the use of expensive specialized equipment, one also needed to be able to see in order to use these text-based forms of CMC. In addition, while the Internet and web are described as being 'worldwide' networks, they are dominated by North America. People without access to these networks, or people who cannot read and type English (who make up the great majority of the world's population), cannot participate in virtual communities of 'shared interest'. Neither can socioeconomically marginalized groups within the US or the UK use CMC (see **digital divide** and **usability**).

Significantly, sociologists such as Barry Wellman began to point to the mixed effects of CMC. By the mid-1990s, it was becoming clear that this was a technology that was both affecting and being affected by society. Rather than producing cyborgs, these new forms of communication were being changed and manipulated by society, including being used to reinforce existing divisions and prejudices.

In addition, as Wellman and others pointed out, there were lots of other changes happening in terms of social relationships that were rather more significant. Many people were moving around rather than staying in a fixed geographical location, and they were maintaining social networks that were often made up of people who were quite geographically remote from one another. True, CMC was sometimes used to maintain and reinforce these social networks, but then so was the telephone, not to mention cars, trains and air travel – and indeed, letters. Rather than having a 'virtual self', it might be the case that you telephone someone one week, visit them another time, email them a further time, 'talk' to them via IRC on yet another occasion, and then phone them to meet for a coffee the week after that. While relationships were clearly starting in virtual spaces for many-to-many or one-to-one CMC, it was also becoming apparent that, as they developed, they started to involve telephone calls and eventually face-to-face meetings.

The other important factor to bear in mind is that the software underpinning much CMC is becoming antiquated, in terms of the life cycle of ICTs, and that it may decline in use or be replaced. As 3G mobile (cellular) phones come into use worldwide, the already widespread use of **text messaging** may start to outstrip the use of email, as is already the case in the UK. Third-generation mobile phones now offer video calls and, at the time of writing, mobile-to-mobile picture messaging is well established in Japan and the UK (sending pictures taken with the phone's inbuilt digital camera to one another). All forms of CMC may also become increasingly visual as bandwidth increases, and it may be the case that the text-based CMC of newsgroups, bulletin boards and IRC are replaced by visual environments in which participants can see one another, in the form of **avatars** or simply as live video. CMC may consequently change very significantly in form over the next decade.

Further sources: Dibbell (1999), Rheingold (1993), Turkle (1997), Smith and Kollock (1999), Wellman *et al.* (2001)

COMPUTER MEDIATED SOCIAL SUPPORT *see* Virtual social support

COMPUTER PROFESSIONALS FOR SOCIAL RESPONSIBILITY (CPSR)

An NGO officially incorporated in 1983 by computer scientists at Xerox PARC and Stanford University to protest against irresponsible uses of computing in military systems such as the Autonomous Vehicle and the Battlefield Management projects that poured large amounts of money into US-based **artificial intelligence** research efforts. The Strategic Defense Initiative (SDI or Star Wars), announced two weeks after CPSR's incorporation, became its first target, the group viewing it as an expensive, dangerous and unreliable weapons system. In the 1990s and beyond, CPSR became increasingly involved in cyberspace issues such as **privacy** and free speech. CPSR chapters now exist in Africa, Asia, Europe and North and South America. CPSR sponsors two bi-annual conferences – 'Participatory Design' and 'Directions and Implications of Advanced Computing' (DIAC). CPSR's Public Sphere Project, a follow-on project to DIAC-2000, was launched in 2001.

Further sources: http://www.cpsr.org, http://www.cpsr.org/program/sphere

COMPUTER SUPPORTED COMMUNITY WORK

An alternative to **Computer Supported Cooperative Work** that shifts the traditional CSCW spotlight by placing *community* as the key focus of the discipline.

Further sources: http://www.scn.org/commnet/cscw-00.html

COMPUTER SUPPORTED COOPERATIVE WORK (CSCW)

The discipline within computer science that studies how computers can be used to support collaborative work, generally white-collar commercial work. Some of the major foci include work flow management, shared applications (groupware), telepresence and document management. The major CSCW conferences alternate between the USA and Europe.

Further sources: Bikson and Eveland (1998)

CONNECTIVITY *see* **Access**

CONSOLE *see* **Games**

CONVERGENCE

A term currently in use to describe the coming together of a range of telecommunications and information technology or multimedia applications. A digital television with hundreds of channels which also offers inbuilt Internet access and the applications now available on home PCs is an example of convergence. Convergence is about the ability of one piece of technology to communicate with others, rather than simply reducing everything that is currently done by several devices into one 'box'. Convergence became possible as technologies such as magnetic tape-based recording or analogue television transmission all started to be replaced with digital technologies. It is also facilitated by the rise of networks that can deliver many forms of digital content (from telecommunications to games, movies, through to network access and applications) **'on demand'** to various household or handheld devices. At the time of writing, a refrigerator that can communicate with one's bank account and then the supermarket to order more milk when one runs out is an oft-cited, although perhaps rather unimaginative and unromantic, example of the kind of communication envisaged. **Wireless** technologies, such as Bluetooth, that can, for example, enable a digital video camera to also act as a web browser and **email** the images it records, are being developed both to facilitate convergence and to profit from it.

COOKIE

A cookie is a small file that a server can write to your hard disk by interacting with your Internet browser. When you next visit a website that has previously sent a cookie to your PC, the site may remember details about you and customize its response to you accordingly. One example of how this works in practice is when someone registers with the online bookshop amazon.com. Amazon's server sends a cookie to the user's hard disk. This cookie is read when the user next visits the site to enable it to greet the customer by name, and the server is enabled to interact with the user, producing worryingly well targeted lists of new products based on past purchases. Cookies are generally designed to expire after a few weeks or months.

COPYLEFT

Copyleft is a general method for making software (and, most especially, its source code) free and readily available. The particular nature of copyleft, furthermore, ensures that all modified and extended versions of the program will be free in the same sense. Copyleft, a brilliant counter to the more familiar copyright, helped earn Richard Stallman, its creator, the coveted MacArthur genius award. Copyleft is the legal – and philosophical – foundation of the **GNU Project**,the aim of which is to give people the freedom to redistribute and change GNU software. Instead of putting GNU software in the public domain, GNU developers 'copyleft' it. To copyleft a program, it is first copyrighted; then distribution terms are added that give everyone the rights to use, modify and redistribute the program's source code or any program derived from it – but only if the distribution terms remain unchanged. While copyleft is a general concept, the GNU General Public License is the specific form of copyleft used in the GNU project.

Further sources: http://www.gnu.org/copyleft/

CORPORATE DOMINANCE

Ever since Ben Bagdikian's *Media Monopoly* (1992) (and others – Herbert Schiller (1989) and Oliver Boyd-Barrett (2003) for example) the idea of 'corporate dominance' or 'media imperialism' as a trend with negative implications for democratic processes has been widely documented and discussed. The question inevitably was raised as to whether cyberspace is subject to domination by commercial interests at all and, if it is, what, if anything, could or should be done to counter those trends. Certainly it is indisputable that cyberspace is more commercial now than it was when commercial activity was strictly prohibited on the Internet (prior to 1995). It is also indisputable that non-commercial interests are well-represented and active in cyber-space (Schuler and Day 2003) now and presumably in the future. Commercial investment is, however, staggering, and time will tell how cyberspace is perceived and used in the future. There is certainly evidence that corporations are interested in developing markets, in terms of both providing network access and providing consumer content **'on demand'** on those networks (see **games**). The critical questions to ask at this time are: what non-commercial activities can be accomplished in cyberspace, and what policy directions should be pursued to ensure that they are not marginalized due to structural constraints?

See also: **Cultural imperialism**, **Globalization**, **'On demand'**

Further sources: Bagdikian (1992), Schiller (1989), Boyd-Barrett (2003)

CORPOREALITY *see* Body

CROSS-DRESSING *see* Cyberfeminism

CROSS-OWNERSHIP

This occurs where one company owns more than one major media outlet, such as television, cable and newspapers, in the same geographical area.

CRYPTOGRAPHY *see* Encryption

CTCNET *see* Community technology centers

CUES FILTERED OUT

For an animal used to seeing the expression, stance and appearance of those it is communicating with, text-based **CMC** creates a number of problems. Much of what is said between people is communicated non-verbally, and these non-verbal 'cues' are 'filtered out' by **email**, newsgroups or **Internet Relay Chat**. Telephones also filter out these non-verbal cues, but many of the messages that can be conveyed simply through the tone of one's voice are still available (although telephone conversations do differ from face-to face-interactions). In contrast, text-based CMC does not allow for either visual or aural cues. Some associate the advent of **flaming** and flame wars with the absence of cues – remarks meant as jokes, or which are at least neutralized by shifts in expression or tone, instead appear as stark and hostile and receive an equally hostile response. Equally, of course, positive or flirtatious comments take on an extra weight without context-setting cues.

Adaptation to non-verbal and non-visual communication happened very quickly. People participating in CMC simply used their keyboards to draw facial expressions, sometimes referred to as 'smileys' or 'emoticons' (a shorthand for 'emotional icon'). Thus, viewed sideways, a semi-colon, a hyphen and a bracket become a smiling, winking face [;-)], while another combination expresses sadness [:-( ], and so forth.

These smileys also feature heavily in text messaging on mobile phones, especially in the UK (these are much more widespread than what are called cellular phones in the US). Use of these symbols as abbreviations for words and phrases, ranges from descriptions of physical attractiveness through to descriptions of states of mind. While smileys are hardly the equivalent of hieroglyphics, there is considerable creativity in the use of a restricted typeset to convey a very wide range of meanings.

Typing can be used to set the tone of remarks in the same way as a facial expression, gestures or tone of voice. When individuals feel the need to emphasize what they are saying, which in another context would be accomplished by raising one's voice or shouting, messages are typed in capitals. The use of capitals in text-based CMC is even sometimes described as 'shouting' by participants.

The absence of verbal and aural cues can also have other effects when combined with physical distance from other participants in CMC. Some find what might be termed the 'remoteness' of communication through typed messages a liberating environment that allows them to explore deeply personal issues in a way they would find difficult in face-to-face interaction. One explanation for this might be that the intimacy of real interaction might involve embarrassment and awkwardness which are avoided by not actually talking face-to-face with another person. The use of what has been termed 'Virtual Social Support' (online self-help and support groups) is now quite widespread and may in some respects be linked to environments offering this sort of communication. Denzin has argued that the North American love of technology and of 'self-help' and analysis were bound to come together (Denzin 1998).

There are other, more contentious arguments about the effects of cues being filtered out by text-based CMC. One of these arguments contends that CMC presents a 'neutral' environment for communication. A host of cues, ranging from physical appearance, ethnicity and gender through to relative wealth, are not available to participants in text-based CMC. Some commentators like Howard Rheingold have argued that CMC creates the potential for communities of 'shared interest' not determined by geographical proximity or who a person appears to be. Those who would not communicate with another – or would communicate in a particular way with one another – because their behaviour would have been determined by visual cues, are now placed in a situation in which they have to assume the other is an equal. There are some difficulties with these ideas. First, they were developed at a time when CMC was very much dominated by the North American middle and upper middle class, the supposedly 'neutral' communication in fact taking place between US middle-class professionals and college professors who had a great deal in common. Second, there are, of course, lots of verbal cues that could give away someone's gender, attitudes and background. Differences in vocabulary, for example, might be used as an (admittedly inaccurate) means of determining broad social class and other variables such as likely income levels.

There is also the issue of deliberate misrepresentation. Most obviously, the mass media has created something of a CMC demon in the shape of the paedophiles and child pornographers who misrepresent themselves online to children. Yet there may be many more subtle and varied forms of misrepresentation, a particular favourite apparently being to change one's gender or to create another identity or series of identities for oneself.

There are a number of difficulties in relation to testing these ideas and hypotheses. Among those that are commonly identified are the sheer scale of CMC and the issue of monitoring what are effectively conversations for the purposes of academic study (see **lurking**). The scale of CMC prohibits a global study and what work has been done suggests the means for text-based CMC are not used in a uniform way. In addition, while online exchanges such as those in newsgroups are 'public' in the sense that anyone can read them, whether those who participate in these exchanges regard them as public property, as opposed to a private conversation, is debatable. Although it is possible to secure the cooperation of those using CMC to observe their behaviour, this may also create methodological problems in that participants in CMC fora will know they are being observed.

Further sources: Denzin (1998), Goodwin (1996), McLaughlin *et al.* (1995), Muncer *et al.* (2000b), Rheingold (1993), Smith and Kollock (1999)

CULTURAL IMPERIALISM

Cultural imperialism is a process of domination whereby the most economically powerful countries in the world attempt to maintain and exploit their superiority by subjugating the values, traditions and cultures of the majority of poorer countries and replacing them with their own cultural perspectives. It is a significant aspect of the way in which advanced capitalist nation-states, such as the USA and others in Western Europe, can be seen to systematically seek to exercise their economic and political interests over less powerful, underdeveloped countries in the Third World. It can thus also be regarded as an integral component of the perceived trends towards **globalization** whereby local cultures become threatened and ultimately displaced by the dominant 'Western' cultural values associated with multinational corporations.

The means by which cultural imperialism can be pursued are varied and have a long history dating back at least to the Roman Empire. In the world today they include the education of the future leaders and ruling elites of the world's poorer countries in Western schools and universities where they are imbued with the doctrines and principles of the free market. More widely influential however has been the influence of US films, TV programmes and global news programmes, such as CNN and the BBC, carrying a Western perspective to world audiences. All of these and related aspects of globalization have led perhaps most significantly to the idea that US English has become the most important language for business prosperity, science and development.

Such processes of cultural imperialism raise important issues for our understanding of cybercultures. The dominant institutional position of the US as the country responsible for the initial development of the **Internet** clearly gives it a cultural advantage over less developed societies. The language, icons and symbols of the **WWW** are predominantly 'Western', indeed overwhelmingly North American, in orientation. For **cyberlibertarians** this domination of the new media is celebrated as a means for individuals to be freed from the oppression of their governments and as an opportunity for them to join the 'American Dream'. In this context the Internet can be regarded as a media technology which is both shaped by the dominant culture of the 'West' and facilitates the processes of globalization consistent with the aims of cultural imperialism.

In recent years however it may be possible to detect the emergence of counter-cultural trends (see **Indymedia**). First, countries such as China which felt threatened by the Internet originally looked to regulation and surveillance as a means to protect their territorial borders. Such strategies, however, are difficult to police, and also they exclude such societies from the potential economic and political benefits of access to **information** flows. Consequently Chinese use of the Internet is rapidly increasing and the Chinese language may soon become the most prolific in cyberspace. Other smaller or newly emerging countries see the potential benefits of using the Internet as a means to showcase their cultures at very little expense. 'Old' languages and customs are being celebrated, and 'cultural battles' are taking place in cyberspace to portray competing national identities and histories.

See also: **Cyberlibertarianism**, **Globalization**, **Hypercasualization**, **Indymedia**

CULTURE JAMMING

This refers to the activities of challenging the imposition of marketing practices in our public spaces by parodying advertisements and hijacking billboards to seriously alter their messages. Often undertaken by highly skilled guerrilla artists, this form of protest is intended to make a contribution to the politics of public space by denying the right of commercial advertisers to dominate the public domain with their messages to the exclusion of others. Increasingly, 'adbusters' argue, our streets, neighbourhoods, schools, sports facilities, public transport, highways and the **Internet** are being submerged beneath a tide of corporate messages and images which no one asked for and few can afford to prevent. Like many anti-capitalist **new social movements**, these activists argue that we should not acquiesce to the commercialization of our public space but rather that we should actively seize it back.

Variously described as *adbusting* or *subverting*, these forms of culture jamming are regarded by their practitioners as the Art of Cultural Resistance. 'A well produced "subvert" mimics the look and feel of the targeted ad, promoting the classic "double take" as viewers suddenly realise they have been duped. Subverts create cognitive dissonance. It cuts through the hype and glitz of our mediated reality and, momentarily, reveals a deeper truth within' (quoted at www.subvertise.org). Yet as Naomi Klein points out, 'the most sophisticated culture jams are not stand alone ad parodies but interceptions – counter messages that hack into a corporation's own method of communication to send a message starkly at odds with the one that was intended' (Klein 2000: 281). It thereby adopts and uses the often highly expensive corporate campaign against itself to highlight what the culture jammers regard as unacceptable corporate practices, such as poor employment conditions, violations of human rights, or health and environmental risks.

A growing network of jammers has emerged in many parts of the world utilizing **cyberspace** as a means to organize campaigns, recruit supporters and activists, and spread their messages of resistance. Websites such as Adbusters and Subvertise use the media not only to further their e-zine publishing and community activism, but also develop and share online culture jamming images. Increasingly **hacktivists** are engaging in reclaiming virtual public spaces.

See also: **New cultural politics, New social movements**

CYBERCAFÉS see **Internet café**

CYBERCRIME

The concept of cybercrime refers to illegal or illicit computer-mediated activities undertaken through the use of global electronic networks. It represents a distinctive form of criminal activity as a consequence of the versatile nature of new **information and communication technologies** (ICTs). Cybercrimes are not simply acts which are labelled criminal because they happen to involve computers. Rather, they primarily refer to activities which are only made possible through the use of ICTs. Global connectivity, for example, enables criminal behaviour to be conducted more easily on a transnational basis. Also, the technologies can be adopted by existing organized criminals to create, for example, more sophisticated techniques to support and develop networks for the use of drug trafficking, money laundering, smuggling and illegal arms trafficking. Increasingly, security and trade secrets can be intercepted and transmitted electronically by those computer **hackers** who are willing to sell such information in a burgeoning market. Moreover, the many-to-many communication which is an essential feature of the Internet enables the relatively inexpensive production and worldwide dissemination of potentially harmful or threatening information and knowledge.

Various types of cybercrime can be discerned. The most common are:

- *Computer network break-ins*, where hackers infiltrate computer systems and networks to steal data or undertake acts of sabotage such as planting **viruses** or **trojans**;
- *Industrial espionage*, undertaken to obtain 'trade secrets', such as information about competitors' product development or marketing strategies, and increasingly conducted by hacking into commercial computer systems;
- *Software piracy*, which results from the capture of valuable computer code;
- *Fraud*, rapidly becoming a significant feature of online commerce and including misrepresented or undelivered goods, specious cyberspace business opportunities, and especially credit card fraud;
- *Pornography*, particularly that depicting children and circulating through paedophile networks;
- *Email bombing*, the process whereby software is written that will instruct a computer to bombard an electronic address with email, flooding the recipient's personal account and thereby threatening to crash the system.
- *Password sniffers*, software programs which challenge the security safeguards of computer networks by monitoring and recording users' identities and passwords, allowing impersonators to access restricted files and documents;
- *Spoofing*, which enables illicit access to networks by electronically disguising a computer to resemble another.

Just as crime has changed with the growth of ICTs, so too have the categories of criminals who engage in cybercrime. There are three basic categories into which we can categorize cybercriminals: hackers and **phreaks**; information merchants and mercenaries; and terrorists, extremists and deviants.

The increasing importance of computer networks to modern organizations and the rapid spread of online commerce have created a corresponding concern among law enforcement agencies and security services about their vulnerability to cybercrimes. This perceived threat of cybercrime to national and international economies, security and social and political relations has questioned the relevance of existing law enforcement practices. The detection of cybercrime often requires a good understanding of the new media and the use of advanced computer skills. Consequently many national and regional law enforcement and security agencies now have specialized units of 'cybercops' dedicated to tackling cybercrime.

Perhaps of even greater significance for the future role of law enforcement agencies in the information age has been the breakdown of the traditional distinction between internal and external security forces. Increasingly, the flexibility of computer networks makes it difficult to distinguish between **information warfare**, terrorism and 'normal' criminal activities. Economic espionage may pose a greater threat than nuclear assault to a nation whose welfare is critically dependent upon its economic security.

The measures used by law enforcement and security agencies to counter cybercrime have led to objections from those concerned about safeguarding **privacy** and the perceived spread of surveillance. Civil rights campaign organizations have argued that mechanisms developed to police the Internet, such as those for accessing **encrypted** messages or tracing communications, are an unacceptable infringement of privacy and freedom. Moreover, the capture of personal data and data-matching with other data sources without permission may represent a move towards a surveillance society.

See also: **Encryption**, **Hackers**, **Information warfare**, **Piracy**, **Privacy**

Further sources: Thomas and Loader (2000), Davies (1996), Lyon (1994)

CYBERFEMINISM

Feminist theorists have made some of the most significant interventions in debates about cyberculture. In part this builds on existing feminist work on science and technology, where there is a long and important tradition of analysis (see, for example, Harding 1986; Wajcman 1991). While much of this work has been critical, in terms of highlighting women's marginalization in, exclusion from and domination by technoscientific culture, it has also opened up a space for feminist writers to engage with the study and practice of science and technology in immensely productive ways. Feminist work on cyberculture includes analyses of the impact of computers and the Internet on women's lives, and this too has included a mix of negative and positive conclusions. For some writers, cyberspace is another realm of heteropatriarchal dominance, structured to exclude female participation – studies of email and bulletin board systems discourse, web design and the computer industry have all highlighted how these exclusions work. However, other writers have suggested that cyberspace provides a new space in which gender relations can be rewired, and that feminists should therefore seize the opportunity to get online in their own terms. Reflecting broader debates in feminist theory and politics, it is therefore more appropriate to talk of cyberfeminisms in the plural, since there are multiple perspectives, sometimes at odds with one another (see Squires 2000).

Feminist interventions in cyberspace are not confined to academic theory, of course: feminist politics have also been shaped by, and had a key role in shaping, cyberculture. Again, there are different threads to consider. Katie Ward (2000) divides feminist cybercultural practice into two categories – online feminism and online cyberfeminism. The first category is using cyberspace to advance a broad-based feminist agenda, through consciousness-raising and so on. The second category has an expressive engagement with cyberspace, perhaps best exemplified by the self-styled 'geekgrrrls', 'nerdgrrrls' and 'replicunts', who are actively claiming cyberspace for women and using it for their own ends. As Sadie Plant (2000: 335) writes:

> The replicunts write programs, paint viral images, fabricate weapons systems, infiltrate the arts and the industry. They are hackers, perverting the codes, corrupting the transmissions, multiplying zeros, and teasing open new holes in the world. They are the edge of the new edge, unashamedly opportunist, entirely irresponsible, and committed to the infiltration and corruption of a world which already rues the day they left home.

There are clear echoes in this quote of one of the most important texts of cyberfeminism, Donna Haraway's 'A cyborg manifesto' (2000). This essay explores the manifold impacts of new sciences and technologies from a feminist perspective, before turning to the **cyborg**, which Haraway seeks to reclaim and rewire as a potentially liberatory figure. As she sees it, the cyborg can act as a troubling 'boundary figure', unsettling the ordering principles of contemporary society: human/ machine, male/female and so on. Haraway has continued to explore the cyborg and other new biotechnological figures, and her work has influenced a great many cyberfeminist writers (see, for example, Gonzalez 2000; Sandoval 2000).

See also: **Cyborg**

Further sources: Bell and Kennedy (2000: part 4), Kirkup *et al.* (2000), Plant (1997)

CYBERLIBERTARIANISM

Cyberlibertarianism refers to a perspective (some would say philosophy) which claims that **cyberspace** and the **Internet** should be regarded as uncontrolled and unregulated electronic spaces where anyone is free to be whatever they wish and express themselves however they like. It thereby shares many of the same principles as free-market libertarian ideologies which regard individual freedom as the primary political aspiration, the unregulated market as the essential mechanism for distributing goods and services, and a loathing of government which is seen as the main obstacle to the achievement of personal liberty. The origins of the term come from various **digerati** the most notable of whom are John Perry Barrow, Alvin Toffler, Esther Dyson, Stewart Brand and Kevin Kelly. In the hands of these enthusiastic proponents, cyberlibertarianism has become a very influential credo which, although subject to much criticism, confronts little in the way of an alternative vision of cyberspace.

The ideological links between cyberlibertarianism and right-wing political theory are perhaps best outlined in an article sponsored by the Progress and Freedom Foundation called *Cyberspace and the American Dream: a magna carta for the knowledge age*, which was written in 1994 by Esther Dyson, George Gilder, George Keyworth and Alvin Toffler and is available online at www.pff.org/position.html. Throughout this treatise the authors celebrate the progressive nature of the new media technology which is said to be heralding the 'Third Wave' of economic development. Knowledge, information and the technological means for their creation, processing and communication are the central resources which characterize this historic stage of human development. Hence '[T]he central event of the 20th century', they argue, has been 'the overthrow of matter. In technology, economics, and the politics of nations, wealth – in the form of physical resources – has been losing value and significance. The powers of mind are everywhere ascendant over the brute force of things.' Cyberspace represents the new **electronic frontier** whereby the dream (seemingly largely American) of pioneers reaching out and exploring this virtual territory of knowledge provides the opportunity for us to realise 'civilization's truest, highest calling'. Its, achievement, however, depends upon the acceptance of the *Magna Carta*, or charter of liberty and individual rights, which challenges existing ideas about property, the marketplace, community and individual freedom.

Cyberlibertarians recognize the importance of property rights for free markets to work effectively, but they propose that the ownership of the emerging electronic frontier should reside first with the people, who are vital for the realization of its potential. In particular they are critical of governments who continue to adopt Second Wave conceptions of property and ownership which the cyberlibertarians regard as inappropriate. In the case of intellectual property rights, for example, patent and copyright protection developed to safeguard knowledge regarded as a 'public good' is being used by governments to develop laws covering electronic property. But this approach, cyberlibertarians argue, is flawed because it does not recognize that the nature of a 'good' is being transformed in the Third Wave as a consequence of the movement from a mass-production, mass-media, mass-culture civilization to a *demassified civilization*. 'The dominant form of new knowledge in the Third Wave is perishable, transient, *customized* knowledge: the right information, combined with the right software and presentation, at precisely the right time. Unlike the mass knowledge of the Second Wave – "public good" knowledge that was useful to everyone because most people's information needs were standardized – Third Wave customized knowledge is by nature a private good.'

The Third Wave also enables the cyberlibertarians to triumphantly proclaim the end of what they regard as the imperfect mass markets of the previous age, characterized by static competition. The 'renaissance of American business and technological leadership' is due, they argue, to the advent of dynamic competition which 'allows competing technologies and new products to challenge the old ones and, if they really are better, to replace them. Static competition might lead to faster and stronger horses. Dynamic competition gives us the automobile ... [It] creates winners and losers on a massive scale. New technologies can render instantly obsolete billions of dollars of embedded infrastructure, accumulated over decades.'

Communities too will be transformed by the technologically-led Third Wave society. 'Cyberspace will play an important role knitting together in the diverse communities of tomorrow, facilitating the creation of "electronic neighborhoods" bound together not by geography but by shared interests.' But this will not produce a common public space; rather, it will enable a global platform for a very loosely networked collection of private cyberspaces. It thereby contrasts with the concerns of Second Wave thinkers who lament the breakdown of **community** and the erosion of **social capital**, and instead celebrates the potential demassification of social life through an explosion of variations on existing customs which are able to manifest themselves in **virtual communities**. Such cyberspaces will be independent of each other, so activities in one will not interfere with what happens in another.

The common thread throughout the *Magna Carta* and other cyberlibertarian pronouncements is a championing of radical individualism which was severely constrained throughout the Second Wave. Now its potential is able to be unleashed in the demassified cyberspaces facilitating dynamic competition between the unfettered creators of customized, transient and ephemeral knowledge. It is a freedom which celebrates 'individuality over conformity, reward[s] achievement over consensus and militantly protect[s] the right to be different.' Above all it is a freedom whose achievement can only be accomplished at the expense of Second Wave bureaucratic big government. This is a point forcefully made by John Perry Barlow, who attempts to portray cyberspace as 'a new social space, global and antisovereign, within which anybody, anywhere can express to the rest of humanity whatever he or she believes without fear. There is in these new media a foreshadowing of the intellectual and economic liberty that might undo all the authoritarian powers on earth' (Barlow 1996a).

The nation–state and government in general represent for cyberlibertarians the single biggest threat to liberty, self-expression and individual prosperity. Through the emergence of new media, however, we have at our disposal both the means and the opportunity of realizing a corporeal existence freed from the politics of the flesh, sovereignty, military coercion and national boundaries (Barlow 1996b). Instead, governance is characterized by self-policing activities, mutual self-help within virtual communities, and liberation through the creation of individual identities and a concomitant rejection of imposed identities and categorization by government officials and statisticians.

The cyberlibertarian ideology continues to be championed by Barlow and others, like the **Electronic Frontier Foundation**, but its arguments have attracted a number of critics (Bennahum 1996; Loader 1997; Winner 1997). Principally it is the assertion by cyberlibertarians that they are creating a new world (Barlow 1996b) without reference to the social, economic and political contexts which act to shape cyberspace that is seen to be the chief weakness of their perspective. By ignoring how the 'real world' has acted to influence the design, use (intended and unintended), diffusion and effects of the new media, the cyberlibertarians do not adopt a crude technological determinism but seem unable to address significant questions about **access**, the **digital divide** and the distribution of power and economic resources. As Langdon Winner remarks in his well-known critique: 'Who stands to gain and who will lose in the transformations now underway? Will existing sources of injustice be reduced or amplified? Will the promised democratization benefit the populace as a whole or just those who own the latest equipment? And who gets to decide? About these questions, the cyberlibertarians show little concern' (1997).

See also: **Access**, **Cyberspace**, **Digital divide**, **Electronic Frontier Foundation**

Further sources: Barlow (1996a, 1996b), Day and Schuler (2004), Loader (1997)

CYBERORGANIZING

Cyberorganizing is a cyberspace policy direction, described by Abdul Alkalimat and Kate Williams, that relies on a conception of information technologies as being potentially socially transformative, and facilitates the self-organizing of marginalized and low-income people in order to be agents for social change.

Further sources: 'Social Capital and Cyberpower: A Community Technology Center in an African American Community', www.communitytechnology.org/cyberpower/

CYBERPET

Cyberpet is the collective name given to assorted computational toys that display animal-like features and which have enjoyed popularity with children since the late 1990s. Early examples included Tamagotchi, Pokemon and similar species, as well as the robot–animal hybrids such as Furby and Poo-Chi. Tamagotchi, introduced by the

Japanese firm Bandai, resembled a digital watch: a small plastic casing with an LCD display screen and buttons on the side. On the screen was an 'egg', which hatched when activated. This virtual pet lived solely on the screen, and was by raised by its owner, who could press buttons to feed, discipline, wash and monitor the progress of the evolving pet. If neglected, the Tamagotchi would 'die'. Tamagotchi were later eclipsed in popularity by Nintendo's *Pokemon*, in which pets ('pocket monsters') were raised and cared for in the same way, but could also take part in gladiatorial contests with other *Pokemon* (see **games**). Early cyberpets such as Furby and Poo-Chi were fairly primitive, little more than mechanized soft toys with a few pre-programmed responses and movements.

More recently, Japanese corporations have begun to develop recreational robots aimed at an adult audience. Sony, for example, markets the Aibo series of 'entertainment robots' (www.jp.aibo.com/ and www.aibo-europe.com/) which employ relatively sophisticated **AI**, enabling them not only to learn tricks but also to develop and exhibit unique behaviour, so that no two Aibo are exactly alike. Giving an Aibo different software can modify its behaviour in the way its owner desires, and enable it to learn new tasks like 'recognizing' its owner through face recognition software. The various models of Aibo are quadrupeds in animal-like shapes.

Aside from their value as toys, cyberpets can be examined as examples of the migration of digital technology into new realms, and as tools to teach both children and adults how to think about cyberculture. Sherry Turkle (1997) has worked with children and computational toys, exploring the ways in which children use them to think through the distinction between 'alive' and 'not alive'. In some senses, then, cyberpets can be seen as primitive **artificial life** (A-life) forms, belonging in a lineage with computer **viruses**, **robots** and intelligent **agents**.

See also: **A-life**, **Robot**, **Virus**

Further sources: Bloch and Lemish (1999), Turkle (1997)

CYBERPUNK

Cyberpunk was a trend within science fiction that began with the publication of William Gibson's **Neuromancer** in 1984. For many commentators, cyberpunk was seen as representative of the postmodern world, and some have argued that the novels of Gibson and other cyberpunk writers such as Bruce Sterling can almost be read as social theory that can tell us what the near future will be like (Burrows 1995; Kellner 1995).

In broad terms, cyberpunk dealt with the impact of technology, particularly networks of computers, **virtual reality** (VR) and biotechnology, on the nature of human existence. It dealt with the nature and essence of humanity in a future in which the use of VR and the ability to extensively change and modify one's own body allowed individuals to constantly re-invent themselves and to avoid dealing with the 'real' world if they did not want to. In *Neuromancer*, a largely urbanized world exists in physical space while its information flows and data are reproduced in **cyberspace** (a term coined by Gibson) – a VR representation of a vast city which is perhaps best described as a totally immersive version of the Internet. Individuals can exist solely in this space, and even continue to exist after their physical death as what Gibson referred to as 'constructs'. Computer code can itself take on an **agent**-like form and act as an intelligent, self-reliant entity. The barriers between human, software representation and reconstruction of human, and humanlike machine are undermined in Gibson's world. In this extract, the main character of *Neuromancer*, Case, talks with the construct (software version) of his dead associate, Dix:

> It was exactly the sensation of someone reading over his shoulder.
> He coughed. 'Dix? McCoy? That you man?' His throat was tight.
> 'Hey Bro', said a directionless voice.
> 'It's Case, man. Remember?'
> 'Miami, joeboy, quick study.'
> 'What's the last thing you remember before I spoke to you, Dix?'
> 'Nothin'.'
> 'Hang on.' He disconnected the construct. The presence was gone.
> He reconnected it. 'Dix. Who am I?'
> 'You got me hung, Jack. Who the fuck are you?'
> 'Ca—your buddy. Partner. What's happening man?'
> 'Good question.'
> 'Remember being here, a second ago?'
> 'No.'
>
> (Gibson 1984)

Biological alteration of the 'real' self is another key theme of cyberpunk, its treatment within the genre being exemplified by the film **Blade Runner** (1982), based on Philip K. Dick's pre-cyberpunk novel *Do Androids Dream of Electric Sheep?* The world of *Blade Runner*, designed by the 'visual futurist' for the film, Syd Mead, set the style for the whole cyberpunk genre. It is an extreme version of contemporary urban space, dirty, polluted, dark and dangerous at street level, yet clean and safe for the economic elite who live in skyscrapers far above the streets. The look of the film greatly influenced Gibson, both in its visualization of the future and in the questions about what is 'real' and what it means to be human, when all that we associate with human life can be produced artificially.

In cyberpunk, not only is it possible to avoid dealing with the 'real', it is also desirable. The world is a harsh, dehumanized place, an extreme manifestation of the least desirable trends in our own societies in which corporations are more important than governments and all the anxieties about the information economy and **globalization** have come true. Society has fragmented into a small global elite of super-rich executives and a mass population of marginalized people who, when not being pacified with advanced multimedia that allows them to escape reality, are busy rejecting society altogether and forming into tribes. The later works of Gibson, particularly *Virtual Light* (1993), draw heavily on the work of sociologists like Mike Davies who wrote about the current divisions in Los Angeles in *City of Quartz* (1992). *Virtual Light* even includes a character who is a Japanese sociologist, investigating the fragmenting and increasingly tribal-like social structures among the marginalized populations of a future Los Angeles. The world of Neal Stephenson's novel *Snow Crash* (1992) is an even more extreme vision, where nations like the US have dissolved into smaller units while international corporations, including a semi-legitimate Mafia, run riot. In *Blade Runner*, huge inequality and division is strongly suggested simply by the way everything *looks*.

It is in this element of cyberpunk that the 'punk' becomes apparent, according to commentators like McCaffrey (1991). Just as the English Punk Rock music explosion of the 1970s, with groups like The Damned and the Sex Pistols, 'rejected' existing society, cyberpunk condemns the way in which it thinks the world is heading. McCaffrey argues that authors like Gibson grew up surrounded both by technology and by counterculture, and in a sense, cyberpunk represents a synthesis of these two influences. The comparison is valid in some senses, but perhaps limited in others, cyberpunk arguably verging on being an intellectual critique of contemporary society at its best, whereas The Damned never really got beyond *Smash it Up* (1979).

Nevertheless, it is the case that cyberpunk has produced something like a social and economic criticism of trends like globalization. The anxieties about the future that feature in cyberpunk are quite different to those of earlier science fiction, because its concerns are more complex and linked to real, recognizable trends. In this sense, cyberpunk does represent something different to the 'Martians equal Communists' simplicities of 1950s US science fiction, or the love/fear relationship with technology found in films like the *Terminator* and its two sequels.

Cyberpunk is generally viewed as having been a short-lived phenomenon which created a context in which new forms of science fiction, fiction and postmodern films could develop. This is perhaps something of an exaggeration, as many current **games**, for example, are highly influenced by the look of *Blade Runner* and by the dystopian world portrayed by authors like Gibson. Recent films, such as *The Matrix*, *The Matrix Reloaded* and *Existenz*, are cyberpunk-like in terms of their plots, which are concerned with the barrier between the 'virtual' and the 'real', and with what it means to be human when the human can exist virtually, in a modified form, or be replicated in **artificial life (A-Life)**. However, it is important not to exaggerate the extent to which popular science fiction explores these themes in depth: a film like *The Matrix*, for example, while superficially dealing with 'what is real', is perhaps as much an excuse for wearing cool black outfits, performing Hong Kong-style martial arts and shooting lots of people as it is an exploration of our place in the near future.

Gibson continues to work on the same themes in more recent novels like *Idoru* (1996) and *All Tomorrow's Parties* (1999).

See also: **Body**, **Cyborg**, **Otaku**

Further sources: McCaffrey (1991), Stephenson (1992), Gibson (1984, 1993, 1996, 1999), Kellner (1995), Burrows (1995), Bukatman (1997)

CYBERSPACE

Cyberspace is a term used to describe the space created through the confluence of electronic communications networks such as the **Internet** which enables **computer mediated communication (CMC)** between any number of people who may be geographically dispersed around the globe. It is a public space (see **public sphere**) where individuals can meet, exchange ideas, share information, provide social support, conduct business, create artistic media, play simulation games or engage in political discussion. Such human interaction does not require a shared physical or bodily co-presence, but is rather characterized by the interconnection of millions of people throughout the world communicating by **email**, **Usenet** newsgroups, **bulletin board systems**, and **chat rooms**.

The term 'cyberspace' was first coined by the writer William Gibson in his novel *Neuromancer*, where he described it as 'a consensual hallucination ... A graphic representation of data abstracted from the bank of every computer in the human system. Unthinkable complexity. Lines of light ranged in the nonspace of the mind, clusters and constellations of data. Like city lights receding' (1984: 51). The origins and use of the concept within this **cyberpunk** literature have been further elaborated and developed by a range of Internet enthusiasts such as Howard Rheingold and **cyberlibertarians** like John Perry Barlow, and the term has now entered into common parlance.

In the hands of John Perry Barlow, who popularized Gibson's term, it came to denote the emergence of an alternative virtual world, an **electronic frontier** (Sterling 1994: 247). In this conception, 'Barlovian Cyberspace' becomes something qualitatively more than a network of computer-linked telephony. The matrix itself gives form to a virtual space behind the computer screen where physical presence is replaced by incorporeal relationships which take place increasingly in computer-simulated environments. Thus Barlow claims that what cyberspace heralds is nothing less than 'the promise of a new social space, global and antisovereign, within which anybody, anywhere can express to the rest of humanity whatever he or she believes without fear. There is in these new media a foreshadowing of the intellectual and economic liberty that might undo all the authoritarian powers on earth' (Barlow 1996a).

This anti-state perspective is particularly pronounced in Barlovian cyberspace. He asserts that 'the internet is too widespread to be easily dominated by any single government. By creating a seamless global-economic zone, borderless and unregulatable, the internet calls into question the very idea of a nation-state' (Barlow 1996a). In this new virtual world, politics is replaced by self-policing, using such activity as **flaming**, placing greater emphasis upon parental control, mutual self-help through **virtual communities** and the emancipation of the national subject by people choosing their own identities.

In his 'declaration of the independence of cyberspace', Barlow (1996b) goes on to suggest a possible fusion of the physical body and mind with the virtual spaces created through the computer network. Thus cyberspace becomes a domain which will eventually replace the politics of the flesh, sovereignty, military force and national boundaries. Barlow thereby proclaims to the old order that 'our identities have no bodies, so, unlike you, we cannot obtain order by coercion. We believe that from ethics, enlightened self-interest, and the commonweal, our governance will emerge.'

Such futuristic depictions of cyberspace continue to have a powerful hold on the popular imagination. This is often emboldened by developments in **virtual reality**, CMC and nanotechnologies. They have, however, also been a source of criticism for mystifying CMC and thereby contributing to a more general misunderstanding of the relationship between **ICTs** and global restructuring (Brook and Boal 1995; Robins 1995; Bennahum 1996). The very discourse of those proselytizing about cyberspace can often be mistaken for a kind of exhortation to enter an alternative reality freed from the encumbrances of a decaying and discredited late modernist society (Rheingold 1991). Such linguistic reverberation between future and present often makes it difficult to distinguish between what is being claimed for current behavioural practice and what is prophesy for a future as yet unrealized. Such ambiguity demands further attempts at clarification.

In the first place, cyberspace is frequently portrayed as a kind of homogenous virtual public or common space. But this is surely to cloak the multifarious usages of ICTs. More accurately, cyberspace should perhaps be regarded as a collection of different multimedia technologies and networks which, while they may be held together by the standard computing protocol (**TCP/IP**), do not necessarily imply that visitors to cyberspace can access all of its domains. Thus while some usages of the **Internet**, such as encrypted person-to-person **email**, invited **IRC** or video conferencing, and password protected **FTP** or World Wide Web sites may be relatively private, others such as email-based distribution lists, **Usenet** groups and WWW pages are more public in orientation (Bennahum 1996).

Moreover, since it is a defining feature of cyberspace that it is a global facility accessible to many millions of people from different countries, it is important to be clear about both the degree to which the Internet may act to homogenize the world's historic cultures and the desirability of doing so. Herbert Schiller (1989), for example, has alluded to the US government's possible role in colonizing global culture through the **Global Information Infrastructure (GII)**.

A further weakness of the Barlovian formulation of cyberspace is the notion that it comprises a virtual reality which is somehow alternative and unrelated to the 'real' world. Yet such an understanding is surely to ignore the fact that the very technologies enabling 'virtuality' have been developed for military, educational, public and – increasingly – commercial use. The Internet itself was the product of the United States's desire to build a military communications system which would be secure from terrorist and nuclear attack. As a research and civilian communications network it continued to be funded directly by the US government through the National Science Foundation until April 1995 and, although now privately operated, it continues to be indirectly funded by public finance. The origins, development and cooperative ethos of cyberspace are therefore directly related to the real world of government policy-making and public expenditure.

Finally, it is necessary to address Barlow's assertion that a world is being created 'that all may enter without privilege or prejudice accorded by race, economic power, military force, or station of birth' (Barlow 1996b). Again, such sweeping assertions surely need to be embedded within the social context of **access** to the Internet. Current data suggests that usage of the Internet is limited to a relatively small percentage of the world's population, and that the majority of users probably come from affluent countries and tend to have professional backgrounds. The degree to which a wider range of people may become 'wired' is likely to be heavily dependent upon public policy-making and corporate planning, which seems to invoke the role of politics in the development of cyberspace.

See also: **Access**, **Cyberpunk**, **Globalization**

Further sources: Gibson (1984), Rheingold (1994), Barlow (1996a, 1996b), Featherstone and Burrows (1996), Loader (1997)

CYBORG

The word cyborg is short for 'cybernetic organism', signalling a hybrid of organic life with cybertechnology. Drawn from the science of space travel in the 1950s, the first-named cyborg was a white laboratory rat fitted with an osmotic pump (Haraway 1995). Much early cyborg research was concerned with equipping animal and human subjects for the demands of space travel; this then was broadened to consider other applications, principally in the military field (Gray 1997). But the cyborg as we currently understand it has a second life story beyond space and war research, although forever ghosted by that context: the cyborg is a product of popular culture, too. Probably the most ready associations of the cyborg come from science fiction, from films like *The Terminator* and *Robocop* and comics like *Captain America* and *The X-Men* (Oehlert 2000). These twin beginnings make the cyborg a powerful yet problematic form of cybercultural body. This status is best captured by American theorist Donna Haraway, whose essay 'A Cyborg Manifesto', first published in the mid-1980s, remains the most significant discussion of the many forms and uses of the cyborg:

> A cyborg is a cybernetic organism, a hybrid of machine and organism, a creature of social reality as well as a creature of science fiction ... [W]e are all chimeras, theorized and fabricated hybrids of machine and organism. In short, we are all cyborgs.
>
> (Haraway 2000: 291–2)

In this dense yet playful articulation, Haraway seeks to explore the ways we have imagined and created cyborgs, to expand our ways of thinking about the **prostheticization** of the body in cyberculture, the comings together of nature and technology. The cruical question Haraway asks is: What are we to make of the cyborgs we have made?

For Haraway, the cyborg is a troubling boundary figure, irreducible to either organism or machine, existing in between some of the most symbolic binaries of modern thought – human/machine, human/animal, nature/technology. In a multilayered formulation, the cyborg resists either/or status, straddling these binary oppositions by being neither/both. A further binary erected in some cyborg theory is also resisted: the binary between science as social reality and science fiction – the cyborg inhabits both worlds simultaneously, our knowledge, experience and imagining of it oscillating between its multiple sites:

> From one perspective, a cyborg world is about the final imposition of a grid of control on the planet, about the final abstraction embodied in a Star Wars apocalypse waged in the name of defense, about the final appropriation of women's bodies in a masculinist orgy of war.... From another perspective, a cyborg world might be about lived social and bodily realities in which people are not afraid of their joint

> kinship with animals and machines, not afraid of permanently
> partial identities and contradictory standpoints.
>
> (Haraway 2000: 295)

Let us unpack this formulation: the first version of the 'cyborg world' that Haraway describes is one familiar from dystopian sci-fi imaginings, emblematized by the narrative of the *Terminator* films. Here, the cyborg is a military–industrial creature, a servant of war. Haraway is acutely conscious of the dangers posed by this kind of cyborgization, of producing new monsters in the service of destruction and domination. Moreover, from the feminist perspective at the heart of 'A Cyborg Manifesto', the gendering of the cyborg as a hardened, masculine war machine can be seen to be particularly problematic. To offset this – but without forgetting it – Haraway juxtaposes a second formulation, stressing the productive possibilities that the figure might offer. Rather than fearing or rejecting the cyborg as inevitably a war machine, Haraway is keen to look for alternatives, to explore the other kinds of cultural work that the cyborg does (or could do). This means looking for other kinds of cyborgs, other places where we might meet cyborgs, and other ways of thinking about cyborgs. Seeing the cyborg as a troubling boundary dweller, a trickster that refuses to be pinned down, suggests a way forward. In this sense, welcoming the cyborg into our 'family' encourages us to recast our relationship to technology, and to join the cyborg in refusing the straitjacket of binary thinking. This is captured in the slogan 'Cyborgs for Earthly Survival!' which Haraway meditates on in another essay (Haraway 1995). As a deconstructive strategy, then, this kind of cyborg thinking takes us into new territories, and offers us the chance for fresh encounters with proliferating cybernetic organisms across diverse domains.

The heat generated by Haraway's manifesto has moved in multiple directions, too. Many of the most important essays are collected together in *The Cyborg Handbook* (Gray 1995), where the full roll-call of cyborgs is mapped and dissected. Gray introduces a four-fold taxonomy of cyborgs, dividing their attributes into (1) restorative, (2) normalizing, (3) reconfiguring and (4) enhancing. In the first two forms, the cyborging intervention is corrective, as in the use of artificial limbs or organs, while the last two produce new forms, such as artificial life or the 'superhuman' space-race cyborg. This classification brings us back to a point made by Haraway, and worked over by scholars ever since: we are all cyborgs. While it runs in contradiction to Haraway's refusal of 'origin stories' of the cyborg, the question of how to define who/what is/isn't a cyborg has attracted a lot of attention. At its broadest, it might be argued that all of human existence has been about cyborgization, since the things routinely (if problematically) taken to distinguish humans from animals – use of language, tools, etc – are all readable as prosthetic enhancements. Certainly, in an age when technology has penetrated so many spheres of all our lives, our lives have been transformed in complex and uneven ways. David Hess (1995) discusses this, arguing that most members of urban societies, at least, can be thought of as 'low-tech cyborgs'.

In a different take on the question, Robert Wilson (1995) suggests that experience is central to answering this question: we are cyborgs only to the extent that we see ourselves as cyborgs, or experience what he names 'prosthetic consciousness'. But this is in itself a paradoxical experience, since the moment of epiphany can usher in an inner struggle to separate the human from the nonhuman – a scenario played out vividly in the movie *Robocop*, where the reawakening of the human side of Robocop leads to a desire to reject cyborgization. Patients fitted with artificial or non-human medical prostheses also commonly experience a similar sensation as they attempt to incorporate the alien into their sense of self. This dilemma echoes perfectly with Haraway's discussion of the cyborg as neither/both, although its outcome at the level of experience might not be so productive while humans continue to hold so tightly to binary thinking. In popular culture, very similar themes have been explored in the **cyberpunk** genre and, most famously, in the film *Blade Runner*.

At the collective level, moreover, the cyborg has been seen as the harbinger of some kind of crisis. In an essay exploring the occurrence of different forms of cyborg throughout history, Jennifer Gonzalez (2000) suggests that hybrids appear when an ontological paradigm shift occurs: when our ways of categorizing the world can no longer hold, strange new beasts emerge to help us move forward. From this perspective, then, our current experiences and imaginings of the cyborg evidence just such a paradigm shift, and it is our job to ensure that the outcome is productive rather than destructive for all concerned – both human and non-human.

Haraway's work on the cyborg has incredible resonances, then, and has spawned its own bastard offspring. It has also attracted its critics, too – some of whom doubt the practical applicability of its call to re-imagine the cyborg (see Squires 2000). Such criticism is, of course, a valuable part of the ongoing lifestory of the cyborg in theory and in practice. Continuing to think and talk about cyborgs from diverse – often contradictory – perspectives is very much in the spirit of the figure itself.

See also: **Blade Runner**, **Body**, **Cyberpunk**, **Prosthetics**

Further sources: Gray (1995), Haraway (2000)

DATABASE

A database is a software system for storing, ordering and retrieving sets of data. In a commercialized and computerized culture such as ours, increasing amounts of personal data are collected, analysed and utilized by corporations, governments and other bodies concerned with better understanding, predicting and exploiting (and some would argue controlling) the behaviour of target populations. In order to theorize the status of the database today, we can turn to Mark Poster's (1995) conceptualization of databases as discourse, which draws on post-structuralist theories of language and identity. A discourse is a body of expert knowledge that both describes and defines its subject. Discourses produce certain subject positions and naturalize them – in an effort to facilitate the domination of the subject. Poster uses the work of French theorist Michel Foucault to think through the function of databases in society. Foucault wrote about systems of surveillance – most notably the prison architecture known as the Panopticon – and about the impacts of surveillance on people (see Bell 2001), and Poster neatly extends Foucault's ideas to consider the ways in which databases produce certain kinds of subject.

As a result of the digitization and virtualization of more and more activities of everyday life for increasing numbers of people – shopping, banking, working – databases can be compiled with ever more detail, building up distinct profiles of our habits, values and tastes. In this way, our personal data become components of our social identities, redefining and reconstituting who we are in terms of the databases' uses. In contrast to the disciplinary regimes Foucault investigated (prison, school, hospital), Poster argues that a distinctive feature of database surveillance is that we willingly submit to it, providing the information necessary through our credit card purchases, loyalty cards, phone banking, web searches and so on. We do not, however, necessarily concur with the uses made of our data, which is often sold on to other agencies. Poster here notes that we live in a climate of increasing 'database anxiety', aware of the fact that we are lodged in countless databases, and that the data we surrender can be put to all kinds of future uses. At the level of social control, databases provide governments with raw materials for policy formulations, and Poster argues that the aim of policy is to produce stability in the population (drawing again on Foucault, this time via his notion of governmentality). And in the commercial environment, databases are bought and sold in an effort to capitalize on identifiable target markets. In the UK, the Data Protection Act marks an attempt to protect some of the rights of individuals who are increasingly reduced to data.

Further sources: Bell (2001), Poster (1995)

DEFINITION TELEVISION *see* Digital television

DENIAL OF SERVICE (DOS) OR DISTRIBUTED DENIAL OF SERVICE (DDOS)

Denials of service are **'hacker'** attacks designed to overwhelm a web server or otherwise render a website inaccessible to users. These attacks include automated, sustained rapid accesses or other techniques that exploit TCP/IP implementation bugs or specification flaws. DOS attacks are often launched from dummy accounts that have been anonymously acquired for this purpose; large corporate websites such as CNN.com, Buy.com, e-Trade, MSN.com, e-Bay and amazon.com have been targets of such attacks.

See also: **Cybercrime**, **Hacker**

DIGERATI

The term 'digerati' refers to the small group of largely self-proclaimed cyber-elite leaders who are influencing the communications revolution. Originally associated with computer **geeks** from Silicon Valley, it has tended to broaden as a term to include a wider range of digital visionaries. These include such notables as Bill Gates, John Perry Barlow, Sherry Turkle and Howard Rheingold.

DIGITAL ART

At its most basic, the term 'digital art' refers to the use of digital technology, such as computers, to produce or exhibit art forms, whether written, visual, aural – or, as is increasingly the case, in multimedia hybrid forms. Beyond this basic definition, however, lies considerable debate. Does digital art have its own aesthetics? What features differentiate digital from analog art, other than the medium of expression? Is writing on a word processor or showing digital photos on a website any different from pounding on a typewriter or putting your snaps in a gallery or a photo album? These are questions for those who make digital art, and for those who consume it. A good example comes in the form of digital photography. Now we live in an age of digital image manipulation, has that transformed the role of the photographer and the way we look at photographs? Some critics argue that we are now in a postphotographic age, since all the old assumptions about photography somehow capturing the 'truth' have been demolished by digital trickery. Digital images are open to endless manipulation, which means that digital art is never finished – it is always in progress. Some artists exploit this feature of digital art, allowing their work to evolve and mutate, and even inviting its consumers to join in to help with the process of change. In fact, the dissolution of the boundary between art's producers and its consumers is another key feature of the digital art world. As an extension of the democratic imperatives of the Internet, for example, the possibilities for participating in Net art offer anyone with access the chance to be an artist. And new media technologies bring techniques within easy reach – we can make music on our laptops, shoot videos through webcams, draw pictures with Paintbox. And we can show off our work all around the world, without the old-fashioned infrastructure of galleries or radio stations or cinemas. Entire new forms of art, such as ASCII art, have grown up around computers, and the imaginative uses to which new media technologies have been put can be truly astounding. Indeed, as Murphie and Potts (2003) suggest, this proliferation of ever more diverse art forms is one of digital art's defining characteristics. The old analog labels we have used to describe different art works – painting, poem, pop song – have dissolved into one another, just as digital technology has spawned new techniques and environments to make and show art: virtual reality programs, mp3s, multimedia DVDs and so on. So, while it may be true that in some cases the 'digital' in digital art is indiscernible, in that we can't always tell if an art work is really made of code or not, this rapid diversification asks whether the 'art' in digital art can be discerned, especially with pre-digital referents. Digital art thus requires careful redefinition.

Further sources: Murphie and Potts (2003), Wilson (2003)

DIGITAL CITY

This is a concept used to describe an online (usually web-based) representation and corresponding set of applications and services based on an existing city (as opposed to a **MOO**, **MUD** or other environment that may employ a 'city' metaphor yet is not associated with an actual geographic city). Amsterdam's Digital City (De Digital Stad, or DDS) – now commercially run – was the first to use the expression 'Digital City' to describe itself. Now other digital cities exist for other cities of the world: Shanghai, Kyoto, Paris, Helsinki, for example. Digital cities, like community networks, have ambitious goals, as they seek to approximate or augment a broad range of 'city' services and encounters. No precise definition exists for a digital city. Digital cities often focus on a representation that bears a physical resemblance to the city (DDS is a major exception). Thus Digital City Kyoto (http://www.digitalcity.gr.jp/index-final.html) features a '2D' city 'walk-through' capability in which users can navigate through photographic representations of various locations in Kyoto. Community networks, on the other hand, rely less on physical verisimilitude with the city and focus more on relationships and connections between the city's residents and services. Questions as to 'ownership' of the digital city are now beginning to be asked: is a digital city a commercial enterprise, a government service, a 'third place' for anybody that wants to be there, or some other hybrid. Several commercial digital cities, including http://www.digitalcity.com/ and http://www.neighborhoodlink.com/public/, now exist. Toru Ishida of Kyoto University has convened several workshops on this topic.

Further sources: Ishida and Isbister (2000), Tanabe *et al.* (2002)

DIGITAL COMMONS

An increasing number of researchers and activists are beginning to identify a conceptual common ground (no pun intended) upon which to form coalitions and leverage their thinking and acting. While traditional commons are physical, such as those related to air, water or land, many nowadays are more abstract realms like information and markets. Knowledge, for example, about drugs whose research and development costs had been borne by taxpayers, has been privatized and sold at a profit. This can result in health catastrophes in developing countries when people cannot afford the drugs originating from the once-public knowledge. A key part of this current effort involves the creation and sustaining of communication 'spaces' in which people can play some role. In the fertile digital environment, a large number of 'digital commons' efforts are being created, many by people who are not aware of the philosophical and political disputes that are surrounding them.

Much of the intellectual support for 'enclosures' or the privatization of commons is based on Garrett Hardin's famous essay 'The Tragedy of the Commons' (1968), which describes how a scarce resource which was open to all was destroyed through neglect and overuse. Elinor Ostrom (1991), on the other hand, has described a great number of commons that have been preserved through various mechanisms, showing that the 'tragedy' of the commons is not an inexorable process that people are unable to prevent.

Further sources: Bollier (2002a, 2002b), Hardin (1968), Ostrom (1991)

DIGITAL DEMOCRACY *see* **Electronic democracy**

DIGITAL DIVIDE

'Digital divide' is a term which refers to the existence of a division between people who have **access** to the **Internet** and those who do not. The digital divide is a major cause for concern both within societies and between different countries and global regions. In the United States, one of the richest nations on earth, there continues to be a persistent social cleavage between the information haves (mainly whites, Asians, Pacific Islanders, those on higher incomes, those more educated and dual parent households) and the information have-nots (largely those who are younger, those with lower income and educational levels, certain minority groups and those who live in rural areas or city centres). This social picture of Internet access is mirrored in European and other economically developed countries. For many poorer countries in the southern hemisphere, however, the extent of online access is even more limited. As the information-rich around the world continue to take advantage of the benefits offered by the new **information and communications technologies**, there is a perceived danger that the divisions will widen still further and lead to greater inequalities between countries, regions and communities.

National policies to tackle the digital divide have largely taken two forms. The first has been policy directives to develop national infrastructures and networks to enable greater access to the Internet. This has involved attempts by governments to negotiate with commercial and civil providers collaboratively to agree the development of advanced electronic networks providing wider access, through more attractive pricing and universal service policies. In the United States one of the primary goals of the Clinton Administration was the development of a **National Information Infrastructure** (NII), or as Vice President Al Gore famously described it, an *Information Superhighway*, which was intended ultimately to provide every American with affordable Internet access in their homes. More recently the Bush Administration has signalled its determination to increase the take-up of **broadband** access (in a Keynote Luncheon Speech by Assistant Secretary Nancy J. Victory to the European Institute Seminar, on 'U.S. and European Approaches to the Future of Broadband', Washington D.C., 19 June 2002).

These policies have only partially addressed the digital divide challenge in developed countries and have therefore been supplemented by the use of community access centres. These initiatives are distinct from the public access to the Internet available through commercial **cybercafés**. In the UK, for example, the **Office of the e-Envoy** is committed to give all its citizens access to the Internet through a national network of UK Online Centres (www.e-envoy.gov.uk). There is less government support in America, where community access is offered through a range of **community technology centers** and other **community networking** initiatives. The intention behind these policies is to enable more disadvantaged groups in society (such as those on lower incomes, the unemployed, educational underachievers and some minority groups) to use such centres for access to computers, training and opportunities associated with online connectivity.

Internationally the digital divide has focused discussion around achieving parity between advanced countries and developing countries. The issue was prominent at the G8 Summit in Japan in 2000, where discussions led to the formation of the Digital Opportunity Task Force (DOT Force) (www.dotforce.org/) later the same year. DOT Force comprised representatives from the G8 and developing country governments, private and not-for-profit sectors and international organizations. In its report *Digital Opportunities for All*, presented to the G8 Summit in Kananaskis, Canada, in June 2002, DOT Force claimed to have 'focused global attention on sustainable, ICT-enabled development, and has encouraged the international development community to mainstream ICTs in its bilateral and multilateral assistance programs'.

See also: **Access**

Further sources: Loader (1998), NTIA (1999), Castells (1996)

DIGITAL LIBRARY

A digital library is a conscious attempt to collect and distribute a large amount of organized information to a large number of patrons using the **Internet**. Some of this information is that found traditionally in non-digital libraries, while some is novel and interactive. Universities, libraries, hospitals and museums are now players in the development of this concept. Commercial search engines (which are subject to a number of constraints that potentially limit their usefulness) currently represent the primary method through which users locate relevant web pages on the Internet. The proprietary nature of commercial search engine weighing criteria tends to retard trends to standardize public indexing systems while, at the same time, making it difficult for website developers to modify their pages to garner artificially high relevance ratings. Major US NSF-funded digital library design is currently being conducted at University of California at Berkeley, Stanford University and several other centres.

Further sources: Williams (2000)

DIGITAL SIGNATURE

A digital signature is specially encoded data that is attached to a given message to uniquely identify the sender. This capability fulfils the same function as a written signature: it guarantees that the 'signer' of the message is in actuality the person represented by the 'signature'.

DIGITAL TELEVISION

Digital television is a means of transmitting high-definition television images, and additional data alongside those images. In both the UK and US, governments have set a timetable for the expansion of digital services, with the UK expecting to cease analogue transmission within 10 years or so of the time of writing. Much more information can be carried via digital transmission than is the case for analogue transmission. The most obvious effect is that high-quality 16:9 ratio images (rectangular in shape), referred to as High Definition TV (HDTV) in the US and simply as 'Widescreen' in the UK, can be transmitted. This allows feature films to be shown in their original format and creates television images that are better suited to our field of vision than the traditional '4:3' ('square') television image. The second most obvious effect is that far more channels can be carried. In Britain, a digital satellite subscriber now has access to hundreds of channels.

In the UK, the British Broadcasting Corporation has already produced interactive documentaries on its digital services, with a choice of commentaries and what is perhaps best described as an accompanying interactive 'website' of images, text and video. Digital services also offer interactive news 'on demand', with digital viewers able to summon text versions of stories, video bulletins of the headlines and other interactive features through their TV remote control unit. This capacity to send data, sometimes called 'data broadcasting' or 'enhanced television' in the United States, creates the opportunity for much denser and more interactive services. This has implications for entertainment, but also for **e-commerce** and **e-government**, as digital television can clearly function as a medium for electronic service delivery. Some British social landlords (providers of housing for low-income families and individuals), for example, are already planning to provide facilities for their tenants to order repairs or pay the rent via interactive digital television. Equally, some British banks are now providing customer services through interactive digital television. The potential of digital TV in this regard is made all the greater by its capacity to transmit large amounts of data comparatively quickly: a US DTV channel, for example, is able to transmit an application of the same size as Microsoft's 'Word' in under five seconds.

The interrelationship between digital television and the Internet will be interesting to watch develop. Digital television offers simplicity, familiarity (in the sense of being an extension of a much-used technology, rather than something new) and high bandwidth. It has the capacity to provide a huge range of entertainment functions, and at least some of the e-commerce and e-government functions that are envisaged for the Internet. The **convergence** of digital technologies and the movement towards computing facilities as integral parts of home entertainment systems may also be important in determining how digital television is used.

See also: **Convergence**

DIGITAL VILLAGE *see* Community informatics

DISABILITY/DISABLED PEOPLE *see* Usability, Virtual social support

DISINFORMATION

Disinformation is false or deceptive information which is deliberately intended to mislead the reader. It is often associated with forms of propaganda which are systematically organized to publicize a particular doctrine or perspective to the detriment of others. With the advent of the **Internet**, a great deal of discussion has emerged about the role of disinformation in the development and practice of cybercultures. Since new **information and communications technologies (ICTs)** enable anyone anywhere (at least in principle – see **digital divide**) to become an information producer, it raises the question about the validation of much information made available in **cyberspace**. How are we to know that information on, for example, health, politics, finance or the environment can be trusted as emanating from reliable sources?

Conversely the many-to-many cross-global **computer mediated communication** available through the Internet also raises questions about its potential to challenge disinformation. Sophisticated, organized commercial or state publicity campaigns can be questioned online, and alternative research and experiences can be posted as counter-claims. At times of national security or even military conflict, disinformation becomes not only a central component for shaping public opinion but also a potential smokescreen for military and political objectives which citizens may not wish to support. The Internet may be one of the few remaining public spaces where citizens, participants or activists can provide alternative perspectives, deliberations and evidence. Many new social movements have also developed websites aimed at providing counterfactual information to the claims of specific corporations.

The use of disinformation has always been an aspect of social, economic and political life. Yet in an information society where our life experiences and opportunities are increasingly becoming influenced by our ability to **access**, validate, manipulate and assess information for life choices, the role of disinformation may become even more important.

See also: **New cultural politics**

DISTANCE EDUCATION

The term 'distance education' refers to the use of advanced electronic networks, such as the expanding range of **wireless** media and high speed **Internet** and **Web** applications to deliver educational services to the household, workplace or other locations remote from the instructor. The potential of flexible educational delivery may have profound consequences for education provision. In some instances it is suggested that, as in examples of business re-engineering using **ICTs**, education may become radically restructured. Institutions such as schools and universities may be reinvented in preparation for a knowledge economy and learning processes may be transformed through computerized distance learning packages.

Distance education has a long history associated with the provision of education in 'off-site' locations, away from schools and university campuses. These might be delivered in isolated rural areas or at 'unsociable' hours of the day. In higher education the UK's Open University, for example, has for many years operated from a central facility where groups of academics produce a variety of print and media materials, in collaboration with expert media developers such as the BBC, for remote students to use. The emergence of new ICTs and their adoption for distance education has led to the creation of new virtual universities such as the Open University of Catalonia, Jones International University and the Canadian Virtual University. In this model the notion of face-to-face classroom teaching is replaced by online communication between students and teachers using electronic forums, websites and individualized tutorial systems.

However, even in traditional institutional settings many of the same courseware applications are being adopted by teachers and lecturers. **Access** to the Internet and Web enable pupils and students to consult class readings, lecture notes, additional information and class discussion forums, and to contact teachers through **email**. Consequently the impact of ICTs on education may act to blur earlier distinctions between distance education and classroom-based education. The Internet has illustrated the exciting prospect of students accessing information which would previously have been difficult, if not impossible. Search and downloading facilities from electronic sources and the use of online catalogues for locating library books are becoming commonplace in the developed world. This information is also being complemented by other educational media. The 1997 landing of the Pathfinder mission to Mars, for example, enabled millions of people worldwide to view images on the Internet relayed from the Sojourn rover to the Jet Propulsion Laboratory in California. In principle, real-time images can be webcast from almost any location using **webcams**, and used as learning resources. Similarly, lectures can be webcast or uploaded to a website.

Further sources: Cornford and Pollock (2003), Dutton and Loader (2002)

DOMAIN NAME

The form by which 'addresses' appear on the Internet is known as the domain name. It offers a simple name for each web address, rather than having to use the full (and cumbersome) IP (Internet Protocol) number – the unique 32-bit number that identifies each host computer on the net. Domain names take the form 'www.staffs.ac.uk', where 'www' stands for world wide web, 'staffs' is shorthand for Staffordshire University, 'ac' denotes an academic institution, and 'uk' signifies the site's location. The national identifier is one of the most contentious parts of the domain name, since names registered in the USA do not have to show their country of origin – seen as an example of America's **cultural imperialism** in cyberspace. Equally significant has been debate about the 'ownership' of names and the commercial exploitation of the domain name system. Advocacy groups like the Domain Name Rights Coalition contest this, while the phenomenon of 'cybersquatting' approaches the problem from a different angle. Cybersquatters register domain names which would potentially be desirable to corporations, celebrities and so on, and then charge huge fees to sell or lease them – a practice seen by some as a form of trademark infringement. The domain name system thus raises crucial questions of the ownership of cyberspace, the rights of individuals, freedom of information and capital colonization.

Further sources: Rony and Rony (1998)

DOT FORCE *see* Digital divide

DOT.COM

A company whose major business thrust is related to the Internet is sometimes referred to as a dot.com. The name stems from the Internet address designation that ends in '.com' (spoken 'dot com')

See also e–Commerce

DOWNLOAD

The act of transferring digital information or files from a network to a local computer is known as downloading. For instance, many email systems download messages from the mail server to the user's computer. Viewing a web page necessitates the transfer of **HTML** or image files from the host computer to the computer of the person viewing the site. Downloading a web page will take longer if the site includes the heavy use of graphics, especially where **bandwidth** is limited.

DYNAMIC HTML *see* HTML

E-BUSINESS *see* e–Commerce

E-COMMERCE (ELECTRONIC COMMERCE)

e-Commerce is a generic term used to describe the buying and selling of goods via the Internet and other interactive networks such as **digital television**. Online **dot.com** businesses such as amazon.com, the Internet bookshop, are able to reduce their costs considerably because they use computerized web-based ordering and the national postal service, rather than retail premises which have to be rented and staffed, as a means of selling to the public. These savings are passed on to the public through reduced prices. In addition, such companies are not restricted by the size of retail outlets, using warehouses to store a much wider range of products than is available in even the largest traditional retailers. Another example of e-commerce is the British company lastminute.com, a wholly web-based travel agent specializing in last-minute holiday deals and cheap flights. Some financial services such as those offered by egg.com in Britain are wholly Internet-based, while Internet **access** to conventional banking services and ordinary accounts has become widespread. The use of web-based consumer services is sometimes referred to as electronic service delivery, and business models of electronic service delivery have been widely adopted by governments as providing a new way to provide public services, forming the basis of **e-government** policies across the economically developed world.

The advantages of e-commerce are obvious. Growth in the sector was initially limited by a lack of consumer confidence that credit card details and other information supplied to a seller would be secure (see **cybercrime** and **encryption**), and in the UK by restricted **bandwidth** for home Internet access. However, by Christmas 2002, UK shoppers buying gifts online spent £1 billion ($1.6 billion), while online sales in the US during July to September period of 2002 were more than $11bn, representing 1.3 per cent of total US retail sales (www.imrg.org/).

The 'dot.com' sector initially benefited from what can be characterized as a kind of 'gold rush' mentality among venture capitalists and investors. Start up dot.com companies were valued at millions of dollars in the US and millions of pounds in the UK. Yet, while e-commerce quite quickly reached the point at which sales were significant in both countries, the explosion of e-commerce as a form of exchange that would start to eclipse shops did not materialize. Confidence collapsed, and took quite a lot of dot.coms of questionable viability with it.

Yet, although even major players like amazon.com are anticipated to lose money for the foreseeable future (although in fact amazon recently started making an operating profit), many analysts remain confident that e-commerce will become a very important mechanism for selling goods and services. Concern has been raised in some quarters that the WWW will become dominated by corporations eager to find new and cost-effective means of selling their goods and services. For some commentators the Internet is now viewed primarily as a new means of economic exchange (Leebaert 1999).

For the true convert, though, e-commerce is much more than a new means of buying and selling. Capitalism has always been constrained by logistics, shops can only be of a certain size, only in so many different places and only offering a limited range of goods and services. Electronic commerce is viewed by some as 'capitalism unbound', a potentially perfect marketplace, in which the buyer has access to the whole globe and can use intelligent **agents** to shop around in search of the best possible product for the best possible price. Some envisage that e-commerce will create highly flexible production facilities that will able to tailor products to consumers' wants, using the perfect information about consumer desires that the electronic market will supply them with.

In reality, these ideas about a 'perfect marketplace' are probably unrealistic, as they pay little or no attention to the domination of global markets by transnational corporations and the extent to which capitalism manufactures demand for its products through advertising. Nevertheless, several factors, such as the falling costs of Internet access, the advent of interactive digital television and busy working lives that leave people restricted time for shopping mean that the convenience of being able to order food from a supermarket website and do the Christmas shopping from home will doubtless fuel the growth of e-commerce. In some urban areas, fear of crime on the part of the middle classes may also bolster e-commerce's development.

Most of those who are inspired by e-commerce pay little attention to a range of possibly negative consequences that might result from it. Some people will not be online, or not have a credit card. The exclusion of poorer people from ownership of the necessary technologies is one of the major concerns of theorists like Castells (1996). If someone has access to the Internet, they can already get cheaper books and cheaper flights than someone without access. It is possible that some of the poorest people in society will not only be excluded from employment, but that their economic disadvantage will be further increased by exclusion from the electronic marketplace. This is not just a problem for individuals: entire nations and their industries might be excluded from the e-commerce network, reinforcing the unequal access to world markets that economically developing nations already face and further compounding their position of disadvantage. In addition, if the evangelists of e-commerce are correct, low-paid jobs in the service sector, which provide much of the employment in post-industrial world – the **hypercasualization** that replaced permanent jobs in manufacturing industry – could start to disappear fast, being replaced by electronic service delivery.

See also: **Access, e-Government, Globalization, Hypercasualization**

Further sources: Leebaert (1999), www.ibm.com/ebusiness/, www.amazon.com, www.lastminute.com, www.egg.com/

ELECTRONIC DEMOCRACY (E-DEMOCRACY)

The innovative use of new media to significantly enhance democratic governance by facilitating more direct participation by citizens in the political decision-making arena is known as e-democracy. Utilizing communications technology to promote more effective democratic politics is not entirely new (Becker 1981; Danziger *et al.* 1982), but the more recent potential of the **Internet** to place greater power in the hands of individual citizens *vis-à-vis* their political representatives, institutions of entrenched interest and even the policy decisions of global corporations has led some to suggest that e-democracy offers the prospect of an entirely new democratic paradigm (Becker 1998). Certainly the capabilities of the new technologies have spawned a worldwide variety of experiments and innovations designed to reinvigorate democratic politics. However, the established institutions of power are thus far proving far more resilient to change than would allow us to proclaim the arrival of a new electronic polis.

Some confusion can arise over the different terms used to describe the enormous range of projects and activities which may be characterized as e-democracy. Thus 'digital democracy' (Hague and Loader 1999) and 'cyberdemocracy' are frequently used interchangeably with e-democracy, which is taken here to encompass these derivatives. The notion of 'teledemocracy' precedes e-democracy and relates to earlier experiments conducted with TV technologies. A more important distinction, however, can be made between e-democracy and the related concept of **e-government**. While the former is more focused upon the emergence of new political cultures where technology enables the empowerment of the people (demos), e-government refers to the attempts to use **ICTs** to restructure existing institutions of government. Thus e-democracy developments can be viewed as attempts to challenge the limitations of traditional representative models of government and replace them with alternative repertoires of democratic expression and activity emanating from the citizen. In contrast, many e-government initiatives have been concerned with re-engineering public administrations through improvements in electronic service delivery, organizational change and cost cutting. Although valuable for most situations, not all developments fall neatly into this categorization between e-democracy and e-government, and it is perhaps the outcomes arising from the tensions between these two approaches which will have the most significant impact upon democratic governance in the future.

The reason for the rediscovered enthusiasm for democratic renewal through the use of ICTs is due to a number of related factors. First of these is the widespread dissatisfaction with modern liberal democratic politics, which is being witnessed in most of the mature democratic nations. In Europe and North America, electoral turnouts have been decreasing (the 2000 US Presidential Election and the 2001 UK General Election both produced their lowest turnouts in living memory), party membership has fallen, and disenchantment with politicians, particularly among the young, is a common concern. This dislocation of the political process from the everyday interests of many citizens is further widened in many countries by the decline in ideological political discourse and a related breakdown of class-based political organization.

Second, this disillusionment with the political system has been further reinforced by a perceived weakening of the nation-state's ability to represent the interests of citizens in the face of the emerging forces of **globalization**. For some commentators (Klein 2000; Hertz 2001), political power has shifted from elected politicians and is increasingly in the hands of global corporate executives whose decisions often have direct significance for the life experiences and opportunities of most of the world's populations. Yet governments increasingly seem to be impotent in the face of such corporate power as a consequence of their desire for inward investment. Thus, together with a largely privately owned mass media, nation-states are often regarded as colluding with corporations to satisfy their business interests rather than the interests of their citizens. Issues of child labour practices, environmental damage or threats to human health and welfare are sidelined in the competitive race between governments to provide tax incentives, deregulation policies and diminished employ-ment protection in order to attract corporate investment.

Third, the disenchantment with existing democratic systems and politicians has in part stimulated the emergence of a new political culture based upon **new social movements** (NSMs) and activity loosely formed around universal values and moral principles such as environmentalism, animal rights and a range of human rights issues. Sceptical of current political rhetoric and the will of politicians to tackle these important political issues, activists have rejected traditional highly organized, institutionalized, class-based politics. Instead they have sought democratic expression through NSMs which foreground lifestyle politics and a politics of affinity which reaches beyond nation-state borders.

e-Democracy initiatives may manifest themselves in a variety of forms which may be regarded as reactions to the disillusionment with democratic politics outlined above. For convenience, these may be grouped into campaigning, citizen forums and NSMs.

The new media are increasingly becoming a significant feature of national and local elections. Political parties and candidates are becoming rapidly aware of the potential of the Internet for canvassing voters, fundraising and motivating supporters (Coleman 2000). However, web-based communication technologies have also been used to challenge the 'sound-byte' media campaigns and make candidates more directly responsive to the voice of the electorate. In the USA, for example, websites such DemocracyNet and Red-WhiteandBlue have attempted to provide neutral sites where citizens can obtain information about the candidates and interrogate them on issues which may influence their voting preference. Furthermore, the technology can be used to verify statements made by political candidates and provide almost instantaneous refutations where appropriate. Tactical voting has also been a feature of web-based campaigning, most notably in the USA with the impact of the 'Nader traders'. Several websites emerged during the 2000 US Presidential campaign (e.g. VoteExchange.com, NaderTrader.com and WinWinCampaign.com), which were intended to enable Gore Democrats in 'Republican' states to pair with Nader supporters in swing states. While the practice caused some controversy, this application of the Internet may prove to be far more significant in future campaigns.

As a means to engender the more informed public deliberation so essential to strong democratic politics, electronic forums have been utilized. Again, these 'citizen forums' take many different forms: they have included locality-based citizen forums such as Minnesota E-Democracy and **Public Electronic Network (PEN)** in the USA, UK Citizens Online Democracy and Amsterdam Digital City. In other guises, such forums may be less directly focused upon geographical places and be shaped by common professional interests such as **CPSR** or the **EFF**. For some enthusiasts the new networked structure of the Internet heralds a return to the direct democracy of Ancient Greek city-states. Citizens connected to an electronic forum are able to have informed debates and make decisions online without recourse to the institutions of representative democracy. However, the practicalities of the modern world make it highly unlikely that we will see the early demise of our political representatives as a consequence of the Internet. More important may be the questions raised by such electronic forums and virtual public spaces for improving our existing institutions of democratic governance. For example: Can electronic discussion groups and forums facilitate more informed deliberation amongst the electorate? How can our politicians use such media to get closer to the people they represent? Do electronic forums enable wider participation in decision-making? How could such electronic networks be used for public consultation?

To date there have been several 'experiments' in the use of the new ICTs to facilitate e-democracy. Limited in number, it is also perhaps too early to draw firm conclusions from such experiments about their capacity to renew interest in democracy and bring governments and public services closer to the people. Research by some scholars has challenged the idea that electronic forums foster more deliberative democratic activity. Instead of reasoned argument, a picture emerges either of like-minded people seeking political solace for their views online or of a few dominant voices taking over discussions (Hill and Hughes 1998). Furthermore, the evidence of many civic networks has been a continued apathy on the part of the public who, if they have participated at all, tended not to repeat the experience (van den Besselaar 2001).

The final aspect of e-democracy, considered elsewhere in this volume, is the use of ICTs by **NSMs** and community activists.

See also: **e-Government**, **New cultural politics**, **New social movements**

Further sources: Hague and Loader (1999), Coleman (2000, 2001), Coleman and Gotze (2001), Jenkins and Thorburn (2003), Schuler (1996) especially chapter 4, 'strong democracy'

ELECTRONIC FORUMS *see* **Virtual community**

ELECTRONIC FRONTIER

This is a term commonly used to refer to **cyberspace**, and in particular to Barlovian cyberspace (see **cyberlibertarianism**). As such it conjures up the analogy of the **Internet** as the virgin 'wild west frontier' of nineteenth-century America with its associated character-istics of lawlessness, freedom of identity and individual innovation. For cyberlibertarians such imagery is obviously appealing in their mission to fight state control and depict the Internet as a medium for self-expression and individual liberty. More critical observers are quick to point out that the frontier of the allusion was in fact already inhabited by Native Americans, whose liberties and lifestyles were destroyed by the white invaders, and that the state played an active role in this genocide through its use of military force. None the less the term has gained common currency among members of the **digerati** such that Howard Rheingold (1993) refers to 'homesteading on the electronic frontier' to portray the development of **virtual communities** while Bruce Sterling (1994) considers 'law and disorder on the electronic frontier' in his book *The Hacker Crackdown*.

See also: **Cyberspace**

ELECTRONIC FRONTIER FOUNDATION (EFF)

The EFF is a **cyberlibertarian** organization formed in 1990 by Mitchell Kapor, John Perry Barlow and others to educate the public, policy-makers and courts about issues related to civil liberties and civil responsibilities. The EFF's first project was funding **CPSR**'s computers and privacy project. Since 1991, the EFF has convened an annual Computers, Freedom and Privacy Conference.

See also: **Privacy**

Further sources: www.eff.org

ELECTRONIC GOVERNMENT (E-GOVERNMENT)

e-Government primarily refers to the adoption of **information and communications technologies (ICTs)** as a means of improving the administration and provision of public services. Around the world, numerous countries are proclaiming the revolutionary potential of the new media to enable government organizations and practices to be restructured in order to get closer to their citizens. At the beginning of the twenty-first century e-government is firmly at the top of many policy agendas and there is almost a global competition between nation-states to be the first to 'put their services online'.

Far from being an entirely new notion, however, in many respects e-government can be seen as the latest initiative in a campaign to 'reinvent government' which goes back at least to the 1970s. Consequently e-government proposals are perhaps best understood when considered against a background of dissatisfaction with the institutions of 'big' government and liberal welfare states which characterized many twentieth-century nation-states. Usually this opposition adopts a perspective which regards government as a competitor, hindering the free market in its function as an efficient means of distributing a country's resources and enabling citizens to satisfy their welfare needs (as such, it shares many of the concerns of the **cyberlibertarians**). The public sector is depicted as 'crowding out' the private sector and being unresponsive to the individual preferences of citizens. For many, the remedy has been to 'roll back' the state through deregulation and privatization policies and thereby enable the commercial and voluntary sectors to deliver more services to the citizen. What remains of traditional government should also be reformed by drawing upon structures and cultures developed in the private sector.

Seen within this context, it is not surprising that e-government strategies are heavily dependent upon models and lessons to be learned from commerce. In particular, the restructuring of many private sector service organizations in finance and banking which adopted ICTs to reduce staffing costs and provide online service delivery offers concrete examples of transformed labour-intensive information industries. Throughout the US and Europe, for example, thousands of banks have been closed and replaced by a combination of ATMs, call centres and **telebanking** facilities. Similarly, government institutions and procedures could be re-engineered to produce new network organizational forms which are more cost effective and should also adopt a customer-oriented approach to service delivery. The World Bank, for example, draws directly upon the analogy with **e-commerce** as a model for the development of e-government. Like e-commerce, which allows businesses to transact with each other more efficiently (B2B) and brings customers closer to businesses (B2C), e-government aims to make the interaction between government and citizens (G2C), government and business enterprises (G2B), and interagency relationships (G2G) more friendly, convenient, transparent, and inexpensive. The scope of e-government, therefore, is fairly broad. Its objectives include: the adoption of ICTs for online service delivery; the development of electronic contractual and procurement networks; the enabling of accessibility for clients to government and personal information; and the creation of better organizational and management practices.

For customers, e-government will be characterized by a 24/7/365 electronic service, provided anywhere in the world. Using whatever channels of communication are convenient and easy, clients will be able to access government portals which will seamlessly guide them to the information, department or service they require. They will need to know nothing about the organizational structure or service responsibilities of particular departments in order to have their online demands satisfied. For this customer service objective to be achieved, government information and services need to be integrated and cost effectively packaged in a manner which is relevant to people's everyday experiences. Many countries, for example, are designing government websites and portals around lifestyles and life episodes as a means to cluster departmental public information and services in a user-friendly and meaningful way.

The integration of electronic services across what are often very large and complex public sectors is no easy task and raises some significant challenges. Its attainment can only be realized through the adoption of remodelled technical infrastructure, common protocols for web use, agreed security criteria, data exchange mechanisms, compatible system design and management and new approaches to organizational governance and management. Consequently a great deal of the development of e-government strategies is focused upon the production of the 'seamless back office'. Its implementation will be shaped by attempts to re-engineer the administration, ethos and professional structure of modern government institutions. While the desire to use ICTs both to keep taxation levels down through cost savings and to open up the public sector to commercial opportunities is a strong one, it may be equally matched by counter-desires to defend privacy, democratic accountability, professional autonomy, probity and administrative impartiality.

If the earliest driving force for e-government has been reinventing the government agenda, it has more recently been joined by concern over the growing disillusionment with democratic politics which has been a feature of many countries at the beginning of the millennium. While one can make a strong distinction between the concepts of

e-democracy and e-government, advocates of the latter have begun to include greater participation by people in government as another important aspect of wired government. This is to be achieved through making government information easier to find, publishing key government information online, and providing multiple channels for contact with government. Online service delivery also allows easier feedback on content, quality and satisfaction of public services. The extent to which it may enable greater consultation and discussion over government policy-making, however, remains less well developed in most strategy pronouncements.

The central importance of e-government strategies remains for most countries as an engine for economic development and competitive advantage. First, it provides an opportunity for governments to be supporting the creation of a knowledge or **information society** as the vehicle for future prosperity. Second, with an increasing amount of public information becoming digital, it provides a market opportunity for the private sector to undertake many government data services. Third, it enables an increasing amount of the cost of public service provision to be born by the citizens themselves through online information search and retrieval.

See also: **Cyberlibertarianism**, **e-Democracy**

Further sources: Fountain (2001), Bellamy and Taylor (1998), Heeks (1999), Margetts (1999)

ELECTRONIC PRIVACY INFORMATION CENTER (EPIC)

Established in 1994 by Marc Rotenberg, the Electronic Privacy Information Center is a non-profit-making educational organization. Its mission is to 'focus public attention on emerging civil liberties issues and to protect privacy, the US First Amendment, and US constitutional values'. EPIC is based in the US, but is also active in privacy and civil liberties issues worldwide, primarily through memberships of coalitions such as the Global Internet Liberty Campaign. Although EPIC has historically been involved in issues related to privacy violations by corporations, the US government has provided it and other civil libertarians with an unprecedented range of important challenges, including **Carnivore**, Homeland Security, the

USA PATRIOT ('Uniting and Strengthening America by Providing Appropriate Tools Required to Intercept and Obstruct Terrorism') Act and Total Information Awareness. The recent Homeland Security Act of 2002 created a cabinet-level Department of Homeland Security, and contains provisions that enhance government surveillance power while weakening open government laws (EPIC Alert 9.23). Much of the legislation in this area that has occurred after the 11 September 2001 attacks on the World Trade Center in New York City has been rushed through Congress with a minimum of debate.

A recent EPIC project, 'Observing Surveillance', documents the surge in the number of video cameras placed in Washington DC's public spaces. Although law enforcement authorities claim that video surveillance helps prevent crime and that there is no expectation of privacy in public spaces, EPIC believes that the evidence has shown video surveillance to have limited, if any, effect on crime prevention. EPIC also questions to what degree surveillance impinges upon free speech and freedom of association – especially when it is used to monitor political protests and rallies.

EPIC is involved in a wide range of activities, including legal challenges such as those that result in disclosure of government documents that EPIC has forced the government to reveal under the Freedom of Information Act (FOIA) including information on the FBI's Carnivore Internet Surveillance System, the Clipper Chip, and on Presidential Decision Directive 29 establishing the secretive Security Policy Board. In 2002, EPIC joined with over thirty groups to stop the Total Information Awareness (TIA) programme. TIA is a program of the Defense Advanced Research Program Agency (DARPA) which, critics claim, is unwarranted and unconstitutional (not to say unreliable and Orwellian), and intended to 'detect, classify, identify and track terrorists so that we may understand their plans and act to prevent them from being executed'. The TIA program is run by John Poindexter, former National Security Adviser to Ronald Reagan, who planned the operation to divert funds from Iranian arms sales to Contra rebels in Nicaragua, and who was subsequently convicted of lying to Congress (www.darpa.mil/DARPATech2002/presentations/iao_pdf/slides/PoindexterIAO.pdf).

Further sources: http://www.epic.org

ELECTRONIC SERVICE DELIVERY *see* **e-Commerce, Electronic government**

ELECTRONIC VILLAGE HALL (EVH)

EVH is a term used to describe a variety of centres which utilize computers and information systems for the social, economic, environmental and political development of communities and neighbourhoods. The activities taking place in EVHs can vary from region to region and from country to country. Typically they may include such things as the provision of training in IT skills (introductory computer courses and distance learning packages), technical and business consultancy, facilities for teleworking, tele-communications equipment to facilitate teleconferences, video links and access to teletex or telefax terminals, and rooms for local meetings and conferences. **Access** can also be a distinguishing feature of EVHs, with some tending to be the preserve of particular communities or groups of interest such as women's centres, while others are more open public spaces. Furthermore their physical location can range from purpose-built public amenities to the adoption and re-utilization of existing public buildings. The precise configuration will be deter-mined by local demand, interests, conditions and, above all, the financial and human resources available. But the overriding intention of using new **information and communications technologies (ICTs)** to empower small communities and foster **social capital** is present in nearly all cases.

While the EVH concept was developed in rural Denmark, its potential value was quickly realized throughout the world, which enabled its spread beyond Europe. This has no doubt contributed to the confusion which can sometimes occur when the term 'electronic village hall' is used interchangeably with *telehuse*, telehouse, tele-cottage, telecentre or even Information and Community Service Centre (ICSC). More recently, **cybercafés** also exhibit many of the same mixes of computer technologies and social activities.

Originally conceived as a 'social experiment' in 1983 in the village of Fjaltring, located in the predominantly rural Lemvig Commune in Jutland, the EVH arose as a response to the perceived centralization of economic, social and cultural life in Denmark. By the mid-1980s a number of EVHs were established to protect remote rural commu-nities from being politically and socially marginalized as a consequence of the economic and social restructuring taking place in Northern Europe. Their strategy to enable members of isolated areas to gain access to the resources of the emerging **information society** was strongly influenced by the democratic traditions of community autonomy and self-help associated with the folk high school and cooperative movements of nineteenth-century Denmark. In particular the philosophy of N.F.S. Grundtvig, who based his liberal Christian enlightenment project on the principles of active participation, collective organization, cultural pluralism, social dialogue and popular mass education, is regarded by some to have been influential in driving the Danish social experiments.

By providing a 'social' space, the most successful EVHs have enabled community members to become empowered through a supportive and shared environment. Thus 'informal' education, whereby community members teach each other how to use the technology, has often been a precursor to further educational attainment for those lacking confidence. Furthermore they have often acted as forums for local democratic debate and social and cultural interaction. While the original EVHs perhaps failed to fulfil the high expectations of their founders, many are still in existence and a number of urban neighbourhood EVHs have proved to be more resilient.

Further sources: Cronberg (1992), Qvortrup (1987)

EMAIL (ELECTRONIC MAIL, E-MAIL)

An abbreviation of 'electronic mail', email describes an application that allows one computer user to send a text message to another computer user elsewhere on a network. Within thirty years of its first use, email had become a major means of communication across the United States. Within the UK, the impact of email as a new form of communication has only been exceeded by the very rapid take-up of mobile telephones and the use of text-messaging on those phones (known more widely as cellular phones in the US). More recent mobiles offer both text-messaging and email, and many of the conventions of communication via both mediums are the same (see **cues filtered out** and **smileys**). The term 'email' has entered English as both a noun and a verb.

The first network email was sent by an American scientist, Ray Tomlinson, in 1971. He had written what he referred to as a 'mail program' some time before, which was in fact two programs, one for sending and the other for receiving messages, the first called SNDMSG (an abbreviation of 'Send Message') and the second called READMAIL. However, this early system was only capable of handling messages sent between the various users of an individual machine. Tomlinson had also worked on a experimental file transfer program called CPYNET that could send and receive files through a network and had the idea of combining the file transfer and messaging programs. In late 1971, Tomlinson used this new combined program to send messages between two machines that were next to each other in his lab. Although these machines were next to each other, they were actually connected through ARPANET, the precursor to the Internet, meaning that the first network email had been sent. Tomlinson cannot remember what the message was, but thinks it was just a few random characters, something like 'QWERTyUIOP'. Tomlinson then decided on a means to differentiate between the network addresses of various machines and adopted '@', creating the now universal convention for email addresses.

In combination with other forms of **CMC** like **Usenet**, email has been responsible for changes in the nature of communication and modifications to the use of English. Since email communication is only text-based, visual and aural cues are not available, which has led to the creation of smileys, 'pictures' that express facial expression made up of keyboard symbols. The use of abbreviations has become widespread, one very well known example being 'LOL' (for 'laughing out loud'). Another important change in communication has been the ability email offers recipients of messages to edit those messages, commenting on them line by line and sending back what can perhaps be described as an annotated and amended version of the original communication. There is a large literature on this and other features of CMC through email, Usenet and **Internet Relay Chat**.

EMOTICONS *see* Cues filtered out, Smileys

ENCRYPTION

This is the process of translating (with an encryption algorithm) a readable message into an unreadable one which can be decrypted or deciphered by the message's intended recipient.

EXPERT SYSTEM

An expert system is a **database** system that uses a series of rules, such as 'if' statements, as the basis by which it provides a user with information. For example, an expert system that was used for diagnosing disease would probably use combinations of symptoms as the basis on which to provide data about possible diagnoses. The system would ask which symptoms were present, thereby generating a list of symptoms that it would then test against its database, selecting the data on diagnoses in which all, or most, of the symptoms were listed.

The term 'expert system' implies intelligence where there is none. The computer is not making any deduction about what information might be relevant; it is merely comparing the information it is provided with against the patterns of information in its database. The machine is matching like with like, although it will often be doing so with a degree of speed that no person could approach, and acting as a valuable tool in the process. The flexibility and efficiency of expert systems can be enhanced by using **fuzzy logic**.

Expert systems are quite distinct from machines with cognitive capacity, or **artificial intelligence**.

F2F

Shorthand for face-to-face, F2F is a term used in **email**, **text messaging** and other digital message forums to refer to the meeting of two communicants **'in real life'** (**IRL**). Although at one level merely a simple abbreviation, also showing the playful use of language symptomatic of these new forms (Shortis 2001), the term carries with it some interesting connotations. For example, the need to meet F2F may be read as evidence of a lingering doubt about online communication – that the 'face work' of interpersonal meeting and communication retains some lustre of authenticity that online communication lacks. It thus says something about attitudes to privacy, honesty and the Internet. The desire to meet F2F is the desire to confirm an impression gained hitherto solely from text-based interaction, and the desire to maintain a separation between online and real-life worlds. This move may be seen as particularly important where the communication has something invested in it, where the risk of deception might be greater. The so-called 'Case of the Cross-Dressing Psychiatrist' reported by Allucquere Rosanne Stone (1995), and other similar cases of online fraud and hoax, perpetuate the fear that cyberspace heightens the possibility of deception, thus encouraging trust only in the F2F confirmation of identity and intent.

See also: **Email**, **IRL**, **Text messaging**

Further sources: Shortis (2001), Stone (1995)

FAQ (FREQUENTLY ASKED QUESTIONS)

An FAQ is a list of questions and answers that has been compiled and is available for public access. The goal of providing an FAQ is to permit context-specific knowledge to be transferred to newcomers (or '**newbies**') easily and in a more automated fashion, so that the same information need not be repeated multiple times. Questions in a newsgroup's FAQ might include information about social norms for the group, or directions for unsubscribing from the group.

FEDERAL COMMUNICATIONS COMMISSION (FCC)

The Federal Communications Commission (FCC) is a US Government agency which is responsible to Congress. Established by the Communications Act of 1934, the FCC is charged with regulating interstate and international communications by radio, television, wire, satellite and cable. The chairman at the time of writing is Michael Powell, an appointee of President George W. Bush and son of current US Secretary of State Colin Powell. Although the public owns the airwaves that radio and TV stations use and profit from, and the FCC is charged with regulating communications in the public interest, there has been little visible acknowledgement of that role lately. Chairman Powell wrote: 'The night after I was sworn in, I waited for a visit from the angel of public interest. I waited all night, but she did not come. I still have had no divine awakening and no one has issued me my public interest crystal ball.' Generally the FCC's interpretation of the 'public interest' coincides with that of media conglomerates. Thus in November 2002 the FCC approved the largest cable TV merger in US history, a $47.5 billion buyout of AT&T by Comcast, the nation's largest and third-largest cable companies respectively. Critics charge that the lack of media diversity concentrates power, marginalizes dissenting political viewpoints and under-represents the interests and perspectives of women, people of colour, labour, environmentalists, disabled people and lesbians, gays and bisexuals.

Critics of the FCC include: FAIR (Fairness and Accuracy In Reporting), www.fair.org; Center For Digital Democracy, www.democraticmedia.org; Independent Media Center Network, www.indymedia.org.

Further sources: www.fcc.gov

FEMINISM *see* **Cyberfeminism**

FILE TRANSFER PROTOCOL (FTP)

The term 'protocol' is used here in the same sense as it would be in diplomacy, as the system or catalyst through which it is possible to communicate. File Transfer Protocol is used to transfer files between computers.

The difference between FTP and **HTTP** is that FTP transfers entire files from one device to another, whereas HTTP is designed to transfer the contents of a web page into a web browser for viewing. An FTP connection also remains open after transferring files, in case the user wishes to transfer more, for at least a short period, although servers will often sever a link after a period of inactivity. In contrast, an HTTP connection closes once a page has been downloaded. An FTP server is distinct from a web server (on which a website is hosted), in that it exists only as a means for transferring files, rather than viewing web pages. Like HTTP, FTP works through the **TCP/IP** protocols.

Further sources: www.w3.org/Protocols/rfc959/

FLAMING

Heated online exchanges in newsgroups and **BBSs** are referred to as 'flame wars' and individual messages containing hostile or abusive language as 'flames'. Flaming, or rapidly escalating hostile language, has been observed since the early days of **computer mediated communication** (CMC). Those who study online communication posit that flaming may be due to the lack of non-verbal communication cues associated with CMC, because when messages are exchanged without the context provided by non-verbal communication, cues such as tone of voice, gesture or inflection, contention can escalate more quickly. Others argue that online social norms make flaming more acceptable, and that the anonymity associated with online discourse is to blame: not being able to associate a face or a person with the messages may depersonalize the recipient in the eyes of the sender.

Some individuals deliberately 'flame' other participants in online fora as a form of recreation. These troublemakers are known as **trolls**.

See also: **Cues filtered out, Troll**

FREE SOFTWARE

This is basically a generic or catch-all expression in a contested and confusing arena. According to the **GNU Project** website:

> 'Free software' is a matter of liberty, not price. To understand the concept, you should think of 'free' as in 'free speech,' not as in 'free beer.'

Some terms in relatively common use denoting ownership status include 'free software, **open source**', 'public domain software', '**copyleft** software', 'non-copyleft free software', 'GPL-covered software', 'semi-free software', 'proprietary software', 'shareware', 'freeware' and 'commercial software'. A diagram by Chao-Kuei on the GNU Project website explains the different categories of software – at least from the GNU Project perspective.

Further sources: www.gnu.org/philosophy/categories.html

FREE-NET

Free-Net is an expression coined by Thomas Grundner in 1985, first for the **Cleveland Free-Net**, and then for the many additional 'Free-Nets' that sprang up, primarily in the US and Canada but also in other places around the world. Free-Nets represented a very popular model for free public access to the Internet and other electronic services, including community-run question-and-answer forums on various topics including health information, automobile repair, and social services, at a time when public access to the Internet was rare. Free-Nets predated the widespread use of the **World Wide Web** and were text-based. A 'building' metaphor was generally employed to organize the information and services on the systems ('the library', 'the schoolhouse', etc.). The term **'community networks'** is a more generic name for a geographical community-based public network. Many of the Free-Nets were members of the now-defunct **National Public Telecomputing Network** (NPTN).

Further sources: Schuler and Day (2003), Kubicek and Wagner (2002)

FREEWARE

Applications that are made freely available by their programmers are known as freeware. The motivation for doing this can be anti-corporate, or simply an attempt to improve the quality of computing or to produce universal standards. One example is **LINUX**, an alternative operating system that is made available by its author.

Freeware is socially significant and potentially economically significant, in that it provides an alternative means by which individuals, organizations and companies can use computers and use the Internet. These alternatives challenge the market dominance of companies such as Microsoft. As well as being anti-corporate (specifically anti-Microsoft) or motivated by a desire to improve computing, the provision of freeware can also underpinned by an ethos that the computing and the Internet should be 'free goods' that are as available to as many people as possible (see **Open Source**).

However, the provision of free, although not Open Source, software has been used very effectively by corporations as a competitive device. Microsoft's browser, Internet Explorer, has always been made available as a free download for anyone using its Windows operating system. Pursuing this strategy from the outset quickly enabled Microsoft to take the dominant 'market' position (in the sense of having the most-used browser) from what had almost become the standard browser, Netscape, a freeware development of Mosaic, the original Internet browser (see **World Wide Web**).

As well as ending the reign of Netscape, pursuit of this strategy also meant potential competitors to Internet Explorer and its companion email client Outlook Express were unable to make a commercial success of selling their software. The US company Qualcomm, which had been making the email client Eudora for a decade, and Norwegian browser company Opera, both recently stopped direct sales of their software, in direct response to Microsoft's strategy. Both deciding to offer free 'sponsored' versions that displayed advertising to those using them, with the option of paying for 'ad-free' versions instead (see **Halloween Documents**).

Perhaps ironically, Microsoft's position in providing the most commonly used browser is built on an application that was based on the original Mosaic, which was made available on an **Open Source** and freeware basis. The latest version of Netscape is still provided in the same way, as an alternative to Internet Explorer. Some other computer companies have tried to use freeware-like arrangements to challenge Microsoft's dominant position, a good example being the Star Office suite which was originally provided as a free download by computer manufacturer Sun as an alternative to the ubiquitous Microsoft Office.

See also: **Free software**, **LINUX**, **Open Source**

Further sources: www.mozilla.org/, www.opera.com/, www.eudora.com/

FUZZY LOGIC

Fuzzy logic extends conventional logic to handle what might be called 'partial truth'. Logic works on a simple 'yes' or 'no', 'true' or 'false' basis. This can make it difficult to emulate the way decisions are taken on the basis of incomplete information, or simple guesswork, since computers are binary systems that work on the basis of something being true or not true (0 or 1).

Fuzzy logic is a mathematical way of handling values that lie between 'completely true' and 'completely false'. It was introduced by Lotfi Zadeh of the University of California at Berkeley in the 1960s, originally as a means to try to model the uncertainty of natural language. While the mathematics are involved are extremely complex, this concept has increasingly become a part of computing since the late 1980s. Code running things as diverse as video cameras and air conditioners employ fuzzy logic as a means by which to increase the flexibility and efficiency with which those systems can react to change in their environment. Fuzzy logic has also been used in the development of **robots** and **cyberpets**.

See also: **Artificial intelligence**

G3

G3 is a shorthand term for mobile (cellular) telephones offering high-speed wireless Internet access.

GAMEBOY

An 8-bit handheld games console produced by Nintendo in 1989 which led the company to dominate the handheld market. The Russian puzzle game 'Tetris', and later the 'Pokemon' series, greatly boosted Gameboy sales. It was subsequently replaced by the Gameboy Color and later by the 32-bit Gameboy Advance and Gameboy SP. Sony has recently announced that it will shortly be entering the handheld market, which may threaten Nintendo's dominant market position, as may Nokia's and Motorola's decision to market mobile/cell phones as gaming platforms.

See also: **Games**

GAMER

A gamer is one who plays computer **games** as a hobby. This is a term of self-identification used by those who make heavy use of games. Gamers can have negative attitudes to what they describe as 'casual gamers'. The industry and some individuals use the term 'hardcore gamers' to describe those who are most committed (see **Otaku**).

GAMES

The first computer game was called 'Tennis for Two'. It was written by an American physicist called William Higinbotham in 1958 to help make the open day at Brookhaven National Laboratory more attractive to the public. The second was called 'Spacewar' and was written by young programmers who were members of a group called the TMRC (Tech Model Railroad Club, although their interests were firmly rooted in computing) at MIT in 1961. By 2001, when total US cinema box office takings were $8.35 billion, US games sales were some $9.4 billion, with a worldwide total of the order of $15 billion anticipated in 2002 (source: *Los Angeles Times*). The UK market alone was worth £219 million in 2001 (source: ELSPA).

In the early 1970s a graduate in electrical engineering called Nolan Bushnell had been sufficiently inspired by 'Spacewar' to hit on the idea of computer games being sold and used in the same way as pinball machines in the US. After a hesitant start with a failed version of 'Spacewar', Bushnell's company, Atari, launched an arcade game called 'Pong', not dissimilar to the original 'Tennis for Two' (two players controlled rectangles, batting a square backwards and forwards between them) in November 1972. The instructions for 'Pong' – 'avoid missing ball for high score' – passed into video and computer game legend. A series of arcade games followed, produced by both Atari itself and traditional gaming machine companies like Bally/Midway.

In 1975 Atari, which had seen initial success wane to some degree, took a very significant step, releasing a home version of 'Pong' in the US that plugged into a television set. The idea was not brand new and there had been earlier experiments, but Atari was the first to begin to make serious money from its home 'video games'. A range of what would eventually be called 'games consoles', such as the Odyssey and Telstar, appeared in the US, but they found only relatively limited markets and were short-lived. Then in 1977 Atari launched the Atari VCS which, unlike some other early US games consoles, also appeared in the UK. Instant programming through hard-wired game 'cartridges' that slotted into the console meant that an initial sale of hardware could be followed by sale after sale of software games cartridges. What would become one of the world's largest entertainment industries was born.

The next significant development was a sudden and massive entry into the arcade games market in 1978 by the Japanese company Taito with a game called 'Space Invaders', designed by Toshihiro Nishikado. The game, involving repulsing wave after wave of on-screen alien attackers, offered simple and addictive gameplay. Crucially, this gameplay was not time-limited: the game lasted as long as the player could hold off each successive wave of invaders. As well as being a huge commercial success, the game was one of the first to create a fan base. 'Space Invaders' had 24-hour arcades dedicated to it in Tokyo and caused a coin shortage. This was among the first indications that, when computer technology was used as a toy, it could produce a fan base that verged on the fanatical and that, 25 years later, the term 'hardcore gamers' would be used in the industry. Soon afterwards, quite rapid technical advances began to be made. While 'Space

Invaders' stretched the available technology, it could only provide limited movement and graphics, while colour was only possible by placing transparencies on the screen. Within a year, another Japanese company, Namco, had produced 'Galaxian' which, while basically the same game as 'Space Invaders', was much more energetic, used primary colours and had enemies that swept across the screen. Meanwhile, in the US, Atari launched classic games using 'vector' (line) graphics, such as 'Asteroids' and 'Missile Command', and Williams released 'Defender'. Each successive game was faster, more dynamic, more complex and more addictive than the last.

While the arcade sector prospered, the home console market began to collapse in the early 1980s. In part, this was because the consoles were being rapidly outmoded by home computers which offered superior games. In the UK, this included the home computers produced by companies like Sinclair and Commodore. The decline was also due to both the hardware and software for the home consoles being expensive and, in the end, to these machines, despite their interchangeable software, being very limited in what they could offer. There was little comparison between what an Atari VCS or an Intellivision console could provide and what was available at an amusement arcade. While home computing could meet the wishes of gamers who were also computer users, it was at that stage a clumsy and relatively difficult technology to engage with.

It was a Japanese company that saw a potential market in more powerful home game consoles that could be operated very simply. In 1985, Nintendo launched its NES (Nintendo Entertainment System). This 8-bit console was way ahead of its predecessors in terms of what it could offer and provided comparable gameplay to a home computer. All one needed to do to program it was simply insert a hard-wired games cartridge. Competition from another Japanese corporation, Sega, arrived with the launch of Master System in 1986. From this point, a war for an ever increasing market broke out between the two manufacturers, with technically superior 16-bit consoles, the Sega Megadrive (called Genesis in the US) and Nintendo's Super NES offering games of ever increasing sophistication and quality from 1989 onwards. In 1994, Sony joined the competition for the home gaming market with the launch in Japan of the Playstation. This 16mb, 32-bit system, which now used CDs rather than cartridges as storage media for its games, eclipsed the competition offered by Sega's 32-bit Saturn console and Nintendo's 64. This was partly the result of Sony's sheer size and marketing power and partly because the choice of software was greater for the Playstation.

Sega, which had dominated home gaming in Europe, released what would be its final console, the 64-bit Dreamcast, in 1999. This console crossed the line between console and computer, having a Windows Communications Electronics (CE) operating system and offering Internet access in addition to gaming. However, the dominant market position of Sony was reinforced with the release of the Playstation II in 2000, which was a 128-bit console offering DVD playback as well as gaming.

Near-total Japanese dominance of video gaming was eventually challenged with the release of Microsoft's Xbox in 2001. This console was a stripped-down Pentium III machine with enhanced graphics, like the Playstation II offering DVD and Internet access and also boasting a hard drive. The other major player in home gaming, Nintendo, released its Gamecube in 2002, this time based around a powerful custom-built IBM processor. At the time of writing, the sales figures for Xbox suggest Microsoft will have a major fight on its hands in challenging Sony, particularly in their home market of Japan, though it has already overtaken Nintendo in the US and Europe. Sega in the meantime has reinvented itself as a software company, supplying games for all its old rivals. Many of the major games companies are Japanese, such as Capcom, Namco and Konami; major US companies include Electronic Arts; and British companies include Rare.

Nintendo dominated handheld gaming following the 1989 release of its cartridge-based Gameboy, which eclipsed competitors like the Atari Lynx and Sega Gamegear, and secured its market position with the 1998 Gameboy Color, the 2001 release of the Gameboy Advance and the smaller Gameboy SP in 2002. Games for PCs also remain a major market, as PCs can offer even more elaborate and sophisticated games than the consoles, provided the machines are fast enough to cope with the latest game releases.

Games will soon be at the point at which their graphics are photorealistic. In some genres of game the complexity with which the player is presented can be much greater than in any other kind of leisure activity which an individual can pursue on their own. Even handheld titles like the fantasy quest/adventure 'Zelda' series on Gameboy machines can present players with a challenge that is in part intellectual and will take many hours to play through, while 'Zelda' on Gamecubes offers even more complexity and depth of play. As the sophistication of the platform increases, so does the potential complexity of the games. Titles like the 'Metal Gear Solid' series or the 'Grand Theft Auto' series for the Playstation II are not quite at the point at which they could be described as an interactive action film (with the player as the hero), but they are getting close to being so, both in terms of complexity and the graphical detail they present.

Games have a cultural significance in the same way that television and cinema are part of culture. They are a mass-market entertainment product used by individuals playing alone, but they are also used socially: consoles have multiplayer facilities that allow several individuals to play against one another – for example, on sports titles. Online multiplayer games like 'Everquest' offer graphical interactive worlds in which players are **avatars** that build upon the original text-based **MUD** experience (in the sense of a Multi-User Dungeon, a text-based Dungeons and Dragons game, rather than as a Multi-User Domain). The game world can be elaborate, and the other players in the game may be numbered in their thousands.

The exposure of children to computers and software as toys makes **information and communication technologies** (**ICTs**) as familiar as television was to earlier generations of children. Some games employ quite advanced graphical user interfaces, almost definable as in-game operating systems. This is necessary because the interaction a player can have with their environment, be it swapping weapons or tools to react to a particular situation, or solving a puzzle, has become ever more complex. To work through a game like those in the 'Final Fantasy' series means using the game interface to control what may be hundreds of in-game commands and settings. This can introduce children to basic computing concepts and conventions as part of their play.

The relationship between the gamer and their games can be a long one. In 2002, a survey by the European Leisure Software Publishers Association (ELSPA) found that the largest game-playing group was not children but adults aged 25–34. This group had grown up with games and now had the disposable income to indulge what is still quite an expensive hobby.

One result of this trend has been the appearance of the 'adult' title. When combined with the graphical detail now available in games, 'adult' themed titles have fuelled anxieties about what effect games might be having on those who play them. One particular genre has caused more worry than all the others: the first-person shooter. The first-person shooter involves a player moving through a series of game worlds, the perspective being what one would see if one were walking around holding a gun – hence 'first person'. The 'gameplay' has little sophistication, one simply kills everything (demons, robots, etc.) – or quite often *everyone* – that one finds.

This genre began with the release of the British-authored 'Wolfenstein 3D' for PCs in 1991, in which the player infiltrated a bunker and shot Nazi stormtroopers. However, it was with the release of the frantically paced and almost maniacally violent 'Doom' and its successors, including 'Quake', that the genre really took off. Hugely violent fantasies could be indulged, players could even attack their adversaries by using a chainsaw on them. Graphical detail increased and increased and so, for some, did the moral questions about some games. Titles like 'Kingpin' and the 'Grand Theft Auto' series, for example, involved the player – in the role of a gangster – working their way up through criminal organizations by way of theft and murder. When a character is shot in one of these games, it can look very similar to actual news footage of someone being shot. The best-selling game on Microsoft's Xbox is the science–fiction first-person shooter 'Halo', while Electronic Arts' 'Medal of Honor' series recreates World War Two from a US perspective, even featuring historically accurate firearms.

These games were looked at as a potential cause when the terrifying social problem of massacres of high school pupils by other pupils began to happen with some regularity in the US. Some evidence suggests that games can produce an increase in violent feelings, but it is not clear at the time of writing whether cause and effect can be demonstrated. It is worth noting that games provide a simple and convenient explanation of the alienation that made some young people act in this way, an explanation easier to grasp than the other potential causes. Games also provide a distraction from the politically difficult debates around the easy availability of firearms in some countries. There is also no evidence that ultra-violent titles like the 'Resident Evil' series ('Biohazard' in Japan), which sell in the millions, have produced any general upsurge in aggression. On the other hand, nor is there evidence to the contrary.

There are related concerns linked to gender. Most titles are aimed at young males, and there are depictions of women within these titles that raise very similar questions to those that are raised about the depiction of women in pornography. Concerns have been raised that this might have an effect on developing male adolescents' attitudes to women (see also **gender**). In addition to giving the world first-person shooters, Britain also scored another questionable first with the 'Tomb Raider' series of games. The hero of this series, Lara Croft, is the embodiment of adolescent male fantasy: an athletic, gun-toting young woman whose chest measurement is anatomically impossible, and who appears to be immune to temperature change and thus able to wear nothing but a pair of shorts and a t-shirt, even in blizzard conditions. While some might argue that the depiction of woman as hero is positive, others might find it difficult to see a crude sexual fantasy like

Lara Croft in that light (see **cyberfeminism**). Other depictions of women as the central character are hardly any more positive (one example would be Joanna Dark in the Rare title 'Perfect Dark' for the now out-of-production Nintendo 64, the player's character in a profoundly violent first-person shooter). The recent purchase of the British company Rare means Joanna Dark is next scheduled to appear in an Xbox title. In Japan, the extreme sexual imagery and including pornographic violence that permeates mainstream comics (**manga**) and animation (anime) is also found in many games (see **Otaku**).

There are 'games for girls', but these are few and far between. There is also some evidence that women also play many of the mainstream genres with cross-gender appeal, such as role-playing games like the 'Final Fantasy' series, or 'Zelda'. The ELSPA survey referred to on page 93 also found a significant proportion of game players in the majority age bracket were women, which has led games companies to begin targeting this new audience. The interest that women and girls have in gaming is demonstrated by several websites, such as www.gamegirlz.com/, some of which are concerned with both gaming itself and the gendered nature of gaming (for example, www.gamegirladvance.com/).

However, while some games do have violent or otherwise-questionable content, many titles feature no real violence or indeed any depictions of recognizable reality. Games can be, at least in part, about nurturing and caring, as in Nintendo's 'Pokemon' (Pocket Monster) series, where players look after a pet monster and train it to compete in sumo-like contests with other monsters (see **cyberpets**). 'Pokemon' has become the **killer app** that, with the Russian puzzle game 'Tetris', helped Nintendo to dominate the handheld market. Similarly, games featuring Sega's 'Sonic the Hedgehog' or Nintendo's 'Mario' are about speed, primary colours and puzzle-solving, and involve no real violence.

Many of the non-violent titles are Japanese, a country which produces a much wider variety of games than do the US or UK. Some of the more unusual Japanese titles reach the European and American market, such as 'Mr Moskeeto' (in which the player is a mosquito flying around a house at night who feeds on the sleeping occupants without getting swatted) or Sega's 'Bass Fishing' (literally fishing). There are also music-based titles, like Sony's 'Parappa the Rappa' which involves the player creating songs. But some titles, such as the arcade game 'Dance Dance Revolution' (in which the game character dances on screen, the user matches their dancing, with everything becoming faster and faster), are rarely seen outside of Asia. Some of most complex games, notably the 'Final Fantasy' and 'Zelda' series, tend to be produced in Japan.

In recent years, the links between the games industry and Hollywood have been deepening. Initial forays into video-game-linked films proved unsuccessful at the box office, such as the *Street Fighter* film based on what was at the time a phenomenally successful 'beat 'em up' (a fist and martial arts) game, 'Street Fighter 2'. However, some titles did prove more successful, with the first *Tomb Raider* film generating enough income to spawn a sequel. It has now become apparent that the most significant opportunities for making money lie with film tie-ins. Lucasarts, the company founded by the creator of *Star Wars*, has created a major market for its various games in which the player can take part in space battles or become a 'Jedi'. The film tie-in for *The Matrix Reloaded* was produced with the involvement of the directors of the movie, which may be the start of a trend for increasingly close links between the 'lean-back' entertainment offered by movies and the 'lean-to' entertainment offered by games.

The games market is also significant because of the ways in which major corporations hope it will develop. It is clear that companies like Microsoft and Sony see their current consoles as first steps towards 'home entertainment centres' that will deliver games, movies, e-commerce, applications and other content **'on demand'** from networks. These companies have an interest in developing their market share in terms of the physical devices consumers use to access networks and in providing content on those networks. These developments could have a profound impact on the way in which networks like the Internet are used (see **corporate dominance**).

Further sources: Burnham, van (2001), Kent (2001), Poole (2000), *Edge* magazine (www.edge.com), www.womengamers.com/, www.nintendo.com, www.playstation.com, www.xbox.com

GEEK

A derogatory slang term that originated in America, the word 'geek' is used by children and teenagers to describe a socially less successful individual who is focused on school work or has a greater than usual interest in science or technology. The term, which is sometimes combined with 'computer' to produce 'computer geek', describes a less alienated or obsessive person than the Japanese terms **hikikomori** or **Otaku**. Another slang term with American origins, 'nerd' is used interchangeably with 'geek'. In Britain, these terms have become commonplace, although there are homegrown slang terms, such as 'anorak'. As **ICT** use becomes commonplace, rather than confined to hobbyists, it will be interesting to see if the use of these terms changes.

GENDER

The implications of cyberculture for gender identities and politics have attracted a lot of critical attention from a range of perspectives. There now exists a large body of feminist theory and research on the topic, ranging from cyberspace as a tool for the perpetuation of patriarchy to cyberspace as a new gender-free environment. To some extent this builds more broadly upon pre-existing work on the relationship between gender and technology, but it also draws in new theoretical and experiential perspectives, making the study of gender in cyberculture one of the most hotly debated subjects in the domain.

The strong tradition of feminist studies of science and technology, which now feeds into work on cyberculture, has many branches, from studies of women's access to technology to the educational opportunities (and barriers) in place for women scientists. Studies of the gendering of technology tend to stress the masculinization of some forms of technology and the feminization of others, as well as highlighting issues of access, inequality and domination. Studies of domestic technologies, for example, reveal the implicit genderings at work in the construction of different artefacts, while work on reproductive technologies places women in a particular role as subjects of (and even subject to) technology. As part of this lineage, then, the computer might be seen as yet another masculine technology; studies ranging from patterns of employment in the industry to the sexism of email talk, and from the hypergendering of characters and formats in computer **games** (Barbie for girls, **Lara Croft** for boys) to the heteropatriarchal structure of global cybercapitalism, have explored the many ways in which computers and cyberculture are 'maled'.

Set against this, however, is a body of work stressing the liberatory possibilities of technology. In this context, cyberculture is seen either as a potentially genderless realm where real-life (RL) identities cease to have any meaning or coherence, or as a space in which women can be full participants and can engage with cyberculture on their own terms. These different perspectives all have their advocates, and there has been considerable debate among people working in this field about the relative merits of different approaches to gender in cyberculture.

Moreover, outside and alongside the academy there are equally significant interventions from activists, stressing the politics at stake in these debates (Harcourt 1999).

For those who would wish to emphasize the productive possibilities of cyberspace for feminist theory and politics, there is a similar range of possible approaches collected under the heading **cyberfeminism**. Sociologist Katie Ward (2000) attempts to order these by making a distinction between 'online feminism' and 'online cyberfeminism'. For her, the term online feminism refers to the use of cyberspace to further 'traditional' feminist issues, such as inequality, consciousness raising and so on – here cyberspace becomes another means of promoting feminism. Online cyberfeminism, by contrast, both makes use of and engages with the technology, in an attempt to recode both cyberspace and feminism. Ward exemplifies this distinction through a discussion of anti-harassment sites (online feminism) set against online cyber-feminist sites such as Geekgrrrl and Nerdgrrl, whose names signal new combinations of computer culture (the words **geek** and **nerd** turned from terms of abuse to badges of pride signalling close engagement with computers) with 'postfeminist' politics (summed up perfectly by Geekgrrl's statement: 'Grrrls enjoy their femininity and kick ass at the same time'). For feminist theorists who share a common vision with the Geekgrrrl ethos, there are exciting new possibilities to be found here in the productive engagement with cyberspace recast as a feminist space, similar trends also being evident in relation to **games**. Sadie Plant (1997, 2000), for example, has applied a playful yet political reading of this online cyberfeminist project, blending it with French feminist theory to explore women's historical, present and future place in cyberculture. However, for some writers this reading is overly optimistic, and needs to be set alongside the material and ideological inequalities that limit women's participation online (see Squires 2000).

An equally large and vigorous debate has been rumbling about the practice and politics of cyberspace as a 'post-gender' domain. Researchers exploring **MUDs,** for example, have described experiments in gender play, most famously on LambdaMOO which offers participants a choice between ten different genders (Kendall 1996). While this might be seen as an exciting development away from the strictures of binary gender – as well as a way of emphasizing the performative nature of all genders, online and off – for some critics the freedom is illusory, as most participants soon fall back on 'traditional', even stereotypical, RL genders – and empirical work suggests that cross-gender identification online is relatively uncommon, and widely perceived as unethical (Roberts and Parks 1999).

The possibility of deception overshadows some contexts of online interaction, therefore, with media-stirred moral panics, particularly those focused on adult males masquerading as teenage girls in chatrooms – a significant component of the broader cyberspace panic about paedophilia. Such riskiness reinstates the necessity of face-to-face (see **F2F**) authentication of identity. This online/RL split, seen here as problematic and the possible source of misuse and abuse, is for other writers an important positive feature of cyberspace, allowing participants the safety to play amongst themselves, to play with others, and to find new ways of expressing identity. Where the online/RL split is rigidly maintained, and there is no possibility of virtual environments bleeding into RL, then new intimacies and identities can emerge. Of course, the 'safety' of this kind of online experimentation has, at some level at least, to maintain a denial of the impact of such practices on the RL **body** and self – and a virtual love (or a virtual rape) may be experienced as profoundly embodied.

As the famous 'virtual rape' in LambdaMOO and the story of the 'cross-dressing psychiatrist' show, creating a supposed free space for gender play can in fact lead to unsavoury outcomes that spill over into RL (Dibbell 1999; Stone 1995). In the former case, the ability of one participant in the MUD to control the actions of another, and to be able to make them engage in non-consensual virtual sex acts, led to a fierce debate around issues of identity play, harassment and the meaning of 'rape' in cyberspace. In the latter, a male psychiatrist who 'passed' as a female online as an experiment and then decided to 'kill' his female persona when he realised the irresponsibility of his actions, brought out in stark relief issues of trust, deception and emotional involvement in online contexts. Both these cases are well known, but less discussed (yet equally important) is the use of cyberspace by transgendered people to explore new identities and to mobilize politically (Whittle 2001). Cyberspace can, therefore, be a 'safe' space in which to experiment with self-identity, to meet like minds, and to build collective projects focused on changing the theory, politics and practice of gender.

See also: **Body**, **Cyberfeminism**, **MUDs**

Further sources: Dibbell (1999), Harcourt (1999), Stone (1995)

GIBSON, WILLIAM *see* **Cyberpunk,** *Johnny Mnemonic,* *Neuromancer*

GLOBAL INFORMATION INFRASTRUCTURE COMMISSION (GIIC)

The Global Information Infrastructure (GII) was proposed by the United States to the other G8 countries in 1995 to secure universal access for the world's population. Its mission is 'to foster private sector leadership and private–public sector cooperation in the development of information networks and services to advance global economic growth, education and quality of life'. This proposal, with its reliance on the 'free market', offers few practical measures for securing its stated goals.

See also: **Cultural imperialism**

Further sources: http://www.giic.org/

GLOBALIZATION

Globalization is thought by many to characterize the current epoch of capitalist development and, as such, it is a highly contested and disputed term. At its simplest, globalization refers to the phenomenon of increased international communication, travel and trade, and the spread of different cultures across national and ethnic boundaries. In the West this manifests itself in the increasingly commonplace experiences of larger numbers of people flying around the globe for business or holidays; a greater choice of 'foreign' products in local shops; the increasingly ubiquitous commercial brand names appearing worldwide; and the mix of ethnic styles in fashions and designs. It is evidence, for some, of the emergence of both a global economy and a global culture. The role of the **Internet** and related global **ICTs** is paramount in this conception of globalization for facilitating the emergence of the informational economy and the network society.

While acknowledging the importance of these global trends and the part played by the new telecommunications media in supporting them, many commentators, academics and activists have campaigned to point out many of the potential negative consequences of globalization. These concerns were firmly placed on the world's political agenda by the protesters at the World Trade Organization's meeting in Seattle in November 2000. The protesters are often described as belonging to the *anti-globalization movement*. More accurately, however, they were not anti-globalization but rather were challenging the neo-liberal economic variant of globalization which they regard as engendering **cultural imperialism** and economic domination by Western capitalist corporations and governments. Perhaps embodying the new cultural politics, the protesters comprise a loose alliance of **new social movements** of environmental, feminist, human rights activists and others sharing a common opposition to the policies and practices of neo-liberal globalization.

The criticisms and concerns about neo-liberal globalization are varied and numerous. In part they stem from the contention that globalization is not *new* at all. Rather it is a concept which stretches back to the trading empires of Britain, Spain, Portugal and the Netherlands. International trade and migration, moreover, were as much features of nineteenth-century capitalism as they are today. In this sense globalization can be seen as in continuity with previous capitalist practices which, despite the protectionist set-backs of the 1930s arising from the Great Depression, have been a common feature of a post-World War Two drive by Western states to strengthen international free-trade relationships.

For the advocates of this economic free trade policy, the benefits of globalization have been considerable. It has, they argue, provided more choice in the shops, stimulated greater affluence and improved living standards, increased international travel, promoted information exchange, led to a greater understanding of different cultures, and enabled democracy to triumph over totalitarianism, communism and dictatorships in many parts of the world.

Opponents, however, point to the unequal effects of neo-liberal globalization whereby Western countries have gained significantly at the expense of developing countries. During the last decade, for example, it has been estimated that the already meagre share of the world's poorest people's wealth actually decreased from 2.3 per cent to 1.4 per cent. Furthermore, the distribution of benefits arising from globalization are not evenly spread within countries. In Western countries, for example, manual labourers have been subject to **hypercasualization**, whereby global corporations move their production facilities to low-wage economies; in poorer countries, governing elites and officials are alleged to be beneficiaries of bribery and corruption as inducements to removing trade barriers.

Of primary concern to the anti-neo-liberal globalization protesters is the way in which the free trade system is structured to support global corporate interests at the expense of local interests. Indeed the post-Seattle mantra has been 'local good, global bad'. Commentators such as Naomi Klein and Noreena Hertz suggest that many transnational corporations now have more power in the world than many democratically elected governments. 'Governments are reduced to playing the role of servile lackeys to big business', argues Hertz (2001). The consequence is that the interests of shareholders are placed before those of communities and even consumers. Faced with the need for inward investment, many governments are powerless to oppose the demands of corporations for a deregulated economy where workers' rights are limited, taxation is advantageous and planning is relaxed. Consequently a situation emerges where global decisions, directly affecting the lives and local circumstances of people and communities, are made by faceless corporate directors who cannot be held accountable for their actions by those most closely affected by them.

The veteran journalist John Pilger, however, even questions this depiction of state impotence *vis-à-vis* corporate power. He argues that 'the illusion of a weakened state is a smokescreen thrown up by the designers of the "new order" ' (2003: 115). Instead, he argues that Western governments have consistently acted in concern with their corporate partners to systematically fashion a world economy which places North American, European and Australasian interests above the rest of the world. Globalization in this context is therefore an exploitative arrangement which seeks to maintain an economic disparity between the rich and the poor countries of the world by ensuring Western corporations have 'unlimited access to minerals, oil, markets and cheap labour'. The mechanism for pursuing this strategy, it is argued, is a combination of the military superiority of the West and the institutions responsible for regulating the global economy such as the World Bank, the International Monetary Fund (IMF) and the World Trade Organization (WTO). Through these instruments a condition of dependency of developing countries upon those in the West is produced. In order to receive financial loans, development aid or corporate investment, developing countries are often first required to deregulate their economies, privatize their public services and adhere to the principles of free trade. Critics of this policy point out that these arrangements are seldom fair. Aid from Western countries, for example, is often in the form of loans to buy surplus Western goods which cannot be sold in the home market. While markets in developing countries are required to be open to foreign competition, Western markets are often protected from cheap produce from developing countries. Agricultural produce grown in poorer countries for Western appetites takes up farmland valuable for indigenous food production and leads to hunger. Moreover, the unregulated operations and practices of corporations have also endangered the health, environment and survival of animal species.

See also: **Cultural imperialism**, **Hypercasualization**

Further sources: Pilger (2003), Greider (1998), Hutton and Giddens (2000)

GNU PROJECT

The GNU Project was launched in 1984 to develop a complete UNIX-like operating system constituted entirely of free software. (GNU is a recursive acronym for 'GNU's Not Unix', and is pronounced 'guh-NEW'.) The project is now actively working on a wide range of projects including utilities for a virtual film studio, libraries for supporting the Java language, the GNU Enterprise for business needs, and GNU Octal for digital music. The Free Software Foundation (FSF) is the principal organizational sponsor of the GNU Project.

Further sources: www.gnu.org

GRAPHICAL USER INTERFACE (GUI) *see* Interface

HACKER

Individuals who use their knowledge to violate security on protected computer systems are known as hackers, but the term is also used as a general description of people with an interest or career in programming. There is a difference between the way in which the mass media defines a hacker, which is someone who breaks into computer systems with malicious or malevolent intent, and the way that some of these individuals portray themselves, as resisting the global domination of companies such as Microsoft. Some hackers would differentiate between actions such as causing damage to major software companies, which are linked to US West Coast anti-capitalist – or, more accurately anti-corporate – sentiments and a wish to maintain the Internet as a playground for those who have a close relationship with computers, and the actions of individuals who commit other **cybercrime**. A hacker is not the same thing as an individual who produces a **virus** which is simply designed to cause damage to computers and networks, as the hacker is in direct control of any actions that she or he undertakes.

See also: **Cybercrime**, **Geek**

Further sources: Thomas and Loader (2000), Taylor (1999)

HACKING

Hacking is accessing a computer-based system without appropriate authorization, which can be unlawful.

See also: **Cybercrime**, **Hacker**

HACTIVIST

This is a portmanteau word, formed from the words **'hacker'** and 'activist', to describe someone who uses and develops Internet software for activist causes.

HALLOWEEN DOCUMENTS

The 'Halloween Documents' refer to several confidential Microsoft memoranda which were leaked, the first being at the end of October 1998. They were generally thought of as Microsoft's first public admission that they felt threatened by **Open Source**. They also present Microsoft's strategy against **LINUX** and Open Source software. The first memo was released to the media, and Microsoft subsequently acknowledged its authenticity. Now several documents are available on the web, annotated by Eric Raymond, author of *The Cathedral and the Bazaar*, which contrasts Open Source and proprietary software development characteristics.

See also: **Free software**, **Freeware**, **Open source**

Further sources: Raymond (1999), www.opensource.org/halloween/

HEALTH *see* **Virtual social support**

HIGH DEFINITION TELEVISION *see* **Digital television**

HIKIKOMORI

Hikikomori is a Japanese term for individuals, mainly young men, who withdraw from social life, confining themselves to a room and refusing to go out. This phenomenon is seen as primarily having social and economic causes, although those who withdraw may exhibit a tendency towards obsessive gaming or using the Internet. The phenomenon is similar in some respects to that described by the term **Otaku**.

HITS

The requests for information received by a **website**. Most hit counters do not count every item downloaded from a website (each graphical element of a webpage can be a separate item) but instead measure the number of times pages have been visited. This is not necessarily the same as the number of actual visitors to a website, as it is an account of how often different sections have been accessed rather than how many people have visited. A separate count, sometimes referred to as 'distinct hosts served', is gathered of the number of machines (identified by their IP number) that have visited a site. Hits on major commercial websites are collected and analysed and, like the Neilson rating for assessing television viewership employed in the US, are the basis for judging site popularity and establishing online advertising rates.

HOMEPAGE

A specific 'page' within a **website**, usually the 'first' or 'front' page encountered, may be designated a homepage. Homepages therefore perform important functions. Whether organizational or personal, the homepage is a crucial location for impression management – for capturing the attention of the casual browser, and leading them further into the website, much like a book cover might catch the eye and persuade you to read what is inside. In this sense, Daniel Miller (2000) has theorized websites as 'traps' designed to catch the attention of the net **surfer** – 'we can describe the homepage as an aesthetic trap or interface, that attempts to capture both the "real self" behind the site and the curiosity of potential visitors.' As the web becomes increasingly crowded with sites, homepages must do increasing work; they must be eye-catching, easy to navigate and use, and not so complex that they take forever to download.

Exploring non-institutional, personal homepages, Charles Cheung (2000) borrows from the sociologist Erving Goffman's concept of 'dramaturgy', which emphasizes the extent to which we play roles in the ongoing drama of everyday life. For Goffman, our interpersonal lives are marked by acting, and life unfolds like a drama, complete with props, cues and scripts. In short, we actively seek to manage the ways others perceive us, and try to present ourselves to them in appropriate and positive ways. For Cheung, this process can be witnessed in the context of personal homepages, which function as a virtual stand-in for the self. Personal homepages often include graphics, images and text, with biographical narratives woven into a gripping story, supported by links to other sites. The choice of sites to link to, in fact, shows an elective ordering of the individual's tastes and interests, as well as displaying what we might call cybercultural capital – showing off one's knowledge of and skill in using the web. Finally, the use of a hit counter, which keeps a running total of the number of visits to the site, displays popularity. As a self-conscious and reflexive articulation of the self, then, the personal homepage carries out a lot of identity work, and is therefore an object worth considerable scrutiny.

The same issues pertain to organization homepages, too – the site should mirror the organization's self image, its place in the world, and serve all potential users. As a promotional tool, the organization homepage now sits alongside other branding devices, similarly operating as a trap for potential customers or clients. Realising the financial implications of this, some individuals have registered the **URLs** of large corporations, celebrities and so on, often in the hope of later being able to sell them back to those companies – a phenomenon known as cybersquatting. Circumventing cybersquatters, or attempting to stand out from the numerous websites with similar URLs, often leads to inventive and attention-grabbing naming strategies.

See also: **URL**, **Website**

Further sources: Cheung (2000), Miller (2000)

HTML (HYPERTEXT MARKUP LANGUAGE)

HTML is the language used to create websites and homepages on the **World Wide Web**; it is not, however, a programming language in the sense of a language that can be used to create applications. In other words one cannot use HTML to create a new wordprocessor or spreadsheet; instead it is designed to 'markup' text so that it is displayed in a certain format. When an internet browser displays the text of a web page in a certain way (bold, italic, as a heading) it does it because of instructions contained within the page's HTML code. HTML can also be used to control the layout of a web page to some extent, though detailed control of the positioning of elements is not really possible.

HTML was invented by an Englishman, Tim Berners-Lee, who worked for CERN (the European High-Energy Particle Physics Lab) in the early 1990s. To promote the use of distributed computing via the **Internet**, Berners-Lee created the first elements of the World Wide Web in 1992. The concept of Hypertext itself predated the development of HTML by some years, having originally been conceived of by an American, Ted Nelson. HTML could not really take off until an easily usable application became available that could interpret and display HTML in the intended format. In 1993, the US National Center for Supercomputing Applications (NCSA) released an application called Mosaic, a web browser which was adopted very rapidly by the then quite small number of people using the Internet. As Mosaic's code was **Open Source**, a host of similar applications arose. Direct descendents of Mosaic include Mozilla and Microsoft's dominant Internet Explorer.

HTML has reached Release 4.01 at the time of writing. Berners-Lee has gone on to become director of the World Wide Web Consortium (W3C), which promotes the use of HTML in a standard and accessible format to ensure that the Web is accessible to as many people as possible. This work has included the consortium launching the Web Accessibility Initiative (WAI), designed to maximize the accessibility of websites to blind and disabled people who are using the WWW. Also of note are XML (Extensible Markup Language), a generic language for creating new markup languages, and the related Dynamic HTML and XHTML. These languages are in a near-constant state of flux because they are very frequently updated and altered, a process that is detailed on the Consortium's website.

See also: **Java**, **JavaScript**

Further sources: www.w3.org/

HTTP (HYPERTEXT TRANSFER PROTOCOL)

The term 'protocol' is used here in the same sense as it would be in diplomacy, as the system or catalyst through which it is possible to communicate. Hypertext Transfer Protocol is used for exchanging hypertext documents across the **World Wide Web**, in other words it is the protocol that allows web browsing to take place.

The protocol is based on the client/server principle. It allows the 'client' computer to contact another computer (the 'server') and make a request for information. An http request tells the server which information the client is interested in and what action to take in relation to the request. The http protocol works with **HTML** or other hypertext web pages, with a click on a **URL** or link on a web page sending an http request for specific information in a format that the client computer can display. This protocol also provides access to a number of other protocols, such as the **File Transfer Protocol**. The http protocol works in conjunction with **TCP/IP** to provide all the information exchange across the web.

Further sources: www.w3.org/protocols

HUMAN/COMPUTER INTERFACE *see* **Interface**

HYPERCASUALIZATION

Hypercasualization refers to changes in the labour market that are related to the rise of **globalization** and the information economy. In essence, hypercasualization refers to the decline of full-time employment in the manufacturing sector and the 'replacement' of these jobs with jobs in the service sector, which are typically low-paid, part-time and quite often on short-term contracts. These changes to the structure of the labour market are perhaps at their most pronounced in the United States, in which service industries predominate, although European countries such as the UK have experienced a very similar shift in their labour markets.

Hypercasualization is seen partly as a consequence of the rise of new capitalist societies that have lower labour costs than post-industrial societies, which has led to the movement of manufacturing out of Western Europe and the USA and towards Asia and, to some extent, Eastern Europe. The rise of the information economy, a catalyst for globalization, has allowed these developments to take place at a greater speed. These processes have made elements of a once secure middle class more vulnerable to losing their jobs, while highly skilled 'knowledge workers' enjoy higher salaries and access to a global job market.

Concern has increased that elements of the working population who would once have been in full-time employment in unskilled and semi-skilled professions in the industrial sector of the economy now find it difficult to secure equivalent work. There is also an increased concern that many may find it difficult to get any work at all, as the industrial work that used to be done by men has moved abroad, while lower-paid, lower-status jobs in the service sector tend to be undertaken by women. In the UK, for example, long-term male unemployment and youth unemployment are seen as major social problems and several government programmes have been created to counteract them. Some of the main policy concerns about hypercasualization are linked to the concepts of social exclusion and social cohesion, which refer to the danger that highly unequal societies are in danger of experiencing instability. Both the current British Government and the European Union have concerns in this respect. Evidence of the consequences of a breakdown in social cohesion linked to extreme inequality is visible in US cities such as Los Angeles, and commentators such as Mike Davies, in *City of Quartz* (1992), have related this to economic change.

See also: **Globalization**

Further sources: Jordan (1996), Castells (1996)

ICQ (I SEEK YOU)

ICQ is a form of **instant messaging** software, which predated AOL's popular service by many years.

INFORMATION AND COMMUNICATIONS TECHNOLOGY (ICT)

ICT encompasses all digital computing and communication equipment. Aside from **computers**, ranging from servers to palm or handheld devices, ICTs include mobile (cellular) telephones and **digital television**. Most academics argue that 'technological determinism' (which holds that society is being changed by ICTs) is too simplistic an interpretation of their social and economic effects and that ICTs are instead shaped and changed by a society that absorbs them. In turn, this absorption of ICTs causes society itself to change shape. One of the key theorists in this area is Manuel Castells, who has detailed his arguments in his three-volume work *The Information Age: Economy, Society and Culture* (1996).

Some argue that ICTs have played a fundamentally important role in the creation of the information economy, **globalization** and **hypercasualization**. ICTs are also expected to have significant effects on commerce and government, in the fields of electronic service delivery, **e-commerce** and **e-government**. At a social level, some argue that high use of ICTs can make people become alienated and socially dysfunctional (see **Otaku**), and there are related worries that some computer and video **games** may also have socially adverse effects.

IDENTITY

Identity has become a contested term in social and cultural theory, at least in part as a result of transformative processes such as globalization and postmodernization. And, in terms of cyberculture, the transformative effects of new information and communication technologies have also reshaped identity at the individual and collective level (see Bell 2001). There has been extensive research into the ways that cyberspace has reshaped some aspects of identity – **gender** is probably the most-researched – and the issue of identity-play has also received a lot of attention. In terms of the latter, the lack of face-to-face (**F2F**) contact in **computer mediated communication** is seen by some commentators as freeing us from the restrictions of our real-life identities and **bodies** – we can endlessly re-invent ourselves, present infinite different selves in different online environments, and experiment with who we are and who we want to be. Cyberspace is seen here as a kind of performance space, where we can utilize props, cues and scripts to enact our virtual identities. Charles Cheung (2000) discusses personal **homepages** in this light, exploring the ways in which homepages are used as a reflection and extension of the self – how the assemblage of visual and textual material, plus links to other sites, works to present the self to net-surfers in particular ways.

Away from a focus on the individual, the broader collective 'axes' of identity – conventionally listed as race, class, gender, sexuality and nationality – have all been reshaped and rethought in the context of cyberculture. However, this should not be taken as meaning that cyberspace completely liberates individuals from their real-life selves. As research by Nakamura (2000), for example, shows, racial stereotypes persist in cyberculture, and inequalities are imported from the real to the virtual world. The implications for gender are similarly mixed, with some writers stressing the new freedoms of a post-gender cyberculture – for example, in some writing on **MUDs** – while others suggest that women remain marginalized in cyberspace and in other spheres such as **gaming**. The same kind of conclusions can be reached about sexuality, perhaps, although most research has focused on gay and lesbian use of cyberspace, often showing the ways in which this produces new spaces for coming out and for community building (Wakeford 2000).

In terms of class, the emphasis of research is different, in that the most prominent issues here centre on questions of access to cyberspace. The economic differentials that structure access have produced a new digital underclass as well as a new information elite (Aurigi and Graham 1998). While these inequalities often mirror those pre-existing cyberspace, the divide between information-rich and information-poor will only get wider as more of life gets lived online – those of us who are forced to remain offline face escalating exclusion. These exclusions are felt at various spatial scales, including the nation: the global map of Internet use shows very starkly who is online and who is not.

For those privileged with access to cyberspace, issues around national identity are also brought into focus. In some instances, we have witnessed a resurgence of nationalism in online contexts, while we can also see the reverse occurring in the form of new transnational identifications freed from geographical limits. Clearly, then, whichever aspect of identity you choose to explore in cyberspace, there are complex and often contradictory forces at work. True, for some people cyberspace offers freedom to become someone new; for others, however, such opportunities remain out of reach.

See also: **Body**, **Gender**, **Homepage**, **MUDs**

Further sources: Porter (1997), Aurigi and Graham (1998), Bell (2001), Cheung (2000), Nakamura (2000, 2002), Wakeford (2000)

INDYMEDIA (INDEPENDENT MEDIA CENTERS)

The first Indymedia Center (IMC) was launched in Seattle during the tumultuous milieu of the 'Battle of Seattle' protests against the World Trade Organization's ministerial meetings in November 1999, and is an excellent example of a new organizational/institutional form made possible (as well as necessary) by new social realities and technological capabilities. In three years, the Indymedia network has grown into a loosely affiliated collective network of over 120 independent but philosophically-aligned local media groups, or nodes, on all continents of the world except Antarctica. Indymedia is, in the network's own words, 'a collective of independent media organizations and hundreds of journalists offering grassroots, non-corporate coverage. Indymedia is a democratic media outlet for the creation of radical, accurate, and passionate telling of truth.' In values, Indymedia's 'principles of unity' emphasize an open network approach to social relations: grassroots democratic discourse, respect for diversity, cooperative coordination and public ownership. In structure, Indymedia is a unique global integration of four types of alternative media modalities, working simultaneously as: a news network for individual media activists and the general public; a decentralized confederation of media collectives; a social-movement media covering the global justice movement; and an alternative media network, serving diverse movements and interests (Morris 2003). The IMCs employ **GNU copyleft free software** and use an open publishing model where anybody can act as a reporter and submit a story to the open newswire. In a newsgroup format, other people can comment on stories. Increasingly, Indymedia journalists pull together and feature various independent and activist-oriented news resources in various print, radio, video and web publications (see, for example, the centre column at the website www.indy media.org). Many IMC local nodes are mostly virtual, meeting occasionally in donated space and operating on donated computer servers. Some more established IMCs, like Seattle Indymedia, do provide a physical space and resources used to produce regular media and to host speakers and meetings.

Further sources: Morris (2003), Schuler and Day (2003), www.indy-media.org

INFORMATION

In discussions of the **information society**, information economy and the importance of **ICTs**, the very idea of information and how to define it becomes of central importance for our understanding of contemporary cybercultures. It is almost an axiom that information has been promoted to occupy a more prevalent role in our everyday lives, whether it is through business transactions, leisure activities or relations with public services and government. There may also be a consensus that we may be threatened by an 'information overload', with greater quantities of it being circulated at ever greater speeds by more sophisticated ICTs. Yet many disputes about the nature of the transforming qualities of ICTs centre upon the fact that information is a highly contested concept.

Broadly speaking, we may identify two perspectives which attempt to understand the concept of information. The first of these is to regard information as a 'resource' which both is quantifiable and has an autonomous existence outside of the social and cultural context within which it is both created and understood. This suggests that information is considered as a stable entity which exists independently of either the transmitter or the receiver. It is a view which is consistent with the idea that information can be measured in 'bits' and is therefore attractive to the communications engineer responsible for the transmission and storage of such symbols. Little or no under-standing of the information is required by those processing it and the information resource is owned by an external agency such as an organization (corporate property).

An alternative and contrasting perspective is to understand information as being dependent upon individual 'perception'. This view draws a distinction between data sets which belong to the organization and information which may use such data but which exists inside people's heads. In this sense, individuals rather than organizations own information. Information does not therefore exist outside of the perception of the receiver. Facts *do not* speak for themselves. Instead they require manipulation and interpretation. Indeed for information to have value it must also have semantic content which has meaning for the recipient. This subjective understanding of information suggests that it is always open to interpretation, misunderstanding and dispute. Individual traits, culture, political structures, economic circumstances and many other factors influence the perceptions of those receiving information.

Why do these competing perspectives of information matter? Arguably the distinctions are important because they may help to explain why, for example, information systems introduced as 'resource'-based may fail as a consequence of different departments or employees interpreting the value of the information in completely different or contradictory ways. In another context the distinction may help us understand how information considered as a resource may be used in a deliberately 'political' manner to limit debate or exclude alternative perspectives. Consider for example the possible transmission of health information between different agencies. The perceptions of health professions, police agencies, insurance companies or employment organizations may give rise to completely contrasting interpretations of an individual's medical records. The value of the information, in other words, will be different for each agency. Its meaning will be shaped according to specific cultural interests. For the health professional it may be a concern with the special relationship of trust between doctor and patient; for the law enforcement agency it may relate to investigative processes; for the insurer it will be interpreted according to risk assessment; for the employer it will be perceived as evidence of occupational suitability. In each case the medical information about the individual will be understood according to the different perceptions of the recipients. Each may attempt to privilege their interpretation and their 'right' to access the information by claiming that it is a vital resource for crime detection, proportional risk allocation or whatever. However, since such claims affect the 'privacy' and 'protection' of the individual, they are likely to lead to considerable political debate about the sharing of information between agencies.

Further sources: Dutton (1999), Lash (2002)

INFORMATION SOCIETY

In the developed world the increasingly ubiquitous diffusion of new **information and communications technologies (ICTs)** into almost every aspect of cultural, economic, political and social life has led to an assertion that we are entering a new epoch in human development: the Information Society. It is a period which is frequently contrasted with the industrial and agrarian societies which are said to have preceded it. The Information Society is usually characterized by the following features:

- Information becomes increasingly important as the economic, cultural and political resources upon which the emerging global information economy and information societies are organized, with the majority of occupations based upon information or knowledge work.
- The dynamic innovation of ICTs is seen to be transforming the potential for processing, storing and transmitting of information in ways previously unimaginable and ICTs are thereby becoming more pervasive in our lives.
- Electronically networked economies and societies fundamentally transform our conceptions of time and space, enabling information flows to transcend temporal and physical boundaries and thereby facilitate processes of globalization and networking enterprise.
- Information becomes culturally more prevalent through multi-media applications, but also more contested and less meaningful, in a world of competing, contradictory and constantly changing images, signs and messages.

As the name suggests, one of the main defining features of the Information Society is a recognition of an 'explosion of **information**' in contemporary life. The creation, ownership and distribution of information is regarded by many as a primary economic activity. Indeed a common measure of the emergence of an Information Society is the extent to which information industries contribute to the gross national product (GNP) of a country. The pioneering work of Fritz Machlup (1962) and Marc Porat (1977) has led to attempts to categorize knowledge work by distinguishing it from non-informational sectors and placing a quantitative measure upon its growth and contribution to national prosperity. Similarly another popular measure of the informatization of society is to examine the proportion of occupations which can be described as 'information' or 'knowledge' work. Daniel Bell, in his famous depiction of the Information Society (1976), pointed to the growth in the number of white-collar workers and the decline of industrial labour as harbingers of profound social and economic change. More recently Robert Reich (1992) and Manuel Castells (1996) have both emphasized the importance of the **globalization** of the information economy and the increasingly prevalent role played by a new kind of informational labour. Reich describes these workers as 'symbolic analysts' who are highly educated, flexible and mobile, and who 'solve, identify, and broker problems by manipulating symbols' (1992: 198). They are seen as the drivers of the emerging information society and are crucial for the development of the global information economy.

It is important to note that, while all of these accounts of the informatization of society offer valuable interpretations of economic and social change, they have also raised much controversy among social scientists (for a good introductory critique, read Webster 2002). In particular, crude employment and GNP statistics are often believed to hide more complex factors which make it difficult for us to say categorically that the Information Society has arrived. For example, studies suggest that, even in the USA, information industries do not yet account for more than 50 per cent of GNP. Moreover, the classification of information workers may owe a great deal more to the personal judgement of researchers than to objective characteristics. Such analysis is often criticized for ignoring 'qualitative' issues, such as whether these perceived changes in patterns of employment have significantly changed the distribution of power and status in societies.

The extraordinary advances of ICTs in recent years, and the breathtaking speed of their development, has led some commentators to describe this process as a technological revolution on a par with its industrial predecessor (Dizzard 1989, Negroponte 1995). At the heart of this transforming capability is the **convergence** between what were once distinct technologies and sectors, whose fusion offers the prospect of profound organizational and behavioural change. Developments in the **computer** industry have seen the decline in importance of mainframe computing relative to the rising importance of microcomputing combined with user-friendly software. The personal computer and the ubiquitous screens of Microsoft and Apple Macintosh software applications, for example, have become commonplace features of many offices and homes around the world. In the field of telecommunications the change from analog to digital signalling, switches and exchanges coincidently provided the opportunities for electronic data transmissions (voice, text, images, data) which use the same binary language understood by computers. More recently this digital convergence has also included the major media entertainment industries, which offer the prospects of further blurring between sectors and the proliferation of multimedia applications (see **games**).

This process of digital convergence between the computer, telecommunications and media technologies has enabled the development of electronic networks such as the **Internet** and the **World**

Wide Web (WWW) whereby computers can be linked and made to communicate with each other. Millions of terminals around the world, whether in homes, offices, shops, banks, schools or elsewhere, can share information at any time of the day. Increasingly other digital technologies such as mobile or cellphones, cable and satellite TV, smartmedia cards and CCTV (closed circuit televisions) are being incorporated into electronic network applications. Such developments in ICTs are seen as supporting the processes of informatization, but they may also be responsible for profound changes to our understanding of time and space.

The network has become the predominant metaphor for the Information Society. Manuel Castells, in his book *The Rise of the Network Society*, remarked that 'as a historical trend, dominant functions and processes in the information age are increasingly organized around networks' (1996: 469). Socially, economically and politically, networking is increasingly regarded as the main form of practice and structure. In part this is facilitated by the transforming capabilities of electronic computer networks such as the Internet. In particular such technology offers the prospect of reconfiguring our understanding of space and the flow of information and communication. Communication between individuals and organizations using 'information superhighways' linking computers is no longer restricted by geographical barriers or time constraints. People can share information across national boundaries twenty-four hours a day.

This has a potential significance for how we think about 'place' and 'space'. Commentators have used the terms '**virtual communities**' or '**cyberspace**' to describe computer-mediated spaces where remotely dispersed individuals can share an interaction through the use of **emails**, **bulletin board systems**, **chat rooms**, forums, **Usenet newsgroups** and other electronic means. Howard Rheingold (1993) famously predicted that people may spend a great deal of their social lives in virtual communities as well as in their geographical neighbourhoods. Moreover, the use of such networked communication may enable the rise of virtual organizations whereby members of an enterprise or public service no longer need to be physically located at the same site. **Network organizations** offer the potential for much more decentralized structures and flexible working practices to emerge.

The final characteristic which is often said to define the Information Society is the emergence of new 'informational' cultures which again are contrasted with the 'industrial' cultures associated with social classes, professional expertise, national citizenship, scientific rational thought and the like. Instead, it is argued, the explosion of information and its increasingly rapid circulation through ICTs and the media has resulted in a fundamental weakening of confidence about what we should believe and who we are. Traditional certainties about personal **identity** are challenged by an enormous array of contradictory and competing messages and styles from radio stations, TV channels, Internet sites, films, newspapers, magazines, advertising billboards, literature, fashions, music and a host of information sources which inform our everyday life experiences.

This informational culture is said to be sustained through the technologies which increasingly pervade our lives, such as telephones, cameras, Walkmans, digital TV, networked PCs and laptops. But the culture also permeates other aspects of our lifestyles, such as the clothes we wear and the body images we wish to project. It is an information-soaked environment in which our lives are almost continually concerned with the process of symbolization – the exchange of meanings about ourselves and others.

There seems little doubt that in many advanced societies people increasingly live in a more information-intensive environment which may often present a confusing set of mixed messages. Indeed, Jean Baudrillard famously suggested that this proliferation of 'signs' has led to a corresponding loss of 'meaning'. Where once signs had a reference – clothes defined a given status, medical advice a scientific expertise, political comments a certain philosophy – they are now replaced by simulations of signs which have no base in reality. For Baudrillard the environment becomes characterized by 'hyperreality' (1983) in which copies and fabrication become reality. Equally, audiences and recipients of symbolization become more self-creative and critically reflective, which leads them to be more sceptical, dismissive and even disillusioned about the intended meaning of the signs.

See also: **Computer, Cyberpunk, Cyberspace, Identity, Information, Internet, Network organizations**

Further sources: Baudrillard (1983), Castells (1996, 2001), Dizzard (1989), Negroponte (1995), Reich (1992), Webster (2002)

INFORMATION SUPERHIGHWAY *see* **Digital divide**

INFORMATION TECHNOLOGY *see* **Information and communications technology**

INFORMATION WARFARE

A concept devised by David Ronfeldt and John Arquilla of the RAND Institute, Information warfare describes a wide range of belligerent activities augmented or made possible via the **Internet**, including propaganda distribution, espionage, **virus** release and computer **hacking**.

Further sources: Acquilla and Rondfeldt (2001)

INSTANT MESSAGING (IM)

IM is a form of text-based, synchronous **computer mediated communication**, originally launched on America Online (AOL). After installing an instant messaging application, users are alerted to messages the moment they arrive, by audio or visual cues. Message exchange is rapid and virtually instantaneous (depending on the speed of the connection). Popular IM services include Microsoft's MSN Messenger, AOL's Instant Messenger, **ICQ** and Yahoo Messenger.

IM offers similar facilities to those found in **IRC chat rooms**, but it is designed for one-to-one interaction. In this sense, it offers the intimacy of one-to-one **email** exchanges but through a CMC medium that offers the capacity to provide the instantaneous feedback of a 'typed conversation' offered by IRC.

Further sources: web.icq.com/, www.aol.com/

INTERACTIVE TELEVISION *see* Digital television

INTERFACE

Defined as 'software that shapes the interaction between user and computer', and the way in which 'the computer represents itself to the user ... in a language that the user understands' (Johnson 1997: 14, 15), the interface (also known as the human–computer interface, or HCI) is what we see on the computer screen. In the not-too-distant past, interfaces were complicated and comprehensible only to computer **geeks**, whereas now, with their clickable icons, decorative wallpaper, desktop and windows, the interface has become a lot more user-friendly. Exploring the look of this Graphical User Interface (GUI) opens up questions of how the computer screen is presented to us, how it works, and how its look impacts upon users. Julian Stallabrass (1999) makes this point in his discussion of Microsoft's multimedia operating system Windows, which he reads as epitomizing a 'rational' aesthetic common to software interfaces:

> Think of its particular features which have become so familiar that we tend to take them for granted; and how familiar it is all designed to be – the files and folders, those little thumbnail sketches which so appropriately bear the name 'icons' ... the sculpted 3-D buttons, the pop-up notices, decked out with instantly recognizable, if not comprehensible, symbols warning of hazards or admonishing the user's mistakes.
>
> (Stallabrass 1999: 110)

In the guise of user-friendliness, Stallabrass argues, this interface represents a dumbing-down of computer use, irritating rather than wooing us with its cheery, matey demeanour. However, this is the whole point of the GUI now commonplace on personal computers – to make the inner workings of the machine transparent by presenting them to users in ways we can understand, complete with pictures and ready assistance. Of course, this does mean simplification – but most computer users do not need (or want) to know about software code, or the actual processes going on inside computers. All we need is to know how to use them. However, this also removes some of the creativity from computer use by only allowing us access to limited, pre-set functions (Cubitt 2001).

Outside of the specifics of Microsoft's Windows, moreover, the general interface practice of 'windowing' has received attention. Sherry Turkle (1999) discusses the windows interface as a tool designed for more effective computing, since it allows users to have a number of applications open simultaneously, stacked up one behind the other, so that we can move from one to the other easily without complex programming or operations. Like riffling through a pile of papers, clicking between open applications offers an experience of computer use that mirrors the complexities of human thinking and working practices. Moreover, Turkle suggests that the windows metaphor extends to the way in which we keep different parts of our own **identity** open, reflecting the postmodern experience of decentred subjectivity.

Furthermore, we need to also consider what we might call networked aesthetics – how the Internet has brought about a restyling of the interface. In particular, the need to depict and present to users the form and structure of cyberspace has had an important impact on issues such as web design – as computers and their capabilities become more complex, so the need to manage the interface between machine and human becomes ever more pressing; at the same time, as computers become thoroughly domesticated and they grow more familiar to us, so the need to demystify them lessens.

In time, interfaces may undergo another transition, through the use of **agents** that enable person-to-(simulated)-person interaction between the user and a computer that reacts like another person. Work on agent software and on 'natural language processing' continues to this end, though the reality of a computer that can actually hold a conversation with its user seems distant at the time of writing. Should such operating systems ever be created, the relationships between a user and a machine that effectively mimics the user may start to become very complex indeed.

See also: **Identity**

Further sources: Johnson (1997), Stallabrass (1999), Turkle (1999)

INTERNET

The Internet is an international 'network of networks' that uses a common set of standards (**TCP/IP**) to permit the interconnection of millions of computers, enabling such services as electronic mail and remote access to information. The **World Wide Web** is built atop the Internet infrastructure.

Millions of computers are linked to the Internet via Local Area Networks (LANs), which are data communications networks usually confined to a limited spatial area, such as a building. These LANs (which are most commonly Ethernet networks) are in turn connected to Wide Area Networks (WANs), physical or logical networks that provide data communications to a larger number of independent users over a larger area (city-wide networks are sometimes called MANs for Metropolitan Area Networks). The Internet is the shorthand term by which we describe these many interconnected networks.

The Internet originated in 1969, as a result of a project of the US Defense Advanced Research Projects Agency (DARPA). The intention was to create a means by which computers – which at that time were hugely expensive – could be contacted by military commanders in the field via a communications system that could theoretically absorb massive damage before being rendered inoperable. The conceptual underpinnings of the Internet had been laid by Paul Baran at the RAND corporation in 1962, when he developed the model of self-routing data 'packets'.

In slightly oversimplified terms, this involved breaking information down into chunks (packets) that might be compared with automobiles on a road network. Like automobiles, packets are 'self guiding', and like automobiles they are able to take alternative routes when the need arises. A data packet travelling across the Internet can be rerouted in face of an obstruction in one part of the network, or take an alternative route if part of the network becomes unavailable. Theoretically, this model made the Internet 'bomb proof', because if one part of the network was lost, the data packets could take another route.

TCP/IP protocols form the basis by which packets are sent. Packets are sent to a 'router', a computer junction that stores each packet and reads its destination, makes reference to its 'routing table', and then sends each one on to another router along the way. The routing tables are updated automatically if congestion or damage occurs, to ensure the most optimal route for each packet. Packets move from one router to another, often via different routes, as the optimal route may change between the sending of one packet and the next, until they all arrive at their destination. The identifiers on the packets are then used to reassemble the entire transmitted dataset. This system is efficient, because breaking data down into small packets allows the most effective exploitation of networks, and because it can cope if elements of networks fail or become congested. The non-proprietary protocols underlying network transactions are key to the Internet's rapid growth and ongoing evolution.

The first civilian use of the Internet was in 1984, when a civilian segment evolved under the auspices of the US National Science Foundation (NSF), which was referred to as NSFNET. This experimental network linked the research computers in universities, industries and government labs. It was at first used for data transfer, but it was also realized early on that messages could be sent cheaply and easily, leading to the development of **email** on these networks.

The explosion in Internet use began with the appearance of the World Wide Web, the basics of which were developed by Tim Berners-Lee at CERN in 1992. Real growth took place when the US National Center for Super Computing decided to make their HTML browser Mozilla available as **freeware** on an **Open Source** basis. The Internet took on its current form in 1995 when the existing ban on commercial activity was lifted and key elements of the infrastructure were sold to corporations. The key physical infrastructure of the Internet is now held by an association of businesses that are represented by an umbrella organization, the Internet Society (www.isoc.org). The great bulk of websites are now commercial, distinguished by the '.com' at the end of their website addresses.

The great increase in home use of the Internet has been directly related to the falling costs of PCs over the last decade or so. Consumers have been attracted by its potential for cheap communication, the huge information base offered by the Web, and, increasingly, by the convenience of **e-commerce**. Since the mid-1990s the Internet has changed, from being a series of networks to which an elite few had access, into a mass communications medium. There is however strong evidence that economically marginalized or disadvantaged people in countries with developed economies, including the US, tend to have less access to the Internet. Most of the world's population has no access to the Internet (see **digital divide**).

See also: **HTML**, **World Wide Web**

Further sources: Gillies and Cailliau (2000), Abbate (2000)

INTERNET BANKING *see* **e-Commerce**

INTERNET CAFÉ

An internet café in which Internet access is available for a fee (generally per hour). Internet cafés are especially popular among tourists. In developing countries internet café rates usually seem quite reasonable to visitors. Internet cafés are sometimes contrasted with telecentres (Robinson 2003), which may have educational and other social goals and are generally non-profit oriented.

See also: **Community technology centers**, **Electronic village halls**

Further sources: Robinson (2003)

INTERNET RELAY CHAT (IRC)

IRC was developed by a Finn, Jarkko Oikarinen, in 1988 while he was working in the Department of Information Processing Science at the University of Oulu. It was designed to provide a kind of 'real-time' **bulletin board** or newsgroup service. From its origins in Finland, IRC spread first to the University of Denver and Oregon State University, and then rapidly across the US and the rest of the world. This spread was facilitated by IRC being made available on an **Open Source** basis with no attempt being made to copyright the software or concept behind it.

IRC is neither written communication nor conversation, although it has features of both. This form of synchronous **computer mediated communication** is perhaps best described as a 'typed conversation'. Users of IRC enter a shared virtual space, usually called a 'channel' or 'room', in which they can engage in conversations with one another (see **chat room**). A line or two of text is typed by a participant and appears instantly on screen, followed by the next person's contribution and the next. Conversations can be just between two people or many, though when a large number of people are present on a channel communication can become difficult. The speed does not match that of speech, not least because everyone is typing rather than talking, but the rate and conversational feel of exchanges can feel closer to being involved in a telephone or face-to-face (see **F2F**) conversation than is the case on **Usenet** or with **email**.

IRC has something in common with **MUDs** in that it allows users to share a virtual space and interact with one another in real time. However, its operating principles are quite different from those of MUDs. Many MUDs are based on a single server (host computer), whereas IRC works on a global basis with its networks often running on a series of interlinked servers. There are many IRC networks around the world, making a global collection of networks of IRC 'channels' or 'rooms' accessible to anyone with IRC software. IRC is also a simple application to use.

The use of **smileys**, combinations of punctuation and letters used as pictograms to express emotion or show facial expression, is common in IRC exchanges (see also **cues filtered out**). **Abbreviations** are also particularly common. Like people who are **text messaging** on mobile phones (cell phones in the US), participants in IRC often wish to convey as much information as possible within a few keystrokes in order to keep up the speed of their exchanges. These abbreviations (e.g. LOL, for 'Laughing Out Loud'), tend to be similar to those used in MUDs, within email or in newsgroups on Usenet.

IRC has become a highly popular means of **computer mediated communication**. Many channels are devoted to casual chatting, **cybersex** or simply to online flirting. It is often particularly attractive to young people. Like MUDs, IRC allows anonymity, role-playing and **gender** and **identity** swapping, any of which may appeal to its users (see **body**). It also offers an environment in which one can experiment with identity, or behave in ways that are not acceptable or tolerated within more traditional forms of social interaction. Different IRC channels vary however. Many are unregulated, while others have operators, or 'ops', who act as regulators and enforce standards of behaviour on participants (with those who do not conform being ejected or denied access to the channel). In some instances, ops can also engage in play, using their authority over a channel to exercise arbitrary authority in a way that they would not be able to in another context.

While IRC is often used for play, it can and has had different uses. Some online 'self-help' resources are based around an IRC channel. In 1991, during the Gulf War, Kuwaitis with Internet connection used IRC to send out information to the rest of the world about what was happening inside their country.

There are a number of quite similar forms of communication. **ICQ** ('I seek you') provides very similar communication between participants on a one-to-one basis (see **instant messaging**).

As **broadband** becomes more widely available, it might be the case that IRC is replaced by video- or **avatar**-based communication, in which users can see one another – or at least representations of one another – and interact in a virtual space that is shown graphically.

Further sources: Danet *et al.* (1998), Reid (1996), Pleace *et al.* (2000)

INTERNET2®

A not-for-profit consortium whose members include 200 US universities, Internet2® is developing and deploying advanced network applications and technology relating to a next-generation Internet. According to their literature, their three goals are: (1) creating a leading-edge network capability for the national research community; (2) enabling revolutionary Internet applications; and (3) ensuring the rapid transfer of new network services and applications to the broader Internet community. There are working groups concerned with applications, backbone network infrastructure, engineering and middleware, each of which is working on a variety of projects.

Further sources: www.Internet2.edu/

IRL (IN REAL LIFE)

IRL is one of countless shorthand forms commonly used in email (Shortis 2001). Things are said either to take place IRL or online, a grammar that makes explicit the split between the 'real' and the 'virtual'. In the same ways that meeting **F2F** is sometimes held up as an important confirmation of identities and relationships established online, so the definitions of real life and virtual life can privilege the real over the virtual. Issues surrounding the status of the **body** and **identity**, IRL and in cyberspace, are raised by the use of this distinction. Perhaps more problematically, it can seem to emphasize the sense that cyberspace is not real, and that therefore no real harm (nor pleasure) can come from online interactions and experiences.

See also: **Body, F2F, Identity**

ISP (INTERNET SERVICE PROVIDER)

An ISP is a company that provides users with **access** to the **Internet**. Examples include America Online (AOL).

JACKING IN

'Jacking in' is a term used in Gibsonian **cyberpunk** to describe the process of entering cyberspace – literally, the uploading of human consciousness into the datascape. In Gibson's novel *Neuromancer*, console cowboys use 'cyberdecks' to access cyberspace (Tomas 2000). In contemporary cyberculture, the dream of uploading in this way, and of thereby separating the mind from the **body**, retains a powerful appeal. In cyberpunk, however, the process is figured as disorienting, dangerous and profoundly ambivalent. In movies such as *Johnny Mnemonic* and *Strange Days*, the direct interfacing of the human mind with data-based simulations can bring thrills and profit, but also carries a price (Cavallaro 2000). The ideal, of course, in part propelled research into **virtual reality** (VR), which attempts to provide an immersive and interactive simulation experientially as close to jacking in as is technologically feasible. However, the experience of 'sim-sickness' associated with VR echoes the ambivalence figured in cyberpunk – that attempting to sever the mind–body split can provoke severe reactions and side effects.

See also: **Body, Cyberpunk, Virtual reality**

Further sources: Cavallaro (2000), Tomas (2000)

JAVA

A programming language developed by computer manufacturer Sun Microsystems, Java is related to the computer language C++ and was originally developed by Bill Joy and James Gosling in the early 1990s. Java is designed as a cross-platform language, which means that any computer with any operating system should be able to run an application written in the language, providing the operating system is designed to be Java-compatible. This, in theory, overcomes the compatibility problems between various operating systems such as **UNIX, LINUX**, Microsoft's Windows and Apple's MacOS, as a Java application should run on any of these platforms. The language uses an application called the Java Virtual Machine which translates general Java commands into instructions that a specific operating system can then make a computer execute. Java has become particularly associated with the **World Wide Web** because it can add functionality to websites without increasing demands on the server on which the website is based. This is because Java code is interpreted and run by the machine that accesses the website rather than the server on which the website is running. Small applications written in Java for web pages are usually referred to as applets, and they can add a range of enhancements to a web page, including animations, multimedia functions and small applications. Java offers multimedia for web pages that is more immediately accessible and quicker to download than some alternative technologies used to provide multimedia functions. Most recent browsers support Java.

Java differs from other languages that are associated with the rise of the WWW because, unlike **HTML** and **JavaScript**, it is a true programming language that can be used to write freestanding applications. The potential for Java is considerable, and it is also being used in mobile (cellular) telephones, digital TVs and so forth.

Further sources: www.sun.com/java/

JAVASCRIPT

JavaScript, originally developed by Netscape, is a language that is designed to be used in conjunction with **HTML**. A web page can have elements of JavaScript mixed in with its HTML that can add a limited range of functions not available through HTML alone. Perhaps the most common use of JavaScript is in the addition of interactive forms to web pages, which allow the use of a web page as a tool by which customers can send comments or requests to a business. JavaScript can also make fine changes to the layout of a page, particularly with regard to the position of page elements, and add limited multimedia functions, such as basic animation and sounds. Like HTML itself, JavaScript is not a programming language, because it cannot be used to create a freestanding application. It is perhaps easiest to conceptualize as a series of commands that enhance and increase the functions available in ordinary HTML, rather than to view it as a separate language.

JOHNNY MNEMONIC (MOVIE)

Directed by Robert Longo in 1995 and based on a William Gibson story, *Johnny Mnemonic*'s eponymous lead character (Keanu Reeves) has brain implants that enable him to upload data directly into his brain. He is a **cyborg** smuggler, reaping handsome rewards for passing corporate data to paying clients – but he has also paid a high price: in order to carry data, he has forfeited some of his own memory, and cannot remember his childhood. His sense of identity is thus radically undermined. Moreover, as the film's plot develops, he is almost killed by the sheer volume of data in his brain. The character can be read as embodying the condition of the decentred self:

> With his head crammed full of data, his loss of memory, and his confused attempts to understand his predicament and the hostile environment, Johnny literalizes a postmodern subject bombarded with information, disconnected from the past in an eternal present, and spatially disoriented.
>
> (Springer 1999: 207)

The film depicts other dangers of cyberculture, in that a new 'plague' – 'Nerve Attenuation Syndrome' – is devastating the world as a result of global data overload. To save himself and the human species, Johnny enters cyberspace with the help of the 'Low Teks', one of the subcultures that populates Gibson's work (Tomas 2000). Cyberspace is thus depicted as both a threat to 'reality' and as the only way to restore 'normality'.

See also: **Cyberpunk**, **Identity**, **Memory**

Further sources: Springer (1999), Tomas (2000)

KILLER APP

A 'killer app' is a piece of software that makes hardware attractive to purchase. When Apple launched the Apple II in 1977, it was one of the earliest incarnations of the spreadsheet Visicalc that made the computer particularly attractive and functioned as its 'killer app'. Subsequently, the spreadsheet for IBM PC called Lotus 123 eclipsed Visicalc in the early 1980s and became one of the main incentives to buy a PC, as well as allowing the development of the Lotus Corporation into a major company. As Lotus 123 showed, software houses that develop a killer app can often become major companies essentially on the strength of that single product. Microsoft's versions of BASIC and DOS, and its Windows operating systems, can be seen as a succession of killer apps that essentially created the company and ensure its continued prosperity. A company that is reliant on one killer app is also one which is vulnerable in a highly competitive marketplace, because there is always the possibility that someone will produce something cheaper and better. In the **games** market, killer apps are equally important. A major company like Sega, Nintendo or Sony (and now Microsoft) can see its fortunes radically altered by a killer app game – for example, Nintendo's dominance of the handheld console market was greatly helped by the puzzle game Tetris and then by the appearance of the Pokemon series on its **Gameboy** and its successors.

KNOWLEDGE SOCIETY *see* Information society

LARA CROFT

The hero of the *Tomb Raider* series of adventure games, Lara Croft recently made the transition to Hollywood film. A female fantasy aimed at pubescent boys, 'she' first appeared in 1996 and has since been taken as a shorthand for describing the inherent sexism and sexual immaturity of some **games**. Lara's image has also been used promote the British software and **ICT** industries.

See also: **Cyberfeminism**, **Games**, **Gender**

LIBERALIZATION *see* Information economy

LINUX

An open source operating system, LINUX has been distributed as **freeware** by its creator, Linus Torvalds. Since it first appeared in 1991, LINUX has been constantly modified and improved by programmers working on its **Open Source** code, producing a highly stable and effective operating system. LINUX, in common with some other software, represents the most serious challenge to the corporate dominance of software provision, by providing an alternative as a free good.

Further sources: www.linux.com/

LISTSERV *see* **Usenet**

LURKING

Passive, non-interactive reading of communication in a **chat room** or newsgroup, lurking is often seen negatively as a form of voyeurism – though it can be an important way to learn the **netiquette** of particular cyberspaces, especially for **newbies**. Lurking is also a favoured research technique for academics wanting to observe online interactions, raising questions about research ethics (see **computer mediated communication**). Other commentators see lurking as a harmless pastime, much like 'people watching'. Attitudes towards lurkers vary considerably between sites, which sometimes have developed protocols for dealing with the 'problem' of lurkers.

Some commentators have become concerned at what might be termed the 'Oprahfication' (derived from the voyeuristic *Oprah* television programme) of newsgroups and chatrooms that are used by vulnerable or distressed people seeking **virtual social support**. The worry is that environments used as a support mechanism by some may simply be used for entertainment by others (see **troll**).

See also: **Netiquette, Newbie**

Further sources: Bell (2001)

MANGA

Manga is the name given to Japanese comics (animated film, TV and video is referred to as anime). Manga comics cover a huge range of topics, from the banal exploits of Japanese workers or 'salarymen' to sexually explicit and ultra-violent sci-fi. Those set in the future are important from a cybercultural perspective for their aesthetic, and for their handling of issues around post-humanism, cyborgs and so on. Aesthetically, there is considerable cross-fertilization between manga/anime, computer **games** and **cyberpunk** films and fiction, and the immense popularity of manga/anime has brought the products and their core concerns to broader audiences – although some critics remain suspicious of the 'Orientalist' appropriation and consumption of manga/anime in the West. Obsessive consumption of manga and anime is associated with **Hikikomori** and **Otaku** in Japan.

See also: **Cyberpunk**, **Subcultures**

Further sources: Levi (1996), Martinez (1996)

MANY-TO-MANY COMMUNICATION *see* **Computer mediated communication**

MARIO *see* **Games**

THE MATRIX (MOVIE)

A hugely successful sci-fi blockbuster, *The Matrix* was directed by Larry and Andy Wachowski in 1999. Heavily indebted to the **cyberpunk** genre, as well as making knowing references to French philosopher Jean Baudrillard's theory of **simulation** and drawing on the aesthetics of computer **games**, *The Matrix* depicts everyday life as an elaborate construct – a datascape in which all human subjects are suspended, living out imaginary lives, when in fact they are being 'farmed', their bodies providing power for the machines that rule the 'real world'. These machines have come to rule following a catastrophic conflict between humans and **artificial intelligences** in the late twenty-second century – although the simulation in which people 'live' is set back in 1999. This virtual world is policed by autonomous intelligent agents (modelled on FBI agents, although the term **agent** is also used to describe independently acting software, which is what the Matrix agents 'actually' are), and the key characters form a band of renegade **hackers** intent on destroying the simulation and 'freeing' humankind (Cavallaro 2000). Laden with religious imagery (which became even more pronounced in the two sequels) about the second coming – the 'hero', played by Keanu Reeves, is named Neo – and with a populist critique of ideology, the film has attracted both praise and criticism. Treating it psychoanalytically, for example, Slavoj Zizek (1999) dismisses it for turning academic theory into populist entertainment, while in a rebuttal of Zizek, McKenzie Wark (1999) describes it approvingly as an 'ontological horror movie' that asks important questions about the status of reality. The second film in the series, *The Matrix Reloaded*, is also of interest as an example of **convergence** in entertainment media, the directors of the film overseeing the development of the tie-in console **games**.

See also: **Cyberpunk**, **Simulation**

Further sources: Cavallaro (2000), Wark (1999), Zizek (1999)

MEMORY

Computers are, in numerous ways, machines for remembering. Most obviously, they store data and programs in a variety of formats, and come equipped with a number of different memory storage devices (on PCs labelled 'A-drive', 'C-drive', etc.). One of the prime selling-points of computational devices is their memory capacity, their RAM size and their gigabytes of storage space. And in everyday use, we often delegate the task of data storage to our computers, filling up their memories with our life's business. We trust our machines to remember for us, and are therefore horrified at the prospect of that memory being corrupted, for example by a **virus**. The extent to which we rely on outside agents to assist our remembrance – not just computers, but also photographs, videos, diaries and so on – is described by some theorists as the prostheticization of memory (see Landsberg 2000). In a mediatized culture, Alison Landsberg argues, we can become confused about the status of our memories: are we remembering 'real' events from our own lives, or just past media constructs? This narrative is vividly played out in sci-fi cinema, in films such as ***Blade Runner*** and ***Total Recall***, both of which explore the idea of prosthetic memory and memory's relationship to our sense of self. How can we know who we are if we can't trust our own memories to be faithful?

But computers are memory devices in other ways, too – not just in their ability to store our files and thoughts, but also in terms of the memories that accrete around them. Like many of the significant objects that we assemble in our lives – houses, cars and so on – computers are woven into our life narratives and accommodated in our life patterns. The computers we have owned and used, our 'rites of passage' into computer culture, and the relationships we build up with these 'intimate machines' are stitched into our autobiographies (Bell 2001; and see **interface**). Moreover, as symbolic objects, computers carry all kinds of associations – often only revealed when we come to replace or discard them. They can be imbued with nostalgia – a facet which in part accounts for the growing interest in computer collecting and retro machines (Finn 2001). While such nostalgia may seem contradictory in a technoculture that is focused on the future, it is easily explainable once we recognize the kinds of relationships that people build up with their closest non-human companions. Under-standing the complexity of the human–computer interaction – and acknowledging that it involves emotion as much as calculation – can give us a much fuller understanding, therefore, of the many memory-making uses of the computer.

See also: **Blade Runner, Total Recall**

Further sources: Bell (2001), Finn (2001), Landsberg (2000)

MOO

MOO is an **abbreviation** for a **MUD** (a Multi-User Domain) that is object oriented. MOOs are thus a sub-set of MUDs, in which participants can actively construct the environment of the domain – building rooms, making objects, and so on. Rather than playing in a pre-set structure, then, participants in MOOs have a role to play in shaping the space in which the online interaction occurs. Lambda-MOO is among the best known and most studied of all MOOs, famous for its multiple gender identities (Kaloski 1999). These text-based environments are currently still in use, but may be eclipsed by graphical alternatives, including online worlds such as those provided by **games** like Everquest.

See also: **MUD**

Further sources: Kaloski (1999)

MOSAIC *see* **World Wide Web**

MP3

The file extension which describes one of a series of software formats that allow efficient compression of digital video and audio data, mp3 stands for 'MPEG (Moving Picture Experts Group), audio layer 3'. MP3 uses 'psychoacoustic compression' to remove all superfluous aural information, including the elements of a recording that a human ear cannot detect, allowing it shrink the size of a music track on a CD by a factor of 12 without noticeably sacrificing audio quality. The availability of music in this format accounts for a high level of web and Internet use by young people (in particular), who can download tracks and albums to highly portable mp3 personal stereos, car stereos and home stereos. Major legal battles have been fought by recording companies over the provision of mp3 files as a free good on the Internet, most notably against the Napster website.

See also: **Piracy**

MUD

MUD is shorthand for Multi-User Domain (or Dimension or Dungeon). Derived from role-playing games like Dungeons and Dragons, MUDs use computer **databases** to construct virtual text-based worlds in which participants interact. Social MUDs are less focused on game-playing, and instead provide a general social setting for interaction, often modelled on a house or a town. MUD owners are known as Gods, since they exercise ultimate authority over what goes on in the MUD; participants granted power to 'govern' MUDs are called Wizards, once more reflecting the origins of MUDs in fantasy role-play gaming. Participants are called MUDders, the practice is called MUDding, and when you've finished you've MUDded.

LambdaMOO is probably the best-known example of an object-oriented MUD, or MOO, where the program facilitates the building of rooms and objects. It was also the site of the infamous case of virtual rape, documented by Dibbell (1999), in which one participant effectively controlled the actions of others in the MUD. LambdaMOO has been the site of extensive academic research into topics such as **gender**-swapping and **identity**-play, and is famous for offering a choice of genders to self-select for online interaction (see Kaloski 1999). Other variants include MUCKs, MUSEs and MUSHs. Graphical environments offered by online **games** and more recent forms of MUD may soon start to eclipse the original text-based MUDs, which date back to the beginnings of the Internet.

See also: **Avatar, MOO**

Further sources: Curtis (1999), Dibbell (1999), Kaloski (1999)

MULTIMEDIA *see* **Convergence**

MUNICIPAL INFORMATION INFRASTRUCTURE (MII)

MII is the technological infrastructure needed to support the digital information and communication needs for a city or town. An MII is frequently conceptualized as a public or public–private partnership, although examples are still far from commonplace. Sometimes such town- or city-wide networks are also referred to as a MAN (Municipal Area Network).

NATIONAL INFORMATION INFRASTRUCTURE

This is a concept popularized by then president and vice-president Bill Clinton and Al Gore for a new digital electronic network – not the Internet – which would provide a communication infrastructure for education and commerce in the United States. An 'Agenda for Action' report was published in 1993 with a variety of recommendations.

Further sources: www.ibiblio.org/nii/

NATIONAL PUBLIC TELECOMPUTING NETWORK (NPTN)

The National Public Telecomputing Network was launched in 1989 by **Cleveland Free-Net** founder Tom Grundner, as the central hub for the growing number of **Free-Nets** around the world and for policy development. NPTN published the 'Blue Book', which contained information on how to start and maintain Free-Nets, and it pioneered the 'cybercast' concept and attempted to define and develop collective projects that would help unite and strengthen the network of Free-Nets – which at one time was the fourth largest network in the world. NPTN content included electronic mailing lists devoted to Free-Net administration, teledemocracy, White House press releases, the TeleOlympics (in which athletes compared achievements via computer) and the Collaboratory (where students worked together on science projects over the Internet). NPTN disbanded in 1996 when it could not obtain adequate operating funds. The Association For Community Networking (AFCN) was founded that year. The Organization For Community Networks (OFCN) was intended to carry over some of the NPTN programmes, including the Medical Center, Academy Center, TeleDemocracy Center and TeleOlympics.

See also: **Free-Net**

NERD *see* **Geek**

THE NET (MOVIE)

Representative of the genre of 'cyberthrillers' (Springer 1999), *The Net* (Irwin Winkler, 1995) centres on the relationship between computer technology and human **identity**. The central character, systems analyst Angela Bassett (Sandra Bullock), has her identity erased by a group of malevolent **hackers**, the Praetorians, who are set to release a **virus** embedded in computer security software. This will give them control over **databases** around the world, and therefore ultimate power. Bassett goes on the run after uncovering their plot, but the Praetorians hack into databases recording her personal identity, and rewrite it. Despite her protestations to the contrary, she effectively becomes someone else – Ruth Marx, a petty criminal. All computerized records have been changed, and anyone who might be able to verify her true identity is either killed or, in the case of her mother, unable to recognize her due to Alzheimer's. Having willingly delegated large portions of her life and her self-identity to computers, Bassett has to turn to now unfamiliar real-life resources in order to regain her self and defeat the Praetorians – though ultimately it is her knowledge of computers that allows her to win, by turning the hackers' virus on their own systems. *The Net* thus tells a cautionary tale about computers, and about the status of self-identity in a computer culture. Like the meditations on memory in *Blade Runner* and *Total Recall*, it reminds us of the risks we run in letting machines too fully into our lives.

See also: **Hackers**, **Identity**, **Virus**

Further sources: Springer (1999)

NETIQUETTE

Netiquette is a set of commonly agreed standards of conduct, or rules of communication, that operate within domains of cyberspace.

Netiquette represents an attempt to lay down loose 'rules' governing behaviour, and these are necessarily evolving as cyberspace itself evolves. Often policed informally from within the particular virtual environment, but sometimes delegated to 'peacekeepers', these rules can include: defining acceptable forms of writing (forbidding swearing, 'shouting', offensive language and so on), regulating the behaviour of **newbies** (not asking too many obvious questions, not spending too much time **lurking**), preventing the wasting of bandwidth via crossposting or **spamming**, and so on (McLaughlin, Osborne and Smith 1995). In many cases, rules and their associated apparatus (laws, police, modes of punishment) have had to be created in an ad hoc way, responding to particular situations – as in the famous case of 'Mr Bungle', charged with raping a fellow participant on LambdaMOO (Dibbell 1999). While these rules are seen by some people as evidence of emerging democracy online, for others they show the exclusivity of virtual environments, especially in their use to police the behaviour of newcomers.

See also: **CMC**, **Lurking**, **Newbie**

Further sources: Dibbell (1999), McLaughlin, Osborne and Smith (1995)

NETIZEN

A netizen is a citizen who employs the Internet for his or her activism. A slightly different perspective suggests that a netizen is a citizen of cyberspace, a person who participates in cyberspace communication – including discussion *about* cyberspace.

Further sources: Hauben and Hauben (1997)

NETWAR *see* Information warfare

NETWORK ORGANIZATIONS

The introduction of networked computer communications into organizations has led to the contention that entirely new forms of organization are now possible which are better placed to survive in the rapidly changing information economy. According to Manuel

Castells, for example, 'it is the convergence and interaction between a new technological paradigm and a new organizational logic that constitutes the historical foundation of the informational economy' (1996: 152). In contrast to the vertically integrated bureaucratic organizations which flourished in the more stable environment of the second half of the twentieth century, these new network organizational forms are both flatter in structure and more flexible in practice. Unlike their modernist predecessors they are, therefore, believed to be more responsive to increasingly dynamic, fragmented and diversified markets.

A number of significant characteristics are believed to enable network organizations to be more adaptive than bureaucratic organizations. First, it is argued that hierarchical structures have become replaced and flattened by more horizontal, decentralized core–periphery networks of semi-autonomous units. The enterprise is thereby directed by a small core of highly skilled and remunerated staff whose role is to strategically guide the organization through the changing informational market. They accomplish this objective by continuously shaping the network through making and severing links with other appropriate organizations, subjects and agencies. The nature of these links is often characterized by negotiated contracts, franchises and service level agreements. Consequently, in their most developed forms it is sometimes difficult to establish where the boundaries of network organizations begin and end.

This trend away from rigid, centralized, hierarchical structures also points to a second related characteristic of network organizations. Instead of vertical control strategies, we begin to see remote control practices whereby resources are devolved to decentralized units while simultaneously making them responsible for managing their own performance. Whether measurement is through comparison with other units, agreed centralized targets or service-level agreements, such remote control is regarded as potentially more effective than the flawed means of bureaucratic surveillance, since it is achieved through consenting self-management.

While the new **ICTs** are not responsible for the origins of the new network organization, it is argued that their transforming capabilities are ideal for fostering flexibility and coordination. The highly competitive global information economy has produced a significant shift away from the mass production of standardized goods and services towards more fragmented dynamic niche markets which require responsive intelligent network organizations capable of continuous innovation. As a consequence the old divisions of labour are replaced by the introduction of multi-skilled or polyvalent working practices. Of particular importance are those positions filled by the imaginative, creative, information- and knowledge-based symbolic analysts.

A central aspect of all network analysis is the importance of trust relationships. An interesting aspect of network organizations may be the extent to which networked coordination of specialized self-directed units may lead to the development, in some instances, of more democratic and participative management based upon high-trust relationships.

While commentators like Castells do not argue that these characteristics lead to a universal model to which all (or currently many) organizations conform, they do suggest that they form a 'common matrix' (Castells 1996: 151) from which a variety of different configurations may evolve depending upon culture, location, technological development or social structure. As such, the network organization represents a new template that challenges the domination of the traditional bureaucratic form of organization.

It is also important to note a number of criticisms which have been made about the cogency of this new organizational form. For some observers these theories are simply constructed at too high a level of abstraction to provide any meaningful explanatory value. Furthermore, they sometimes appear to be drawn from a very small number of high-profile examples such as Benetton and Toyota, and consequently it is not clear how widespread they are in practice. Moreover, by often being couched in the logic of capitalist development, they also run the risk of being technologically deterministic and ignoring the possibility of human agency and resistance to such organizational forms. Lastly, other commentators have been at pains to suggest that such organizations have more in common with past practices and cannot be considered as new. Certainly remote control strategies focusing upon performance measurement, for example, seem to have much in common with the scientific management theories of the early part of the last century.

See also: **Information society**

Further sources: Castells (1996), Clegg (1990), Webster and Robins (1998)

NETWORK SOCIETY *see* Information society

NEUROMANCER (BOOK)

First published in 1984, William Gibson's *Neuromancer* is probably the best-known and most influential **cyberpunk** novel. It helped secure Gibson's reputation as the star writer of the genre, and contains the famous coining of the term 'cyberspace', described in one of the most-quoted passages of any sci-fi text. The first part of his Sprawl Trilogy, *Neuromancer* was followed by *Count Zero* (1986) and *Mona Lisa Overdrive* (1988).

Neuromancer's impact extended well beyond the world of sci-fi readers, and is argued by some critics to have had a profound impact on the development of computers and cyberculture. It described the experience of entering cyberspace – the world of data between the screens arranged like an urban landscape – and imagined a future **information society** dominated by corporate capital. Gibson also populated the novel with a new breed of 'hero' – based on **hackers** and phone **phreaks**, he described the console cowboys and cyberpunks who engage in renegade activities when **jacked in** to cyberspace, as well as a whole range of new tribes or **subcultures**, all trying to claim space in the new world order (Tomas 2000).

The legendary status of *Neuromancer* extends to the myths of its creation – that Gibson banged it out on an old manual typewriter, that he derived his inspiration from watching kids play arcade games, and that he had only very limited knowledge of or contact with the computer culture (Davis 1998).

See also: **Cyberpunk, Hacker, Jacking in, Subculture**

Further sources: Davis (1998), Kneale (2001), Tomas (2000)

NEW CULTURAL POLITICS

This is a symbolic politics which embraces new repertoires of political activity designed to circumvent established interests, social elites or corporate power, and to appeal directly to the public. Such (dis)organized political activism which characterizes many contemporary social movements (SMs) appears to have a strong affinity with the non-hierarchical networks of **virtual communities** which exist through the **Internet** in **cyberspace**.

Through their symbiotic relationship with the world's mass media, SMs are able to portray their message through a fusion of symbols, images, icons and drama which proclaim their anxieties, values and concerns more effectively than participating in political parties, elections or traditional campaigning. The convergence of old and new media, offering as it does the opportunity for many-to-many communication across a global network which transcends parameters of both time and space, is likely to have still further significant implications for these SM-driven cultural politics. In particular is its potential to collapse the social and political spheres by creating new forms of discourse outside the ambit of traditional politics and which deal with such matters as global justice, environmentalism, intimate relationships, different sexualities, frailty and personal risk, and which prioritize lay experience over professional expertise.

See also: **New social movements**

Further sources: Webster (2001)

NEW SOCIAL MOVEMENTS

Social movements may be described as informal networks of people and groups who share a common identity and are capable of mobilizing resources for protest on issues of conflict. Some notable examples include the Labour Movements, Women's Movements, Environmental Movements, Social Welfare Movements, Animal and Human Rights Movements and, more recently, a host of global justice movements. The **Internet**, with its transnational many-to-many communication facility, offers a revolutionary potential for social movements to go online and circumvent the 'official' messages of political and commercial organizations and the traditional media, by speaking directly to the citizens of the world. Furthermore, the use of email, mailing lists, websites, electronic forums and other online applications provides powerful media tools for coordinating the activity of often physically dispersed movement actors. Moreover, **ICTs** may also contribute to the important function of social movements in shaping collective identity and countering the claims and arguments of established political interests. This potential was dramatically demonstrated in the use of the new media both to help coordinate the diverse protest groups against the World Trade

Organization's ministerial meetings held in Seattle in 1999 and the worldwide dissemination of their arguments.

The new media can be of value to social movements in a number of significant ways. First, email offers the prospect of high-speed and cheaper communication between social movement actors. This can enable members to communicate more frequently between local branches and national, or even international, parts of the same organization. It can also facilitate communication between coalitions of social movements, both within national boundaries and across them. Through the further development of electronic discussion forums, it is much more possible for movement actors to participate in debates around particular issues. Such interactivity fosters two-way discussion between members and organizers, and can thereby strengthen the building of shared identities through inclusiveness.

Second, websites can also be powerful and cost-effective communication tools for social movements. They enable movements to have a worldwide visibility and make information resources available to members to download. Campaigns can be launched and supported through websites, enabling financial donations, electronic petitions and notification of demonstrations. Recruitment of new activists may also be undertaken through websites, as well as providing existing members with up-to-date news and events.

Finally, **computer mediated communication (CMC)** is a potentially powerful means to aggregate geographically dispersed aggrieved individuals into a group capable of purposive collective action. It can thereby contribute to the 'mobilization' of social movement actors.

The subversive networking potential of the new media may have particular appeal to what some commentators have described as New Social Movements (NSMs). These groups are distinguished from earlier forms of social movement by their rejection of class-based materialist demands, such as the redistribution of resources within and between societies. Instead, they are characterized by their interest in lifestyle conflicts and campaigns of affinity. Movement identity is oriented around universal principles and moral values such as animal rights, environmentalism, sexuality, gender differences, and human rights and dignity. In contrast to social class solidarity, NSMs can be seen as loosely-coupled networks of people comprising a plurality of meanings and orientations. Such social network structures may be significantly facilitated through ICTs which enable individual activists to express their multiple identities and allegiances to several social movements instead of one collective identity.

The use of ICTs by NSMs may also be influenced by the latter's adoption of new repertoires of action which replace or combine traditional protest with leisure activities and playful mass spectacles. Such activism is regarded as important for demonstrating a **new cultural politics** and lifestyle choices. Through the creative use of new media, NSMs attempt to combine traditional aspects of political discourse and analysis with captivating drama, images and symbols as a means of illuminating concerns and issues of conflict.

A brief look at the use of websites by global justice movements may help to illustrate the foregoing description of online NSMs. A number of distinct types of website can be identified, including **culture jamming**, **Indymedia**, single anti-corporation, brokerage, and global network. Culture jamming developed as a protest against the commercialization of public spaces through what is seen as the increasing domination of highways, public transport, schools, neighbourhoods, sports facilities and the Internet by corporate advertising and logos.

The Internet has also been used by activists to focus upon what they believe to be the unacceptable practices of particular corporations. Numerous sites now document the commercial activities of global brands in order to make the public aware of what they regard as unfair employment practices, cruelty to animals, environmental damage, or untruthful advertising campaigns. The intention is to empower consumers and the shareholders of such corporations by placing the evidence of such malpractice in the public domain. Similarly, there has been a growth in the number of websites devoted to promoting fair trade for small producers in developing countries. This again provides an online opportunity for poverty to be tackled and sustainable development to be achieved through the actions of consumers after they are informed and made aware of the power of their collective choices.

Another interesting innovative use of the Internet to empower the consumer as a political activist is to be found at the RTMark website. This group of largely digital artists have established a brokerage whereby citizens can promote and discuss concerns about corporate products and receive funding from investors to campaign for their abolition. A notable past example was the Barbie Liberation Organization, a project funded by a group of military veterans to replace the voice boxes of three hundred Barbie dolls with G.I. Joe voices, the purpose being to highlight the gender-based stereotyping of children's toys. The adapted G.I. Joe doll subsequently said 'I love school. Don't you?', while the liberated Barbie remarked that 'Dead men tell no lies.'

The Internet and the **World Wide Web** clearly offer NSMs a powerful set of communication tools with which to network, campaign, recruit, protest and challenge corporate, state and media institutions and practices. They are a valuable addition to political activism and provide an online presence with which to communicate directly to millions of citizens worldwide. What is less clear, however, is the extent to which we will see the emergence of virtual social movements whose existence is wholly dependent upon networks of non-**F2F** communication between geographically dispersed activists. The high degree of trust needed for long-term commitment and collective action may not yet be generated through computer-mediated communication alone.

See also: **Culture jamming**, **Indymedia**, **New cultural politics**

Further sources: Donk *et al.* (2004), Diani (2000), Webster (2001)

NEWBIE

'Newbie' is an online slang term for a newcomer, particularly someone with little technical competence or knowledge of the rules and norms of a particular virtual forum. On **MUDs** and in **chat rooms** or online **games**, newbies can feel like outsiders, unable to participate in the codified conversations of longer-established participants. Those who choose to stay online but not risk participation until they are more familiar with the social codes or **netiquette** of the forum can also be accused of **lurking** – a kind of virtual voyeurism treated with disdain by veterans. One way of catering for newbies is via the creation of **FAQ (Frequently Asked Questions)** lists, where basic information can be accessed prior to participation. Nevertheless, newbies are often made to feel their outsider status, either by being ignored or by being belittled, so the term itself functions almost as a form of abuse.

See also: **FAQ**, **Netiquette**

NEWSGROUPS *see* **Usenet**

NICK

Pseudonyms used in **MUDs**, **IRC**, **email** and other communications forums are referred to as 'nicks' (shorthand for nicknames), or sometimes as 'handles' (a term borrowed from CB radio). Where users may choose their own nicks, we can see them as forms of self-identity not unlike the personal **homepage**. They might also be seen as attempts to grab the reader's attention, in the same way as the 'Subject' header on an email (Lee 1996). As a badge of personal identity or individuality, then, the nick attempts to communicate in a few characters something about the person behind it; to give off the 'right' message to those that receive it, in the absence of the usual **F2F** cues. Participants with multiple email accounts may also use different 'nicks' to communicate with different networks (for example, with work colleagues and friends), echoing the point made by Sherry Turkle (1997) about cyberspace enabling a 'distributed self' split between different domains and contexts.

See also: **Email, F2F, Homepage**

Further sources: Lee (1996)

OFFICE OF THE E-ENVOY

The Office of the e-Envoy is focused on the promotion and adoption of **e-government** throughout British central and local government. Its role extends to each central government department, as well as the services provided by the elected local authorities throughout England. Separate arrangements are in place for Scotland and Wales, since those countries took control of large parts of their own governance. The e-Envoy is responsible for ensuring that all government services are available electronically by 2005, with key services achieving high levels of use, a target that looks increasingly optimistic as 2005 draws closer. Within the Office of the e-Envoy, the e-Economy group provides strategic support to the e-Minister and the e-Envoy on developing **e-commerce** within the UK, there being a government objective to develop the UK as the 'best environment for electronic business'.

Further sources: www.e-envoy.gov.uk/

'ON DEMAND'

The concept that lies at the root of the delivery of digital content over networks is known as 'on demand'. The **convergence** of media into digital formats allows for the possibility of creating devices, ranging from **G3** mobile (cellular) phones through to enhanced **digital televisions** and handheld and tablet PCs, that can download and use software applications, **games**, movies, music and other material in a digital format from a network. Only that content which a user or consumer wishes for is downloaded from the network, 'on (their) demand'.

ONLINE

An American, Doug Engelbart (inventor of the computer mouse), demonstrated what he referred to as an 'oNLine System' (an NLS) in December 1968. NLS had **hypertext** browsing and editing and **email** capacity, and it is from this system that we took the term 'online'. The term now generally refers to the act of using a computer network, such as the **Internet**, in the sense that browsing the **World Wide Web** is an 'online' activity.

OPEN SOURCE

'Open Source' is a designation for a class of software in which both compiled and source code software is readily available (generally by downloading it from the Internet without charge). This designation is less constraining than **copy-left** software, as Open Source software can be freely incorporated into other software without the restriction of copy-left. A popular website for tech-heads, particularly aficionados of Open Source software, is Slash dot. Its motto is 'News for Nerds. Stuff that matters'. Slash dot employs an interesting model, as the vast majority of the content on the site is contributed by people from outside the site itself. Virtually all stories are submitted via a form at their website. Readers can add their comments to the articles which sometimes can number in the thousands. Topics mostly focus on technology, but also include a number of other less 'techie' topics such as 'The Almighty Buck', 'Censorship', 'Media' and 'wine'.

Further sources: freshmeat.net, slashcode.com

OPERATING SYSTEM *see* Interface

OTAKU

Otaku is a Japanese slang term used to describe someone with an obsessive interest. It differs from the English slang terms **geek** and **nerd**, in that it describes a socially deviant obsessive, rather than merely denoting someone whose interest in science or **ICTs** reflects a lack of success in forming friendships and sexual relationships. In Japan itself, the term is often associated with people who have a fanatical interest in adult animation and comics, known respectively as anime and **manga**, material which often employs strong sexual images, including violent pornographic content, and which is strongly influenced by (and in turn influences) **cyberpunk**. Japanese computer **games** are full of the imagery (and sometimes the characters) of manga and anime. Equally, however, a fixated fan of something as innocuous as a pop singer can be described as an Otaku (although some pop singers in Japan adopt the highly sexualised pubescent schoolgirl image that permeates manga and anime).

Whether this is really a 'group' of Otaku within Japanese society or whether they are something of a media invention is perhaps debatable. The mass media's archetypical Otaku, a lone male who is not only an obsessive consumer of manga and anime, but also a fanatical gamer and Internet user, whose relationships are all conducted through **CMC**, emphasizes an unhealthy relationship to technology.

In this sense, the Otaku are a manifestation of Japanese and Western anxieties about what our relationship with ICTs might mean. Rather than the enhanced, improved and enriched **cyborg** versions of humanity that some sociologists and others predicted, the Otaku are instead alienated and deviant. The height of this anxiety found expression in some particularly violent murders that were described in the Japanese and Western media as having being committed by 'Otaku' in the early 1990s (see *Wired* 1.01: Mar–Apr 1993: www.wired.com).

More recently, although the term was not used, anxieties like those about the Otaku were focused on the obsessive use of ultra-violent games by schoolchildren who were later responsible for high-school massacres, like that at the Columbine school in Denver in the United States.

There has also been renewed interest in an 'Otaku'-like phenomenon, the discovery by Japanese sociologists of **'hikikomori'**, young people who are socially withdrawn and spend a lot of their time in lone use of ICTs or games. Interestingly however, the hikikomori are characterized as being individuals reacting to the social and economic pressures of Japanese society, not as young people who have become deviant through their sometimes obsessive relationships with technology, manga or anime. Similar themes and anxieties about potentially unhealthy relationships with technology are examined in science fiction cinema and literature, particularly within the **cyberpunk** genre.

See also: **Cyberpunk**, **Geek**, **Nerd**

PACKET SNIFFING

This is the act of examining ('sniffing') the stream of digital information, dispatched in packets (see **Internet**), from and to an address on the Internet. Encoded information can be sniffed in this way, but its meaning cannot readily be discerned. Although their use is disavowed by legitimate system administrators, packet-sniffing software is readily available to the unscrupulous sniffer.

See also: **Encryption**, **Internet**

PHREAK

Someone who breaks into the telephone network illegally, typically to make free long-distance phone calls or to tap phone lines, is known as a phreak. The original phreaks were a kind of evolutionary step towards the **hackers** who would appear later. The term is still sometimes used to describe anyone trying to break into any network.

PIRACY

A major element of **cybercrime**, piracy refers to the illegal copying of software and **games**, movies, music and other digital media. Piracy is relatively easy to undertake, quite often requiring no more than a CD-RW or DVD-R/RW drive that can replicate the original CDs or DVDs on which a particular application is stored. Applications, games, music and movies can also, of course, be simply copied onto the Internet for download. As **convergence** takes place, with all media becoming digital, copying itself and the production of copies of the same quality as the original has become much easier. Equally, the availability of the **World Wide Web** makes the sale and distribution of pirated material a much simpler matter than was previously the case. Further, web-based sales or distribution of pirated material can make it harder to track those perpetrating the piracy. The rise of digital media and networks has, for all its benefits, also acted as a catalyst for a new criminal industry.

According to some estimates there are thousands of websites offering illegal copies and downloads of digitally copied software, games, movies and music. According to the US International Intellectual Property Alliance (IIPA), an umbrella organization of several bodies representing companies working in media and software, including the Business Software Alliance (BSA) and the Motion Picture Association of America, the US economy 'lost' $9.2 billion (in potential earnings) through copyright breaches in foreign countries in 2002. In 2001, the BSA estimated that software piracy in the US *alone* was costing the industry more than $1.8 billion.

The famous Napster case in the US, which took place during 2000/01, highlighted problems faced by the music industry. The Napster website was providing copyrighted music as **mp3** files on its website, it being an easy process to copy CDs into this downloadable digital format. In 2001, Napster negotiated a deal with songwriters and music publishers that Napster would pay $26 million to them as well as a percentage of the money it took as a service that now charged users for downloading its mp3 files. By some estimates there are a great many websites offering illegal mp3 files across the Internet.

Losses to piracy from the **games** industry are similarly gigantic. According to the European Leisure Software Publishers Association (ELSPA), games publishers lose some £3 billion to piracy in Britain alone every year. By some estimates piracy of games in areas like Russia and Asia far exceeds legitimate sales. Games companies have attempted to counteract piracy by launching new formats that are more difficult to copy, as well as by using sophisticated encryption and copy protection. However, even difficult-to-copy media, like disks that can only be used in a console and not read in a standard CD or DVD drive, and complex encryption are overcome in time.

Piracy can be used to raise or invest money from more serious criminal activities such as illegal drug distribution, and there is some evidence that it may also support the activities of political extremists and perhaps even terrorist groups. Some piracy is, however, under-taken by individuals.

Software pirates sometimes use the term 'warez' to describe software that has had its copy-protection removed and has been made available on a website or elsewhere on the Internet for downloading. Pirate sites are thus sometimes called 'warez' sites.

See also: **Convergence**

Further sources: www.siia.net/, www.idsa.com/, www.elspa.com/

PLATFORM

Platform is another term for operating system or make of computer.

See also: **Interface**

POKEMON *see* **Games**

PORNOGRAPHY

It has been argued that pornography in its myriad digital manifestations is the **killer app** of the **World Wide Web**. As of 1999, Internet-related annual sales in the legal sex/pornography industry was estimated to be about one billion US dollars out of an estimated 56 billion dollars (Morais 1999). There are an estimated 30,000 pornographic websites in the US alone (Diamond 1999; Lane 2000). Pornographic web pages worldwide are thought to number about 12 million or about 1.5 per cent of the estimated 800 million pages on the web (Lawrence and Giles 1999) and online pornographers are among the most innovative and successful **e-commerce** entrepreneurs.

Cyberspace, of course, offers great advantages to a consumer of pornography (Cronin and Davenport 2001). Cyberspace allows for easy and discreet delivery to a consumer's own desktop, removed from a geographically red light district or local pornographic outlet. Privacy, also, is presumably an important factor, although cookies, packet sniffing, credit card purchases, as well as voluntary provision of personal information on the net, point to the dubious nature of this assumption of privacy. The net, of course, also – at least for now – allows consumers of pornography to bypass local restrictions on their access to pornography. e-Pornographers, according to Cronin and

Davenport (2001) in their discussion of pornography in the digital economy, are among the most entrepreneurial of the content-providers and are exploring many new avenues towards legitimizing their industry.

The Internet has also facilitated access to disturbing and illegal material, including images aimed at a paedophile audience. However, although the Internet offers the attraction of apparent anonymity to those individuals who seek this sort of material, ignorance of the ways in which individual users of the Internet can be traced and located has enabled the detection of some paedophiles. A US Federal Bureau of Investigation revealed visits to a child pornography site by some 6,000 British citizens, 1,300 of whom had been arrested by the beginning of 2003.

See also: **Cyberfeminism**, **Gender**

Further sources: Cronin and Davenport (2001), Diamond (1999), Lane (2000), Lawrence and Giles (1999), Morais (1999)

PORTAL

A portal is a website on the **World Wide Web** that is used as a major access point to a large number of other websites and services. The portal is one of the key concepts in developing **e-government** services, providing a simple navigable **interface** that enables the citizen to easily locate the public services they desire. The UK government portal http://www.ukonline.gov.uk/ is organized around 'life events', such as 'having a baby' or 'moving home', to simplify the process by which a citizen can find services, enabling them to search for what they want without having to know which section or department of government provides it.

PRIVACY

The state that exists when information about an individual or corporate entity is confined to that entity. Historically, privacy concerns have been associated with the state and the conflicting needs and desires of the state to gather information on individuals and organizations and their opposing desire to restrict the flow. Increasingly, the concern is with commercial entities, as virtually all information has some commercial value. The advent of cyberspace has raised privacy concerns to unprecedented high levels. Computers (the engines of cyberspace) allow (and promote) the storage of vast amounts of information and the rapid transmission of data. The increasing use of cyberspace means more data is available. Computers, finally, can be set to comb through large amounts of data and to accumulate collections of data from numerous smaller chunks.

PROSTHETICS

Prosthetics is the term used for artificial augmentations to the body – most often in medical science to describe replacement body parts such as limbs or heart pacemakers. Prosthetics are taken by some critics to signal the transformation from human into post-human or **cyborg** figures, mixing biological 'meat' with high-tech metal. The extent to which we use technology to augment human capabilities beyond replacement limbs leads some writers to suggest that we live in a prosthetic culture – that objects such as cars and computers become extensions of the self. Moreover, these additions can extend our abilities rather than make up for deficiencies – a theme played out in the *Six-Million Dollar Man* TV series, which centred on the use of 'bionic' prostheses to turn its protagonist into a hybrid superman. For some, this is to be celebrated as the next phase in (post-)human evolution (Stelarc 2000), while other commentators worry about the implications of letting technology invade our bodies and lives so totally. The prostheticization of everyday life extends to the use of computers as **memory** machines, although other more mundane artefacts, such as photographs, play a similar role – as portrayed in the film *Blade Runner*, what we think we know of our own past may in fact be prostheticized (Landsberg 2000).

See also: *Blade Runner*, **Cyborg**, **Memory**

Further sources: Gray (1995), Landsberg (2000), Stelarc (2000)

PUBLIC ACCESS *see* **Access**

PUBLIC BROADCASTING

Not-for-profit radio and television broadcasting by non-commercial organizations is known as public broadcasting. The exact definition of what constitutes public broadcasting varies between countries. Public broadcasting organizations may be supported or enabled by governments, but they are distinctive from state-controlled media because they retain editorial independence. The role of public broadcasting centres on the provision of responsible, editorially balanced programming which has a 'beneficial' purpose. Public broadcasting, which is also sometimes called public service broadcasting, usually has a stated objective to inform, educate and generally promote civilized values, rather than simply to entertain.

There are radical differences between European nations and the USA in public broadcasting. Public broadcasting in countries like France and the UK has a very significant presence within the mass media. Probably the best known example of public broadcasting in the world is the British Broadcasting Corporation (BBC). Within the UK, the BBC competes with analogue and digital commercial television broadcasting and retains a mass audience, often outperforming commercial stations in the ratings. Supported by an annual, legally enforced, licence fee, effectively a flat-rate dedicated tax that every citizen who watches television has to pay (on a per-household rather than per-television basis), which was £112 at the time of writing, the BBC has resources that most public service broadcasters can only dream of. Some US public service broadcasters, in contrast, have to devote considerable portions of their airtime to fund-raising.

These resources have enabled the BBC to move into digital services on a very considerable scale. From a base of two national analogue television channels and five national radio stations (plus many regional and local stations), it has expanded into free-to-air digital broadcasting with the introduction of eight additional channels, plus a range of partnership projects with other broadcasters. Digital radio stations have also been introduced. The BBC has pioneered the use of interactive **digital television** services, beginning a process that will provide online services that rival websites in their interactivity and depth of content. The BBC has also developed one of the most extensive web presences in the world, with a website that offers online versions of its broadcast services (and online broadcasting of its radio and television services). The BBC website is one of the most visited in the UK.

Questions are sometimes raised about the extent to which the BBC has embraced digital television and the Web. Expenditure on its websites and digital channels is considerable, but, even by 2002, the majority of its audience was not able to access either of these services. However, this strategic decision was taken in the context of British government plans to auction off analogue television frequencies, which could be used for high-**bandwidth** hand-held devices such as enhanced mobile (cellular) phones and other **wireless** devices.

The **Web** is increasingly a virtual space that is characterized by corporate dominance (see **globalization**). Most of the people who connect to the Web from home do so through the services provided by a major corporation. Alternative voices may always be present on the Web, but as the Web itself is increasingly promoted as a product, through which users are 'guided' by commercial **ISPs**, those alternative voices may require more and more effort to find. The web itself is increasingly characterized by **e-commerce**. The presence of organizations like the BBC, with a public service remit, as opposed to a commercial one, may help counter corporate domination of the Web. However, there are questions as to how far organizations like the BBC are sufficiently different from the commercial mass media that they imitate in many respects to really provide an outlet for alternative, or minority, views and perspectives. Certainly, alongside its traditional role, the BBC has entered into direct competition with commercial mass media in the UK and produced a large amount of poor-quality, mass-market programming that cannot be distinguished from the output of commercial broadcasters.

Further sources: www.bbc.co.uk/

PUBLIC ELECTRONIC NETWORK (PEN)

The Public Electronic Network (PEN) in Santa Monica, California, launched in 1987 by Ken Phillips, Director of the Information Systems Department of Santa Monica, California, and Joseph Schmitz of the USC Annenberg School of Communications, was the first city-sponsored, public-access computer system in the world. PEN served as one of the most important arenas for understanding issues of 'electronic democracy' as it is actually practised, and provided several early cautionary tales in relation to citizens' use of new technology. In addition to providing free access to each other for Santa Monica citizens via various forums, PEN provides access to city government information (such as city council agendas, reports, public safety tips and the library's online catalogue) and to government services (such as the granting of permits or the reporting of petty thefts). Citizens can converse with public officials and city servants as well as with each other, using email and electronic conferences. Each city organization in Santa Monica is online. PEN also provided the communication infrastructure for one of the world's first political action campaigns at a local level to be carried on electronically. In August 1989 Bruria Finkel, a Santa Monica resident, posted an idea to the Homeless Conference on PEN based on discussions she had with homeless residents. The concept, dubbed SHWASHLOCK (for SHowers, WASHers, and LOCKers), was intended to help homeless people find and maintain jobs by providing them with morning showers, laundry facilities and lockers for their belongings. The Santa Monica City Council ultimately allocated $150,000 for lockers, showers and a laundry facility, demonstrating the potential of using online resources for community organizing.

See also: **Community informatics**, **Electronic democracy**, **Electronic government**

PUBLIC POLICY NETWORKS

Public policy networks (PPNs) are a recent organizational hybrid that engages a diverse group of people who have common interests but sometimes conflicting values, perspectives, agendas and ways of doing things (Reinicke 1999/2000). Although possibly subject to manipulation by the PPN's sponsor, these networks offer an interesting new organizational form that relies on cyberspace. They typically address broad issues that cut across traditional national and other boundaries like climate change, trade, food security, pollution and poverty.

Public policy networks, according to the GPPN Resource Group, have four central attributes:

● Multi-national: Global PPNs (GPPNs) attempt to address issues where no national government has clear authority;
● Policy action-focused: GPPNs work within the full range of policy tasks, from problem definition through to solution implementation;
● Network structure: actions and decisions are made without dependence upon formal hierarchical authority;
● Boundary spanning: GPPNs typically bridge problematic tradi-

tional divides such as sectoral (business–government–civil society), cultural, disciplinary, north–south and rich–poor.

Further sources: Reinicke (1999/2000), www.gppnresearch.org/about

PUBLIC SPHERE

'The public sphere' is a concept developed by the German philosopher Jurgen Habermas (1989) to express his idea of settings where people can freely enter and discuss issues. Habermas's concept also connects to power structures and can thus contribute to social change. Although an English translation of his book *Structural Transformation of the Public Sphere* wasn't available until 1989, the concept soon became one of the most important in communication studies. In contrast to other concepts in communication studies (such as **cultural imperialism**), the concept of the public sphere is posited as a positive one, a mode of communication seen by many to be a desirable and attainable state of affairs.

Since a 'public sphere' is abstract and imprecise, its best use may be as an indicator for direction and as a metric for criticism and action. Whether the idea of an equitable and universal public sphere becomes a reality will depend on how effectively people can organize around this issue. The idea of a public sphere can help people to evaluate the communication systems that currently exist. It can also help them to imagine – and create – better ones.

Further sources: Habermas (1989)

ROAD WARRIORS

This is a term used in *PC Magazine* to refer to people whose work is undertaken on the move between locations and who are heavily dependent upon networked computer communications to undertake their business. Professionals, managers and technicians of various sorts are to be found in transit all over the world in corporate hotels, bars, restaurants, airport lounges and the like. These road warriors typically spend several days a week moving between offices, conference venues or other work locations. Their work practice is supported and shaped by their almost constant use of laptop computers, checking emails and text messages, and discussions with other dispersed colleagues via mobile telephony.

See also: **Wireless**

ROBOT ('BOT')

A robot or 'bot' can be a software tool that is used for searches or data mining. The bot can be given directions as to what to search for and then left to get on with it, responding to its user when it has found the required answers.

At present, perhaps the best example of bots are the 'spiders' or 'web crawlers' that some of the **search engine** companies employ to catalogue websites and web pages. Such applications can be triggered when someone enters a new **URL** for a website and the bot initiates a process of indexing the site on the search engine.

The bot is also envisaged as being a key tool for **e-commerce**. According to some thinkers, the bot will evolve into a tool that can search for the best 'deal' for its user on a given product or service and report back to them. This will facilitate the generation of perfect or near-perfect markets, by automating the kind of comprehensive searches that users would not undertake for themselves.

A robot can, of course, also be used in the sense employed by popular science fiction. Beyond the long-standing and widespread use of industrial robots on production lines, there are now interactive robot 'toys', such as the Sony *Aibo* series, that have elements of **artificial intelligence** (see **cyberpets**).

Honda produced an 'intelligent humanoid robot' called ASIMO (Advanced Step in Innovative Mobility) during the early 2000s. The company claimed that it was capable of interpreting the postures and gestures of humans and moving independently in response. ASIMO could 'greet' approaching individuals, follow them, recognize their faces and address them by name. ASIMO, which was due to be made available for corporate rental during 2003, could also provide people with information via direct wireless Internet access, while acting as a receptionist. Honda have emphasized the 'humanity' of ASIMO, which emulates both the human form and human movements, in that it walks, climbs stairs, waves and reacts to people it 'knows'. These kinds of development raise questions about how we will relate to changing technology in terms of how we view machines that emulate us and how our self-conception may change as a result.

See also: **Artificial intelligence**, **Body**, **Cyborg**, **e-Commerce**

Further sources: Leebaert (1999), www.jp.aibo.com/, world.honda.-com/ASIMO/, asimo.honda.com/

ROBOT EXCLUSION STANDARD

WWW robots (or 'spiders' or 'wanderers') are software programs that automatically traverse pages on the **World Wide Web**. As a result of various unwelcome visitations, a standard method for denying entrance to web pages was devised, known as the Robot Exclusion Standard. The method relies on the existence of a 'robots.txt' file at a specific location on a web server that is checked for general or specific disallowing strictures before accessing web pages.

See also: **Robot**

Further sources: www.robotstxt.org/wc/norobots.html

SEARCH ENGINE

A search engine is a tool (often a website or web **portal**) whose primary purpose is to help users to locate web pages, generally through the use of search terms. Search engines represent the most common means through which people find web pages and, as a result, are accessed hundreds of millions of times per day. The major online search engines are Altavista, Google, Lycos and Yahoo. No search engine has over 30 per cent of the **Web** indexed. They are subject to many limitations and, unlike the Dewey Decimal System and other public approaches, and Internet protocols in general (for exchanging mail, fetching web pages, etc.), commercial indexing schemes are proprietary and, hence, not available for public use.

See also: **World Wide Web**

SELF-HELP *see* **Virtual social support**

SEMIOTICS

The so-called science of signs, semiotics (also known as semiology) is concerned with the relationship between things and meanings. It is an important element of Cultural Studies, since meanings are made by culture. Among its key thinkers are Ferdinand de Saussure and Roland Barthes. The foundation of semiotics can be defined in terms of this equation: 'signifier + signified = sign'. Another way of putting this is 'thing + meaning = thing-with-meaning'. The signifier is the thing before it is given meaning or is named – the thing as it exists, in the 'real world'. The signified exists only in our minds, as the meaning we give to the thing, and the two together represent the sign – the thing plus its meaning. To convey the sign (to talk or write about it) we have to use a signifier (e.g. a word) – but this can be misunderstood as we can't directly convey the signified. Meaning is therefore never fixed. The sign's meaning is ever-changing as the link between signifier and signified shifts. Ultimately, each signifier can only be known in relation to other signifiers – they exist in an unending chain of signification. Moreover, signification works on two levels, denotation and connotation. Denotation is the literal meaning of something, its name or dictionary definition. Connotation is the associative meaning – what we feel when we think of the thing. So, a computer might have connotative meanings of technological progress, or of technophobia. In a media-saturated culture, some critics argue, the meaning of things becomes completely disconnected from the things themselves – so the things cease to exist. The term 'simulacrum' is used to describe this disconnection of image from reality – a concept readily applied to cyberculture, where virtual realities exist independently of 'the real' (Cubitt 2001).

See also: **Simulation**

Further sources: Cubitt (2001)

SERVER *see* **World Wide Web**

SEXISM *see* **Cyberfeminism, Games, Gender, Pornography**

SILICON VALLEY

Silicon Valley refers roughly to the geographical region in California, south of San Francisco, that includes San Jose, Mountain View, Santa Clara, Cupertino and Palo Alto. The region is home to a very large number of software and hardware companies and research institutions.

The proximity to US government aerospace research and development establishments helped establish the region, which is considered the birthplace of the computer industry.

Further sources: Chong-Moon *et al.* (2000)

SIMULATION

In contemporary philosophy and social theory, simulation is a key concept with a complex meaning and history. It is defined in Sean Cubitt's excellent guidebook, *Simulation and Social Theory* (2001), as follows:

> Simulation: a copy without a source, an imitation that has lost its original. The theory of simulation is a theory about how our images, our communications and our media have usurped the role of reality, and a history of how reality fades. Though it speaks at length of our mediated world, at its heart simulation is a philosophy of reality and our changing relations with it.
>
> (Cubitt 2001: 1)

Simulation rolls together an assortment of theories and ideas, including **semiotics**, psychoanalysis, information theory, ideology and postmodernism, in order to explore the terms of our relationship to 'reality'. Although Cubitt points to its breadth, he also signals the close link between the mediatization of our lifeworld and the experience of simulation. As more and more of our lives are mediated, so we are increasingly distanced from 'the real', until ultimately we become totally disconnected from it. This escalation is most famously summarized by French theorist Jean Baudrillard, in his book *Simulation and Simulacra* (1983). Baudrillard describes the 'precession of simulacra' – the increasing distanciation of the image from reality – like this: the image begins as a reflection of reality; it then covers over reality; next it masks the *absence* of reality; finally, it has no relation to reality whatsoever – it is a copy of a copy *ad infinitum*, with no 'original'. Reality therefore disappears, and the real is replaced by the hyperreal, the copy-without-original that is more real than reality itself – a theme Baudrillard famously explores in his discussion of Disneyland as the hyperreal simulation of America (Baudrillard 1988).

In terms of cyberculture, we can see first how computers introduce new forms of simulation, furthering the precession of simulacra by producing virtual realities, artificial life-forms, and by converting reality to code. The increasing computerization of everyday life accelerates the process of simulation, as Cubitt's (2001) discussion of computers in the workplace shows. And the theme of reality's substitution by simulated or virtual is a common scenario in films and fiction about cyberculture – perhaps most vividly seen in *The Matrix*. The film's central character, Neo, even hides computer disks inside a hollowed copy of *Simulation and Simulacra*, making the connection explicit – and the simulation is stripped away in one key scene to reveal 'the desert of the real'. As Cubitt says, the film itself toys with our ambivalence about simulation – we enjoy the simulation that the movie creates while accepting its critique of simulation.

See also: **Cyberpunk**, **Cyborg**, *The Matrix*, **Robot**, **Semiotics**

Further sources: Baudrillard (1983, 1988), Cubitt (2001)

SMILEYS

'Smileys' are text-based symbols usually inserted into email or other forms of **CMC** in order to provide contextual information which would otherwise be communicated using non-verbal cues (such as tone of voice, gesture or physical expressions). The 'happy face' icon [:-)] is probably the best-known, but there are many, many other examples. Smileys (also called 'emoticons', a shorthand form of 'emotional icon') are used to convey the spirit in which a message is meant, for example to communicate a sense of irony or light heartedness ('I'm just joking').

See also: **Abbreviation**, **Cues filtered out**, **Email**, **Flaming**, **Usenet**

SMS (SHORT MESSAGE SERVICE)

SMS is a technology used for **text messaging** on mobile or cellular phones.

SOCIAL CAPITAL

Social capital is a term popularized by Robert Putnam in 1995 that represents the latent capacity of a community to support and sustain itself (through community organizations and the skills and interests of community members, for example.) Social capital is often characterized as having three components: trust, norms, and reciprocity. Social capital can be divided into 'bonding' social capital, in which social capital exists within a community, and 'bridges' social capital, that stretches across communities and is similar to Granovetter's (1973) concept of 'weak ties'. Putnam's research reveals a steady erosion in social capital in the US over the past forty years by a broad range of indicators, and some researchers assert that the Internet will further the erosion. Commercial broadcast television is often singled out as a major culprit in this erosion.

See also: **Access**, **Digital divide**, **Otaku**, **Social exclusion**

Further sources: Granovetter (1973), Putnam (2000)

SOCIAL INFORMATICS

This, according to the definition on the Social Informatics Home Page (http://www-slis.lib.indiana.edu/SI/), 'refers to the body of research and study that examines social aspects of computerization – including the roles of information technology in social and organizational change and the ways that the social organization of information technologies are influenced by social forces and social practices'.

See also: **Community informatics**

Further sources: Kling (1999)

SOCIAL SHAPING OF TECHNOLOGY

A commonplace way of understanding the relationship between technology and society is labelled 'technological determinism'. In this formulation, technology exists outside of the social, and produces effects in society. Against this viewpoint, the 'social shaping of technology' perspective argues that technology is social; that it emerges in particular contexts, as a result of social imperatives, and moreover that technology has a social – and we can add cultural – life. Indeed, the ways in which we incorporate technology into our lives can be seen to resist determinism. Thinking about how computers have ended up on our desktops, doing the jobs they do for us, has to involve thinking about society, not just as the 'victim' of technology but as its producer. Society and technology exist in a complex, adaptive relationship, therefore, each shaping the other. This does not mean rejecting the view that technology has a role in how society works; it means balancing that with an understanding of the role society has in how technology works. User groups can, in fact, significantly influence the forms and uses of technology, often in unforeseen ways. For example, email was originally added to the functions of the evolving Internet almost as an afterthought, but users quickly saw its usefulness and encouraged its development. In much the same way, the text-messaging function of mobile phones took on a much more significant social life than the industry predicted, spawning an entirely new repertoire of cultural practices. Critics have suggested that we need to make sure we do not lose sight of deterministic perspectives totally, however − that we must acknowledge that technology does shape society. Maintaining a balanced perspective in this equation offers us the most fruitful way to understand the human–machine interface.

Further sources: MacKenzie and Wacjman (1999)

SOFTWARE AGENTS *see* Agents

SPAM

Spam was originally a slang term used to describe the deliberate crashing of a computer application by overloading a fixed-size buffer with an excess of data (also known as a buffer overflow). It was then adopted as a way of describing the repetition of newsgroup posts on Usenet. Spamming can mean repeatedly posting the same message in one newsgroup, but it can also refer to what is also sometimes called Excessive Multi-Posting, or EMP, which involves sending the same post to many newsgroups. 'Spam' is also often used to describe any sort of unwanted post on a newsgroup or any unwanted email message, including unsolicited commercial email (UCE) and un-solicited bulk email (UBE). Those who send spam are sometimes known as 'spammers'.

Various explanations of the origin of the term exist. The most commonly accepted is that it is derived from a sketch from the 1970s

British TV series *Monty Python's Flying Circus*, in which two people try to order food in café and are confronted with a menu entirely made up of Spam, a type of tinned luncheon meat. It is the repetition in the sketch, with the participants saying 'Spam' to one another almost endlessly as they discuss the menu, that seems to be the origin of the term.

Spam is objected to on the basis that it takes up valuable **bandwidth**, slowing down networks and filling up valuable hard disk space. It may also cost the recipient money to receive spam. In 2003, Microsoft claimed that its filters on the servers at MSN and Hotmail were blocking more than 2.4 billion spam emails a day and the company also launched legal action against several major 'spammers'.

Mechanisms have been developed to block spam. Most email clients have the ability to block or instantly delete email that originates from senders on a list that the user can specify. However, mechanisms to counteract such measures have of course been developed by those sending spam, such as never using the same email address more than once. Some organizations have been sufficiently annoyed and inconvenienced to develop a range of anti-spam resources, and a number of companies offer products that claim to block spam.

From a sociological viewpoint, spam is interesting because of the reaction it can generate among those who are long-term users of the Internet and **computer mediated communication**. It is a violation by mass marketing of what had been quite a rarefied space. It is perhaps no coincidence that spamming is quite often associated with **newbies**, new users of virtual spaces who can be viewed negatively because they do not know, or do not respect, rules that were established when access to computer mediated communication was much more restricted.

Further sources: spam.abuse.net/, www.cauce.org/

SPIDER *see* **Robot**

STEPHENSON, NEAL *see* **Cyberpunk**

STRANGE DAYS (MOVIE)

Set at the turn of the new millennium, Kathryn Bigelow's *Strange Days* (1995) stars Ralph Fiennes as Nero, an ex-cop making a living from selling illegal digital recordings of other people's experiences –

known as playback. Like a mind-altering drug, playback enables its users to see, hear and feel everything that the other person experienced. In one of the key scenes of the film, a gang robs a restaurant and has a fatal gunfight with the police – and the whole experience is recorded by one gang member, to be sold on. Shot with extensive use of hand-held cameras, and using rapid editing, the film attempts to convey the acceleration and disorientation of life in a digital media culture.

Nero begins to receive playback of brutal murders, recorded from the victim's perspective, and the film revolves around his attempt to locate the killer, and to protect his own ex-girlfriend from becoming a victim. The central theme of the film, however, is the addictive experiencing of other people's lives – though most commonly it is sex and death that are made into playback. *Strange Days* thus offers a commentary on **simulation** and **virtual reality**, and on the status of experience in a mediatized world. However, as Claudia Springer (1999) argues, the film is keen to retain the authenticity of the real – a motif played out through the romantic relationships between Nero, Faith (Juliette Lewis) and Mace (Angela Bassett).

See also: **Simulation**

Further sources: Springer (1999)

SUBCULTURES

The term 'subcultures' has a long history in Sociology and Cultural Studies, and is used to describe social groups, often of young people, who forge a collective identity in opposition to the 'mainstream' or 'parent' culture. In Britain, the classic groups studied from a subcultural perspective include mods and rockers, punks, bikers and football hooligans. The focus of attention is often on the groups' reworking of existing cultural materials to create new styles – of dress, of music, of speech – referred to as *bricolage* (Hebdige 1979). Also significant is the use of media forms to circulate 'insider' information to other members of the subculture – things like fanzines are important here.

In terms of cyberculture, there are number of significant subcultural formations that have emerged. We can divide these into two groups: the first uses cyberspace primarily as a communications medium, much as it uses other media forms. Many of these groups existed before cyberspace, and have expanded into it, taking advantage of the opportunities it offers for worldwide communication. In this category we can include fan groups (of bands, movie stars, TV shows) and what we might describe as 'fringe' groups – alternative and marginalized religions, political organizations and worldviews. Here we can include things like conspiracists, anti-capitalists, UFOlogists and far right-wing groups (Bell 2001). Websites and **bulletin boards** are used to convey each group's or individual's opinions, and the decentralized network of cyberspace is used to circumvent censorship and build transnational coalitions. These groups have proliferated in cyberspace, but by and large they are not subcultures *about* cyberspace.

The second category we can label as cybersubcultures, or hi-tech subcultures: these are groups who are signalling an expressive engagement with new technologies (Terranova 2000). Here we can include hackers, anti-technological neo-Luddites, cyberpunks and other groups on the hi-tech fringes (such as those experimenting with new technologies outside of mainstream, state-sanctioned contexts). These subcultures have arisen in direct response to cyberspace, either to make non-mainstream or alternative use of its resources, or to challenge its dominance in our lives. Some groups use it stylistically, in an act of bricolage, while others are concerned with its technological rather than aesthetic potentials (Dery 1996). In either case, cybersubcultures remain fertile grounds for invention and imagination, showing the creative possibilities of cyberspace as well as critiquing its increasing mainstreaming and homogenization.

See also: **Cyberpunks**, **Hackers**

Further sources: Bell (2001), Dery (1996), Terranova (2000)

SURFING

Commonly used to describe 'travelling' on the web, surfing derives from the couch potato's hobby, channel surfing – meaning the passive and often rapid movement through different TV stations, looking for something attention-grabbing. Web surfing as a term has therefore been criticized as sounding too recreational and passive, and as referring to the consumption of websites as a form of entertainment. The term also conjures images of surfing waves on the ocean – an image often used in advertising to depict the act of web surfing (usually drawing on images borrowed from the comic book *Silver Surfer*, with the cityscape representing the datascape). Even this is criticized by some for its recreational, beach-bum connotations – though this downplays the level of skill involved in surfing (both in cyberspace and on the ocean).

TCP/IP (TRANSMISSION CONTROL PROTOCOL/ INTERNET PROTOCOL)

TCP/IP is a collection of protocols that govern the way data travels from one machine to another across networks. The term 'protocol' is used in the diplomatic sense, meaning a set of rules that are designed to facilitate communication between parties, or, in this instance, computers. The **Internet** is based on TCP/IP.

The Internet works by breaking data into manageable blocks or packets of data. These packets of data can be sent more quickly than can one large block of data. The Transmission Control Protocol (TCP) divides data into packets that a network can handle efficiently. It also ensures that the packets all arrive at their intended destination and is used to reassemble the data at their destination. The Internet Protocol (IP) addresses the data, i.e. it labels it so it is clear where it is going, and then places it in packet. It also enables a network to read the packet and forward the data to its destination. The IP protocol also defines how much data can fit in a single packet. As the two protocols are interrelated, they are generally referred to as TCP/IP.

TECHNOLOGICAL DETERMINISM *see* Social shaping of technology

TELEBANKING

Telebanking is the use of interactive networked services, allowing transactions with banks to be undertaken online from the home or office.

See also: **e-Commerce**

TELECENTER *see* Community technology centers

TELECONFERENCING *see* **Network organizations**

TELECOTTAGE *see* **Community technology centers**

TELEPRESENCE *see* **Virtual communities**

TELESHOPPING *see* **e-Commerce**

TEXT MESSAGING

Text messaging is the use of mobile telephones (often abbreviated to 'mobiles' in the UK and called cellular or cell-phones in the US) to send and receive text messages. In the UK, which has one of the highest levels of mobile phone use in the world, use of text messaging, particularly among young people, is very widespread. Just as someone can 'email' or have 'emailed' someone else, one can now 'text' or have 'texted' another person. In the UK, use of text messaging is probably more widespread than the use of email, reflecting near-total market penetration by mobiles and a lower (though still significant) level of home Internet access. Text messaging uses many of the conventions of **CMC**, including **abbreviations** and **smileys**. The small size of mobile phone screens, however, has led to greater use of acronyms, smileys and abbreviations than is the case for CMC.

See also: **Cues filtered out**, **Email**, **Flaming**

TOTAL RECALL (MOVIE)

Starring Arnold Schwarzenegger as Douglas Quade, Paul Verhoeven's *Total Recall* (1990) centres on the possibility of having **memories** implanted into the human brain, as a form of virtual tourism. Quade buys memories of a trip to Mars – and in the memories he is a secret agent. However, the implanting procedure goes wrong, and other memories appear to Quade – memories of having actually been a secret agent, called Hauser. Hauser/Quade then encounters recordings left by his former self – an image that says to him 'You are not you. You are me' – and he spends the film trying to separate 'true' memory and identity from the **prosthetic** memories he has had implanted in his mind (Landsberg 2000). Ultimately he chooses to be Quade, regardless of the status of that identity, and despite the efforts of the film's villain, Cohagen (Ronnie Cox), to convince him that he's *really* Hauser. The film's plot concerns the oxygen supply to a colony of mutants on Mars, which Cohagen controls. Quade uncovers an ancient alien generator deep within the planet, which creates an inhabitable atmosphere on Mars. Like *Blade Runner*, then, *Total Recall* asks important questions about memory, **identity** and machines: how do we know who we are? What makes up our sense of self?

See also: *Blade Runner*, **Identity**, **Memory**

Further sources: Landsberg (2000)

TRANSNATIONAL ADVOCACY NETWORKS

This is a term developed by Keck and Sikkink (1988) to describe how activists form and use networks of people that extend across national boundaries to define, discuss and develop campaigns. It is conjectured that the existence of an inexpensive networked communication and increasing numbers of international NGOs will contribute to the continued influence and growth of these networks.

See also: **New cultural politics**, **New social movements**

Further sources: Keck and Sikkink (1988)

TROJAN

A Trojan is a type of computer **virus**. Trojans originally took their name from 'Trojan Horses', as they were malicious and destructive viruses that 'hid' in files that were disguised as games or software upgrades. More recent Trojans do not attempt any such subterfuge, but they are still regarded as a separate class of viruses because they are designed to be destructive. Whereas some other viruses, such as **worms**, might merely spread themselves, a Trojan is intended to delete files, undermine operating systems, compromise system security or generally damage any computer or network that it infects.

See also: **Virus**

TROLL

Troll is a slang term originating in **Usenet** newsgroups, and also used in **IRC** rooms or channels to describe an individual or group of individuals who deliberately cause trouble with other participants. In some instances a troll may be making fanatical religious or fascistic statements. In other instances trolls will behave in a insulting way for reasons that are not really clear, other than perhaps a need for attention that they cannot get any other way. The term comes from the American English for deep-sea fishing with large nets (trawl in English), the meaning being that individuals of this sort 'troll' around newsgroups looking for trouble and the resulting attention they will get.

See also: **Cues filtered out**, **Netiquette**

2001: A SPACE ODYSSEY (MOVIE)

Directed by Stanley Kubrick and released a year before the Moon landings (1968), *2001* is a landmark sci-fi movie, not least for its depiction of **artificial intelligence** as embodied in the form of HAL 9000, the computer on board the spaceship *Discovery*.

The film comprises three acts, all linked by mysterious black monoliths. In the first segment, primitive humanoid-apes apparently 'learn' from the monolith (which has strangely materialized on the African savannah) how to use bones as weapons, with which they kill members of an opposing tribe. The second, longer act concerns the voyage of astronauts Dave Bowman (Keir Dullea) and Frank Poole (Gary Lockwood) on the spaceship *Discovery* to Jupiter, following the uncovering of a monolith on the Moon which is emitting a radio signal back towards Jupiter. The third part of the film focuses on Bowman's trip to Jupiter space through a strange, hallucinatory realm, his encounter with the monolith, with his own, rapidly ageing self, and with the foetal 'Star Child' floating alongside an image of Earth from space – an enigmatic yet utopian final sequence.

The depiction of HAL, which is said to have taken its name from the letters in the alphabet before 'IBM', draws on common themes of machine intelligence as a potentially destructive force. HAL is initially depicted as a servant to the human crew, but the computer becomes obsessive, even delusional, and kills all the crew except Dave – partly as it believes itself more rational than and superior to the humans. Eventually, HAL is shut down, regressing to 'infanthood' and singing the children's song 'Daisy, Daisy' – the first song ever played by a computer, in 1957 (Edwards 1996). In common with later representations, such as the 'Terminator' series of films, and indeed earlier representations of advanced technology bringing destruction that date back to *Forbidden Planet*, HAL reflects anxieties about machine intelligence and the effects of technology, also seen in popular media representations of social phenomena like the Japanese **Otaku**. However, HAL has also evolved into something resembling a goal in terms of the development of improving **interfaces** between humans and computers. Microsoft, for example, is devoting its resources to the creation of Natural Language Processing, with the theoretical goal of a computer that can understand and, perhaps, reply in English and other languages. The development of **agent** software also has a similar goal, creating a person- or character-like interface, with which the user can 'converse'.

See also: **Artificial intelligence**, *Blade Runner*

Further sources: Edwards (1996), Stork (1998)

UNIVERSAL ACCESS

Universal access is the US policy objective of ensuring that all citizens have access to communication capabilities. Originally this meant setting up a cross subsidy in which profits from urban telephone use were employed to provide rural telephone services at a rate less than actual costs. Many people have attempted to apply this concept to the Internet. The presumed need to develop policy to this end has been roundly criticized as unnecessary in nearly every location where it has been proposed, because 'market forces' would soon allow every citizen access.

See also: **Access**, **Public broadcasting**

UNIX

UNIX is an operating system that provides a multi-user **interface**, allowing many people to use a computer simultaneously. According to some definitions, UNIX originally stood for UNiplexed Information and Computing System (or Unics), which was a wordplay on Multics, the name of an earlier, similar, operating system. UNIX is a significant operating system in its own right, but doubly so because it forms the base for **LINUX**, one of the most important pieces of **Open Source** software available, as well as for Apple's OSX.

URL (UNIFORM RESOURCE LOCATOR)

A URL is the **Internet** 'address' of any piece of data, such as a file or web page on the **Web**. A URL takes the form: 'protocol://host/ localinfo'. The first part identifies the 'protocol' that will be used to fetch a given piece of data, which for a web page will be the HyperText Transfer Protocol (http). The 'host' identifies the server on which the data are held, and the remaining part gives its specific address on that server.

See also: **HTTP, TCP/IP, World Wide Web**

USABILITY

As text-based mediums require the use of a keyboard and mouse, **computer mediated communication** (CMC) such as **email**, discussion forums and online self-help like that provided on **Usenet** and the **World Wide Web** itself can all be inaccessible to a significant proportion of the population. Poor **access** to the new technologies is often discussed in terms of the digital divide, but there are many people who are not able to use orthodox means of interacting with **ICTs** because these have tended to be designed by young, white, male, North American engineers.

Human–computer interface design can be confusing, counter-intuitive, over-complex and difficult to engage with for those outside the industry. Of course, there have been massive advances: operating systems have gone from using largely incomprehensible typed commands to the graphical user interfaces of such systems as Windows that are far more accessible. There may also be further significant advances, particularly around natural language processing (voice command using ordinary language) and in the use of **agents**, to enable someone using a computer to interact with it on a 'person-to-person' basis. These developments, if they come to fruition, will replace what we currently understand as operating systems with a human–computer interface that is similar to interaction with another person. At the time of writing, however, computers remain difficult for many people to engage with, particularly at anything above a very basic level. This is best demonstrated by the high levels of need for technical support from people using computers at home and in the workplace.

Language can be a major boundary to usability. The web, far from being actually 'worldwide', is a largely American network. Apart from the difficulties for the bulk of the world's population to gain access to ICTs in the first instance (see the **digital divide**), someone who speaks and writes only Mandarin or Gujerati, for example, may not find their language and culture well represented on the web, although the presence of other nations and cultures on the web is increasing.

Language may cease to be as important a barrier to usability as it is at the time of writing when and if reliable translators for resources like web pages become available. Many of the mainstream software packages can already cope with the various character sets required by the world's languages and also provide their commands and help systems in those languages. However, representation of the world outside the US will also depend on the extent to which the current global digital divide can be addressed.

Anyone whose main language is English but who is illiterate or sub-literate will not be able to engage with a resource like the web, or use many applications. Education is often linked to social and economic exclusion and is part of addressing the digital divide. As already noted, the human–computer interface may also become more speech-based over time, potentially opening up access to people with a learning difficulty who may never be able to acquire sufficient literacy skills.

Older people with arthritis or other conditions may find it difficult to control a mouse accurately or to use a keyboard. Others will not be able to use these established ways of interacting with ICTs at all. Many people may find a computer screen difficult to read because they have a visual impairment, or will not be able to read it at all because they are blind.

There are many means by which hardware can be modified, including pointing devices other than mice and alternatives to a keyboard. Combinations of software and hardware can be used to provide modifications to standard operating systems and applications, particularly voice commands (although this still may not be usable for some people with disabilities). Web browsing and computer mediated communication can also be provided through talking browsers or email clients that do not require physical interaction with the computer.

There are essentially two problems for people who need access to these sorts of modifications. The first is cost, in that disabled people may often find it more difficult to secure work, while welfare or benefit systems will often not be prepared to fund the modified computers that people with disabilities need for Internet access and for an opportunity to engage with ICTs. The second is that insufficient thought, in fact often no thought whatsoever, has been given to the needs of people with disabilities in the basic design of hardware and software.

The web is, again, a good example of how inaccessible ICTs can be to people with disabilities. Many sites are designed with an emphasis on visual appearance, often at the expense of easy navigation, which can make them awkward for anyone wanting to use them, but particularly awkward for someone who cannot use a computer in the orthodox way. A great many sites are unintelligible to a talking browser used by a blind or visually impaired person. Others may employ interfaces that are hard to navigate for someone who cannot easily use a pointing device like a mouse with a high-enough degree of precision.

As a response to the inaccessibility of the web, the World Wide Web Consortium has launched the Web Accessibility Initiative (WAI) which is designed to promote accessibility of the web through five primary areas of work: technology, guidelines, tools, education and outreach, and research and development. In essence, this involves the provision of web pages that are easily navigable and as usable as possible for anyone who wishes to use the web.

See also: **Access**, **Digital divide**, **HTML**

Further sources: Nielsen (2000), www.w3.org/WAI/

USENET

The Usenet is a system of **computer mediated communication** invented in North Carolina in the USA in late 1979 by three postgraduate students, Tom Truscott, Jim Ellis and Steve Bellovin. The news reading and organizing software was to be enhanced by a number of other programmers, and several different versions became available.

Most email clients (software for reading and sending emails) can access Usenet, and web-based access is also available.

Usenet is usually defined as a worldwide distributed discussion system which plays host to many thousands of electronic fora called newsgroups. Newsgroups are an asynchronous form of CMC, which means that participants cannot 'talk' directly to one another as they can in a system like **Internet Relay Chat (IRC)**. A newsgroup works as if it were an electronic version of a notice board or **bulletin board**. An individual can 'post' a message which other visitors to the newsgroup can read. The difference between a newsgroup and a notice board is that anyone who reads a message on a newsgroup can post a response, which can also be read by anyone visiting the newsgroup.

As soon as one or more messages have been posted in response to an original post, the software sorts them into chronological order and places them together in a 'thread' of posts all on the same subject. The sorting mechanism is the title of the original post, which responses to that post need to retain if they are to be placed in the same thread.

This organization of messages into threads is very important because it brings some order to busy newsgroups, which might have hundreds of posts at any one time, and allows a visitor to select the subjects they are interested in and read all the posts on those subjects. Most busy newsgroups have their older posts periodically deleted or archived.

Usenet is an open system that anyone can enter and use. However, certain aspects, particularly the creation of new groups, are controlled to some extent. An individual who wants to create a newsgroup cannot simply do so, and has to contact the appropriate individuals, who are referred to as 'news administrators'. This contact can be made via a newsgroup maintained by the news administrators. There are also rules about how to behave on Usenet; these are generally referred to as **netiquette**. In practice, once a group is established, netiquette may sometimes be ignored unless the group has a moderator who prevents certain posts from appearing. Abusive messages that appear on newsgroups are generally known as **flames**. Individuals who visit newsgroups and deliberately start fights or arguments are usually referred to as **trolls**.

Newsgroups on Usenet are organized by their broad subject, which allows individuals to search through a list of newsgroups easily to find ones they might be interested in. These classifications by broad subjects are referred to as 'Newsgroup Hierarchies', and the hierarchy in which a newsgroup is located forms the first part of its name. There are quite a large number of hierarchies, but some of the more commonly used ones include: alt. (alternative); biz. (business); comp. (computer); misc. (miscellaneous); rec. (recreational).

In addition to including a hierarchy name that identifies their broad subject, newsgroups based outside the USA will also include a hierarchy name that identifies the country in which they are located. These hierarchy names are self-explanatory, such as 'uk.' for Britain and 'jp.' for Japan. A newsgroup name will also explain the subject of the group in more detail, as in the following examples:

- uk.people.disability (a newsgroup located in Britain for disabled people);
- alt.support.depression (an 'alternative' newsgroup offering support for people with depression and, because its name contains no country identifier, it is US-based);
- rec.arts.books.tolkien (a US-based recreational newsgroup for people interested in J.R.R. Tolkien's novels):
- alt.animals.breeders.rabbits (a US-based 'alternative' newsgroup for people interested in breeding rabbits).

Newsgroups that are not moderated allow full freedom of speech, and in consequence there is a range of very offensive material available within certain newsgroups, including the views of racist, misogynist and fascistic individuals. This same unregulated quality is of course found on other networks, such as the **World Wide Web**.

Further sources: ftp.faqs.org/faqs/usenet/, www.usenet.org/, www.usenet.org.uk/

VALUE-ADDED NETWORK

A value added network is an enhanced service built on the basic telecommunications network, such as **email** and **telebanking**.

VCHAT *see* **Internet Relay Chat**

V-CHIP

This is an electronic device that can be installed in a TV set to block out 'objectionable' material, which is detected by a rating encoded in the television signal.

VIDEO GAMES *see* Games

VIRTUAL CHAT ROOM *see* Chat room

VIRTUAL COMMUNITY

'Virtual community' is a term conceived and popularized by Howard Rheingold to describe how online technologies helped facilitate the creation of communities whose bonds were mostly or entirely *virtual*.

Further sources: Rheingold (1993)

VIRTUAL ORGANIZATION *see* Network organization

VIRTUAL REALITY (VR)

'VR' is the term used to describe computer systems that create a real-time 3D audio and visual experience depicting a simulation of reality or an imagined reality. The term originally referred only to environments in which one could genuinely immerse oneself, and a user could only see and interact with VR by using a headset and a data glove. During the mid-1990s, VR was seen as the next step in human–computer interfaces. It could simulate a reality that an individual could experience in a similar way to moving around the real world. However, early experiments with VR in **games** proved a major disappointment to those who had advocated the technology. The headsets needed to use a VR game were heavy and awkward and the experience of VR itself made a lot of people feel disoriented and nauseous. Early VR games, although they demanded a lot of computing power, were prone to produce rather dull and featureless environments. These same issues arose with regard to using VR for other applications.

The term is now used in a much wider sense to describe 3D modelling and simulations, as well as imagined 3D environments: large devices like flight simulators use advanced 3D modelling for example, as do military simulators. On the **World Wide Web**, **HTML** is quite often used in conjunction with Virtual Reality Modelling Language (VRML). VRML can be used as a   multi-platform language for publishing 3D Web pages. It tends to be used when whatever is being displayed has to be shown three dimensionally, although in fact it presents a 2D illusion of 3D. Common uses include online games, engineering and scientific models, 3D educational sites and 3D architectural models.

The term is also used to describe other 3D modelling systems that are used in a wide range of applications. For example, an application that creates an on-screen studio set for television programmes, showing the viewer a presenter in front of a lavish set when in fact they are just sitting in front of a blue screen, would sometimes be described as a VR application. The concept of genuine VR, in which all the senses are taken over by the computer and there is a real 3D representation, is widely used in descriptions of imagined computer networks by **cyberpunk** authors.

Further sources: www.web3d.org/, www.vrs.org.uk/

VIRTUAL REALITY MODELLING LANGUAGE (VRML) *see* **Virtual reality**

VIRTUAL SOCIAL SUPPORT (VSS)

The use of **computer mediated communication** for self-help and social support by people with support and health-care needs is referred to as virtual social support. The easiest way in which to understand virtual self-help is to imagine an online version of a 'support group', made up of people with the same needs as one another, who offer each other social and practical support, similar to a local Alcoholics Anonymous meeting. Rather than meeting on a weekly basis in a venue to which they all have to travel, online virtual social support groups instead meet virtually, in a newsgroup on **Usenet**, or on an **IRC** channel or in a **chat room**. In some instances, they may use other types of shared virtual space, such as a **MUD**.

Self-help is grounded in shared experience rather than professional expertise or opinions. It offers the support of other individuals who share the same health problem, or have had the same experiences as oneself. This access to other individuals who have the same needs and experiences can potentially mean access to a level of understanding and support that professionals, however good they are, cannot really ever hope to emulate.

Social support is sometimes discussed in terms of either the 'buffer' theory, in which social supports are held to have a positive effect when individuals are confronted with illness and stress, or the 'main effect' model, in which social supports are held to have a constant and generally beneficial effect. A range of social resources are held to act against stress and in turn both reduce the likelihood of the onset of health problems and aid recovery if health problems develop. Cohen and Wills (1985: 313) list *esteem support*, information that a person is esteemed and accepted; *informational support*, help in defining, understanding and coping with problematic events; *social companionship*, spending time with others in leisure or recreational activities, and *instrumental support*, the provision of financial aid, material resources and needed services, as the main forms of social support.

Virtual social support differs from traditional self-help or support groups in a number of important respects. Virtual self-help is global, in the sense that anyone with **Internet** access can use these online groups. This access is currently heavily skewed towards higher-income households in North America, the UK and other West European nations (see **digital divide**). This has made the use of virtual social support something of a middle-class pursuit at the time of writing (Burrows and Nettleton 2000). These groups are also accessible at any time, with internationally-used groups sometimes having at least some participants online on a 24-hour-a-day basis. The logistical considerations in setting up a self-help group, from finding members to getting hold of a suitable venue, do not arise when setting up an online group. An online self-help group is probably just a couple of mouse clicks away for people with most health-care or other support needs.

Virtual social support offers a qualitatively different form of social support to that which can be provided by a 'real' self-help or support group. Muncer *et al.* (2000b) have argued that, while virtual self-help can provide social companionship, informational support and esteem support, it cannot deliver instrumental, or practical, support. In part, this reflects the rather obvious point that group members do not actually physically meet one another. Equally importantly, however, it also reflects a finding that these virtual self-help groups often do not have a stable membership, so relationships cannot form in the same way as they might between participants in a 'real' support or self-help group.

For commentators like Denzin (1998), the enthusiasm for virtual self-help is about the natural merging of the North American love of self-help with their love of technology. However, research in Britain also found that virtual social support was being used by people there, sometimes by visiting North American groups and sometimes by establishing their own online support groups. For commentators like Burrows and Nettleton (2000), it is the context of the use of virtual self-help in the UK that is of the most interest. They view virtual self-help as a reaction to new levels of uncertainty in day-to-day existence. As faith in professionals declines, including medical professionals, the relatively new phenomenon of what doctors in the UK sometimes call the 'netty' patient (as in internet-user) has arisen. These are middle-class professionals who arrive at the surgery with a stack of printouts, some from the web and some from virtual self-help groups, wherein the patient has exchanged views with other people with the same health problem. For a doctor, this can mean dealing with a patient who has a very firm opinion about how they should be treated.

Once this starts to happen, virtual social support could be seen as representing a potential threat to professionals' roles. Virtual social support may cause individuals to question what might be an inaccurate diagnosis by their doctor, which is obviously a positive development. However, of course, there is already evidence of low-quality or incorrect information on health issues being found on the Internet and being disseminated through virtual self-help groups. This raises the danger of professional medical advice being ignored and patients potentially endangering themselves.

The other issues that can arise in relation to virtual social support include the unregulated nature of the Internet and most computer mediated communication. Vulnerable users may visit online environments offering virtual social support and have negative experiences, for example such groups might be targets for abusive individuals (see **trolls**). They may also potentially endanger themselves in such environments, raising the same sort of fears as accompany children's use of the Internet. Equally, virtual self-help and support groups may be used by voyeurs who do not share the health problems or support needs being discussed, and who might use the groups in much the same way as some popular television shows present individual misery as mass entertainment.

The significance of virtual social support is not clear at the time of writing. There are online versions of Alcoholics Anonymous meetings, online groups for survivors of child abuse, for disabled people, for people with arthritis and a host of other groups across the Internet. It is apparent that people establish and use these groups. Yet they appear to represent only a minority among the many bulletin boards, newsgroups and IRC channels available on the Internet. The survival of virtual social support in the form in which it exists at the time of writing may be closely linked to the survival of existing forms of computer mediated communication. Part of the current attraction of virtual social support is its anonymity, something that has arisen through technological limitations rather than by deliberate design. As the technology changes, these groups may have to change with it. There is also the point that these groups seem to be used largely by the relatively educated and affluent middle classes, something which may limit their appeal to other groups of people.

Further sources: Burrows and Nettleton (2000), Denzin (1998), Pleace *et al.* (2000, 2001), Muncer *et al.* (2000b)

VIRTUOSITY (MOVIE)

In the sci-fi thriller *Virtuosity* (Brett Leonard, 1995), a composite serial killer combining characteristics drawn from Hitler, Charles Manson, John Wayne Gacy and Jeffrey Dahmer has been put together in cyberspace for use in police training simulations. The construct, Sid 6.7 (Russell Crowe), escapes from cyberspace and finds a way to inhabit the borderland between the real and the virtual. A former police officer, Parker Barnes (Denzel Washington), is brought out of jail to pursue Sid 6.7. Barnes has himself been subject to **virtual reality** experiments in improving police effectiveness, while imprisoned for killing the murderers of his wife and child, and in those experiments he was pitted against Sid 6.7 in simulations. Barnes enlists the help of psychologist Dr Madison Carter (Kelly Lynch), and together they ultimately contain Sid 6.7 in his 'proper' (virtual) place.

As Claudia Springer (1999: 209) writes, *Virtuosity* simultaneously demonizes cyberspace as unleashing the evil embodied in Sid 6.7, and celebrates the potential of fluid **identities** and boundary states – Crowe plays Sid 6.7 as 'a flamboyant merrymaker who luxuriates in his simulated life ... frolic[ing] through actual reality, overturning all norms and conventions'. It thus encapsulates the anxieties and excitement that surround cyberspace, and that recur in a whole series of 'cyberthrillers', notably **Strange Days** and **Johnny Mnemonic**.

See also: **Identity**, **Virtual reality**

Further sources: Springer (1999)

VIRUS

Computer viruses are programs that produce particular effects when they are run on a computer. Most simply, a virus is a piece of software capable of reproducing itself. Viruses are transmitted from computer to computer on 'infected' disks, or more commonly today via email (see **worm**). The term has come to be associated with programs that cause some kind of 'damage' to host machines (see **Trojan**), is often aligned with **hacking** activity, and is subject to the same kinds of moral panic. An entire anti-virus industry has evolved to help computers and their users deal with the negative effects of these programs – virus scanning software, equivalents of inoculation and antidotes, and so on.

As well as affecting computers, viruses also produce particular effects in computer users – most frequently, panic. Viruses make very visible our anxieties about computers, also revealing how poorly we understand the insides of our machines. But for some commentators, viruses have a vital function to perform in cyberculture – and a creative rather than destructive one. However, the most common portrayal of viruses and their writers emphasizes destructiveness.

The 'Love Bug' worm, which spread around May 2000, brought home forcefully the possibilities of putting the Internet to malicious use. The Love Bug was an email virus carrying the header 'I Love You' and promising a seductive attachment: the message read 'kindly check the attached LOVELETTER coming from me'. Who could resist opening up such an email? From the evidence of those few days in early May, not many people: the Love Bug caused upwards of US$1bn worth of 'damage' before the warnings came out and the anti-virus industry stepped in. Its effects were felt all around the wired world, and it spread with amazing rapidity.

The panic surrounding the Love Bug was obviously very real. Computers were infected and affected, business was halted, money was lost, lives were disrupted. Moreover, the media coverage around the Love Bug re-animated debates about hackers and viruses, and about security and anxiety in computer culture. Deborah Lupton (1994) has deconstructed previous media coverage of computer viruses, reading them as examples of 'panic computing'. For her, the designation of rogue programming as a 'virus' has a lot to tell us:

> The nomination of a type of computer technology malfunc-
> tion as a 'virus' is a highly significant and symbolic linguistic
> choice of metaphor, used to make certain connections

between otherwise unassociated subjects and objects, to give meaning to unfamiliar events, to render abstract feelings and intangible processes concrete.

(Lupton 1994: 557)

For Lupton, the use of the term 'virus' carries a moral agenda with it – the morality of danger, risk, trust and protection, spilling over from the other global viral crisis, HIV/Aids. Tracking parallels in health discourse and computing discourse, she identifies the same logic at work: imperatives about safe sex are rewritten around safe software (see also Ross 2000), and computer users are drawn into a discourse about safety, risk and contamination. The Love Bug reinforces the sexual motif by tempting us into 'risky' behaviour on the promise of romance – tapping knowingly into the widespread use of workplace emails for personal, even intimate, messaging. Moreover, this virus showed the vulnerability of the Internet, subverting its decentralized character – which simultaneously facilitated the rapid networked spread of the virus and allowed its writer to hide, at least for a while. Once uncovered, of course, the virus's writer was subject to the now familiar demonization process that attempts to mark hackers as deviants (Ross 2000).

Against the tide of media panics, however, other commentators take a more productive view of viruses. In his essay 'Viruses are good for you', for example, Julian Dibbell (1995) attempts to offset viral panic by recasting viruses as 'autonomously reproducing computer programs' – as artificial life-forms existing and mingling in the 'ecology' of computer networks. As he says, the aim of this move is to refute the 'mix of bafflement and dread' that marks our current response to viruses: 'Overcoming our fear of computer viruses may be the most important step we can take toward the future of information processing'. Like other countercultural elements within cyberculture, virus writing is here reworked as a creative activity that can produce positive benefits – innovations in software, for example. Mark Ludwig (1996a: 19) similarly argues that 'computer viruses are not evil' and that 'programmers have a right to create them, possess them, and experiment with them', adding that 'viruses can be useful, interesting, and just plain fun'. His expanded definition of viruses works to shed them of their malevolent image:

> ... *computer viruses are not inherently destructive.* The essential
> feature of a computer program that causes it to be classified as
> a virus is not its ability to destroy data but its ability to gain

control of the computer and make a fully functional copy of itself. It can reproduce. When it is executed, it makes one or more copies of itself.

(Ludwig 1996a: 29; emphasis in original)

In order similarly to broaden our view of the world of computer viruses, Dibbell sketches the motives of programmers – motives a long, long way from the popular image of twisted or vengeful hackers. He reiterates that the moral panic around hackers covers over the central role of hacking in the evolution of computing, and also notes that most viruses have no destructive aim – they are a way of demonstrating programming skill and also of testing and refining current systems. Destructive applications or pranks embedded in viruses often only really serve to give the virus 'character'. One hacker, Dibbell described viruses as 'electronic graffiti' – sometimes prankish, sometimes malicious, but more often just a powerfully symbolic way to display programming skill and inventiveness in cyberculture, to show who you are, that you're there, and that you know what you're doing.

Other virus writers have different motives, of course. There are those with an interest in **artificial life** (**A-Life or AL**), for whom viruses are a first step towards creating new life-forms in cyberspace. Collecting and observing computer viruses 'in the wild' thus gives these virus watchers insights into computing, into evolution and into the possibilities of A-Life. Others 'breed' viruses, letting them mix and mingle in quarantined machines (like virtual safari parks), watching the programming solutions that evolve in these ecologies, and looking for evolutionary leaps that might be harnessed for new uses – for example to create intelligent **agents** or other software solutions.

However, in an essay on computer viruses and evolution, Ludwig (1996b) presents a slightly more pessimistic or at least cautious scenario about the outcome of creating self-replicating, evolving programs in cyberspace. As he asks: 'What would a virus that had become what it is primarily by evolution be like?' (Ludwig 1996b: 243). Applying Darwinian logic to computer viruses, Ludwig suggests that self-serving viruses could easily destabilize the matrix of computers in the same way that biological viruses can over-run their hosts. As with other fears over computers running amok, Ludwig worries that we might unwittingly unleash viral life-forms that could turn against us. Using the analogy of the Cambrian 'explosion' in biological life-forms, Ludwig concludes:

> Right now there is no reason to believe … that a similar flowering will not take place in the electronic world. If it does, and we're not ready for it, expecting it, and controlling its shape, there's no telling what the end of it could be. … We often imagine that computers will conquer man [sic] by becoming much more intelligent than him [sic]. It could be that we'll be conquered by something that's incredibly stupid, but adept at manipulating our senses, feelings, and desire.
>
> (Ludwig 1996b: 246)

Learning from the Love Bug, for instance, a computer virus could find the emotional buttons it needs to push to get a needed response out of humans, just as biological viruses ingeniously utilize our foibles to create opportunities for replication and transmission. A relatively 'primitive' virus could therefore produce catastrophic effects.

Ultimately, viruses will always engender panic, because the only time most of us think about them is when we receive an emailed virus warning, or when the mass media covers the more spectacular viruses like the Love Bug. Attempting a more generous understanding of the different forms and roles of computer viruses in the wake of such panic logic is difficult, but – as Dibbell and Ludwig both argue – necessary if we are to enjoy the benefits while also being mindful of the risks that computer viruses bring.

See also: **A-Life**, **Hacking**

Further sources: Dibbell (1995), Ludwig (1996a, 1996b), Lupton (1994)

VISIBLE HUMAN PROJECT (VHP)

The US National Library of Medicine's Visible Human Project (VHP) represents the coming together of biomedicine and cyberspace in a unique and extraordinary way. The project arose from the NLM's interest in producing a digital archive of the human body, to function as a biomedical resource for research and teaching, and as an aid in the development of telemedicine techniques. The productions of the project, the Visible Man and the Visible Woman, are complete, anatomically detailed, three-dimensional virtual renderings of human corpses, constructed using an array of medical imaging and computational technologies. The donated corpses (having been selected to represent 'typical' or 'normal' bodies) were MRI scanned, frozen in gelatin to −85°C, quartered, scanned again, sliced through (into thousands of slices between 0.3 and 1mm thick) and photographed repeatedly, as each layer of their bodies was planed away, turning to dust. The digitized images thus produced can be infinitely reassembled and manipulated by computer programs. Animated 'fly-throughs', cross-sections at any chosen plane, patholo-gical reconstructions, explorations of particular parts or systems within the body (the skeleton, the circulatory system) – all of these and countless more applications are possible, and many examples are available online. Accessible in cyberspace, the Visible Humans are eternally available for scientific and educational (not to mention recreational) scrutiny and use.

The story of the VHP has another, potentially even more sensationalist, dimension to it. The donated corpse of the Visible Man turned out to be that of a murderer, Joseph Paul Jernigan, executed by lethal injection in Texas in 1993 (after twelve years on death row). This biographical information brought out issues of the status of the criminal body as biomedical norm, questions of prisoners' rights, and so on (Cartwright 2000). The Visible Woman has not attracted the same level of posthumous celebrity, and is known only as an anonymous 59-year-old Maryland housewife who died of a heart attack.

The VHP has led to panics about scientists 'playing god' or 'meddling with nature', and has prompted Frankensteinian readings of the project as yet another attempt at parthenogenesis (male self-reproduction without women). Sarah Kember (1999), for example, offers this kind of analysis. Of course, in the realm of popular culture, Frankensteinian fears are a commonplace reaction to science, and the VHP's arrival in cyberspace coincided with a slew of Hollywood 'cyberthrillers' addressing questions of virtual **bodies** and **identities**, including *Strange Days*, *Johnny Mnemonic*, *Virtuosity* and *The Net* (see Springer 1999). In this sense, the VHP brings sci-fi to life, and has to be read in relation to popular culture as well as biomedicine. As an extraordinary manifestation of cyberspace's reconfiguring of the human body, it belongs in a lineage that also includes **cyborgs**, posthumans, and forms of **artificial life** (**A-Life**). Indeed, as Waldby's (2000) excellent book on the VHP shows, these databodies offer us numerous ways to think about the status of the body in cyberculture.

See also: **Body**, **Identity**

Further sources: Cartwright (2000), Kember (1999), Waldby (2000)

VOICE MAIL

Voice mail is the means by which spoken messages may be stored on a network for subsequent retrieval by the recipient.

VOYEURISM

Webcams, with their ability to send static and moving images across the Internet, have helped create a bizarre new activity. A few individuals have added cameras to one or more rooms in their home and started to broadcast, unedited, images from their daily lives. One of the first and perhaps the best-known of these sites, called Jennicam, was set up by a female American student. An anecdotal story, which may be the Internet equivalent of an urban myth, relays that when she was scheduled to make love in front of the cameras, the server crashed because it received so many **hits**. Although the sexual content is doubtless a motivation for visitors, it is important to draw a distinction between something like Jennicam, which shows sex because it shows almost every aspect of someone's existence, including images of their sleep, and the much more widespread use of webcams for **pornography**.

The voyeurism found on the **World Wide Web** has now made the leap to mainstream media. The best example of this is the television show 'Big Brother', in which game show contestants were placed in a 'house' under constant surveillance, their continued residence in the 'house' being determined by votes from the public. Originally developed in the Netherlands, this is a concept that has since been adopted and extended by television networks throughout the world. In Britain, the television coverage of the Big Brother house was complemented by constant website based surveillance and, of course, 'Big Brother' led very quickly to 'Celebrity Big Brother'. The appeal of these shows, in which wholly unremarkable people are temporarily elevated to celebrity status, probably lies in the extent to which those who are on screen are seen as a reflection of themselves by the social groups who are drawn to this sort of programming.

The possible effects of Internet-based voyeurism will depend on how widespread and significant this sort of activity becomes. The transition to mainstream media may be important, particularly if

digital television begins to take over from analogue television; as important will be cheap **broadband** Internet access, when that becomes widely available.

There are obvious concerns as to whether this sort of activity is conducive to mental health, both for the watched and the watchers. Voyeurisms like Jennicam and 'Big Brother' raise similar, though perhaps more profound, concerns to those raised by the onset of television, as expressed by thinkers such as Baudrillard about how our relationship with images and simulacra changes and perhaps undermines our relationship to the real. This in turn links with arguments about the role of new media (alongside a range of other factors) in reducing **social capital**.

Further sources: www.jennicam.com/, www.channel4.com/bigbrother/

WARE

The mechanical and electronic parts of computers, the silicon chips and screens, keyboards and disks, are referred to as hardware – the material objects of cyberculture. Programs, files and so on are the software. These things exist in or on the hardware, but also enable it to operate and enable us to use it: a computer is useless until it is programmed. Software that enables people to share documents and work collaboratively is known as groupware. Programs distributed freely on the Internet are sometimes called shareware or **freeware** – the idea of information freedom is an important if controversial element of cyberculture. **Pirated** software can be called 'warez'. And in certain circles, particularly those sympathetic to the **cyberpunk** or post-human ethos, the brain is described as wetware.

See also: **Cyberpunk**, **Piracy**

WAREZ *see* **Piracy**

WEB *see* **World Wide Web**

WEB BROWSER *see* **World Wide Web**

WEBCAM

Webcams are digital cameras designed to capture moving and still images in a format that is suitable for sending across the Internet. A number of webcam sites simply show streets in different towns and cities and a host of other different subjects and locations. One of the earliest experiments in sending images through the Internet was at the Department of Computing at the University of Cambridge, which sent images of its Trojan Room coffee machine across the Internet. Some individuals have made a decision to broadcast some or all of their lives across the Internet using this technology, creating an industry based on **voyeurism**. Webcams are also used extensively in the production of online **pornography**.

Further sources: A brief history of the Trojan Room coffee machine can be found at www.cl.cam.ac.uk/coffee/coffee.html, although the coffee machine itself was finally switched off, after distinguished service, on 22 August 2001.

WEBMASTER

The person who runs a website is known as the site's webmaster.

See also: **World Wide Web**

WIKI

According to Ward Cunningham's original description, a Wiki is 'the simplest online database that could possibly work'. Wiki is a type of server application that allows people to create and edit web page content using web browsers. Wiki supports hyperlinks and has a simple text syntax for creating new pages and crosslinks between internal pages. Wiki supports an 'open editing' approach in which users can modify the organization of contributions in addition to the content itself. Although the basic model allows anybody to edit any content on the Wiki, there are restrictions which can be enabled to help reduce the possible mischief resulting from a completely open editing policy. The first Wiki site was launched in 1995 as an automated supplement to the Portland Pattern Repository (c2.com/cgi/wiki?PortlandPatternRepository), which was used by the object-oriented programming pattern language community to post and review their pattern ideas.

Further sources: Leuf and Cunningham (2001), wiki.org/

WIRED (MAGAZINE)

Wired is an American magazine that documents, details and extol the virtues of **ICTs**. In some senses its editorial line reflects the approach of the early Internet optimists like Howard Rheingold (www.rhein-gold.com/), who saw in the Internet the possibility of new forms of social interaction and community. The online world was seen by these early Internet optimists as an equal world, in which the barriers to communication that were raised by time, space and convention could be overcome, and communities of shared interest could be developed. While it would be an exaggeration to view *Wired* as simply expressing these sorts of views, it can present a mix of Californian and right-wing attitudes to individual freedom, alongside quite a keen interest in business and ICT markets, within its pages. Almost every aspect of what might be defined as cyberculture has been discussed in *Wired* at some point, and the magazine and its online archive at www.wired.com/ represents a significant resource in documenting changing attitudes and trends in our relationships with ICTs. *Wired* describes itself in the following way:

> Wired magazine is the journal of record for the future. It's daring. Compelling. Innovative. Courageous. Insightful. It speaks not just to high-tech professionals and the business savvy, but also to the forward-looking, the culturally astute, and the simply curious.

Further sources: www.wired.com/

WIRELESS

Wireless is a generic term used to describe technologies that enable devices and **ICTs** to communicate with one another without the need for connection to a cable. The devices currently use the IEEE 802.11b standard. Technologies like Bluetooth enable connection to networks like the **Internet** by devices that merely have to be in broadcast range of a 'hotspot' (the area covered by a service providing wireless connection to a network). Wireless connection to networks is seen as creating the possibility of the increased use of handheld devices such as **G3** phones and in allowing network access by groups of people like **road warriors** from anywhere. The potential of these technologies may be greater than that of mobile cellular telephony, although, at the time of writing, some hesitancy has arisen as to whether or not technologies like G3 have quite the marketing potential they were thought to have, a worry fuelled by the bitter experiences of the **dot.com** boom and bust.

Further sources: www.bluetooth.com/

WIRELESS APPLICATION PROTOCOL (WAP)

WAP, like other protocols such as **HTTP** and **FTP**, provides a set of universal instructions that cover a process of transferring digital information. In this instance, the protocol covers the delivery of wireless content to mobile phones and similar mobile devices. WAP was developed following a joint initiative between Unwired Planet, Motorola, Nokia and Erickson. Wireless Markup Language (WML) is very similar to **HTML** and the associated language for creating interactivity, called WMLScript, has connections with **JavaScript**. The main differences between these languages and those used on the Internet are that the former are designed with compression in mind, in order to save **bandwidth** in a wireless environment. WML creates a 'deck of cards' (each card equivalent in size to a mobile phone's screen) rather than the 'pages' created by HTML for a full-sized computer monitor. WMLScript also works in a slightly different way to JavaScript in that, rather than embedding the commands in a page (a deck of cards), it only adds links to WMLScript **URLs**.

At the time of writing, WAP looks as if it may become something of a dead-end development. Third-generation (**G3**) mobile telephones, tablet PCs and handheld computers offer rapid access to the web in the same way as a browser on a desktop machine. That said, most of the mobile phones on sale at the time of writing have WAP capacity. Whether extensive low-bandwidth WAP services optimized for the small screens of most mobile phones will be developed remains to be seen.

Further sources: www.wap.net/, www.wapforum.org/

WORLD WIDE WEB (WWW, OR JUST 'THE WEB')

The Web is a vast collection of hypertext documents that are accessible via the **Internet**. In 1945, the American Vanevar Bush published an article in *Atlantic Monthly* about a device called a Memex (for memory extension) that could make and follow links between documents on microfiche (a variant of microfilm used by libraries before the advent of computers). This article set out some of the fundamentals of hypertext, which allows one document to be linked to another document. A hypertext link within a given document enables the reader to jump to another document with more details about a particular subject. A page written in hypertext about the films of Alfred Hitchcock, for example, might talk in general terms about his career and offer hypertext links (hyperlinks, or links) to other documents that offer more detail about a particular subject. An extract might look like this:

> During the 1950s, Hitchcock made a number of classic films such as Vertigo and Rear Window, establishing a close working relationship with the actor James Stewart.

Each underlined section of text provides a link to a more detailed document on this subject, so someone reading this hypertext page has the option to jump to detailed documents on *Vertigo* and *Rear Window*, and on James Stewart.

During the 1960s, the next step towards the development of the Web was made by Doug Engelbart, another American, who created a prototype of something called an 'oNLine System' which was referred to by the initials NLS. This system, as well as giving us the term 'online', could undertake hypertext browsing and editing and send email. In addition to creating the NLS system, Engelbart also invented a device called a 'mouse' to be used with it.

In March 1989, an Englishman called Tim Berners-Lee, working at CERN (the European Particle Physics Laboratory in Geneva), circulated for comments a document called *Information Management: A Proposal*. The memo proposed a system that would use hypertext on computers as a way of organizing and accessing CERN's data. The memo had to be re-circulated in May before Berners-Lee was allowed to buy the computing equipment necessary to undertake his proposal, a NeXT box, in September. Working with Nicola Pellow and Bernard Pollerman, Berners-Lee had a workable hypertext browser and editor working by Christmas of 1989. The first elements of the World Wide Web were available on certain CERN machines by May 1990, and by August 1990 they were available on the Internet, but only via **FTP.** Berners-Lee then invented the conventions and protocols and most of the related software, including URI, **URLs, HTTP** and **HTML,** that enabled the Web to develop.

In April 1993 a landmark decision was made by CERN that WWW technology would be **freeware** (made freely available to anyone). The first true browser, called 'Mosaic', was completed by Marc Andreessen at the US National Center for Supercomputing Applications (NCSA) in February 1993 and released by NCSA for PCs, Apples and UNIX in September 1993. The first signs of mass media interest began in the UK and US late in 1993.

From a situation in October 1993 when there were 200 known HTTP servers in the world, the Web expanded to reach a vast scale. However, at the time of writing, the Web is more accurately described as a 'US web', rather than a genuine 'World-Wide' network. Entire continents, languages and cultures, indeed most of the world's population, have little or no presence on the supposedly 'World Wide Web' (see the **digital divide**, **e-commerce** and the **information economy**).

Berners-Lee now heads the World Wide Web Consortium (W3C), which promotes and develops what it refers to as 'interoperable' technologies designed to encourage universal standards and a high degree of accessibility across the Web. More generally, W3C supports Berners-Lee's original intention that the Web be a forum for information, commerce, communication and 'collective understanding'. Recent work by W3C has included the creation of the Web Accessibility Initiative (WAI), designed to ensure maximum access to the Web.

Further sources: Berners-Lee (1999), www.w3.org/

WORM

In computing terms, a worm is a type of **virus**. Worms spread by attaching themselves to **email** messages. Once a worm has gained access to a computer, it will begin searching for new machines to infect, spreading itself. Some worms merely replicate themselves as much as they can, others also cause damage to the computers that they infect. Worms can spread rapidly between computers permanently connected to the Internet because they require no user intervention to function. Worms sometimes have the capacity to 'spoof' email addresses, so that an email appears to come from one sender but has in fact been sent from another sender who has that email address in their address book.

BIBLIOGRAPHY

Abbate, J. (2000) *Inventing the Internet*, Cambridge, MA: MIT Press

Acquilla, J. and Rondfeldt, D. (1997) *In Athena's Camp: preparing for conflict in the Information Age*, Santa Monica, CA: RAND

—— (2001) *Cyberwar is Coming!*, Santa Monica, CA: RAND

Alkalimat, A. and Williams, K. (2001) 'Social Capital and Cyberpower in the African American Community: A Case Study of a Community Technology Center in the Dual City', in L. Keeble and B. Loader (eds), *Community Informatics: Shaping Computer-Mediated Social Relations*, London: Routledge

Aurigi, A. and Graham, S. (1998) 'The "crisis" in the urban public realm', in B. Loader (ed.), *Cyberspace Divide: equality, agency and policy in the information society*, London: Routledge

Bagdikian, B. (1992) *Media Monopoly*, Boston: Beacon Press

Barlow, J.P. (1996a) 'Thinking locally, acting globally', *Time*, 15 Jan.

—— (1996b) 'A Cyberspace Independence Declaration', *Cyber-Rights List*, 8 Feb.

Bassett, C. (1997) 'Virtually gendered: life in an on-line world', in K. Gelder and S. Thornton (eds), *The Subcultures Reader*, London: Routledge

Baudrillard, J. (1983) *Simulation and Simulacra*, New York: Semiotext(e).

—— (1988) *America*, London: Verso.

Becker, T. (1981) 'Teledemocracy: bringing power back to the people', *Futurist*, December 6–9

—— (1998) 'Governance and electronic innovation: a clash of paradigms', *Information, Communication and Society*, 1, 3: 339–43

Bell, D. (1976) *The Coming of Post-Industrial Society: a venture in social forecasting*, Harmondsworth: Penguin

Bell, D. (2001) *An Introduction to Cybercultures*, London: Routledge.

Bell, D. and Kennedy, B. (eds) (2000) *The Cybercultures Reader*, London: Routledge

Bellamy, C. and Taylor, J. (1998) *Governing in the Information Age*, Oxford: Oxford University Press

Bennahum, D. (1996) 'Call for comments from around the world', *MEME*, 2 March

Berners-Lee, T. (1999) *Weaving the Web*, London: Orion Business Books

Bikson, T.K. and Eveland, J.D. (1998) 'Sociotechnical reinvention: implementation dynamics and collaboration tools', *Information, Communication and Society*, 1, 3, 270–90

Bloch, L. and Lemish, D. (1999) 'Disposable love: the rise and fall of a virtual pet', *New Media and Society*, 1: 283–303

Bollier, D. (2002a) 'Reclaiming the Commons: Why we need to protect our public resources from private encroachment', *Boston Review*, Summer: http://bostonreview.mit.edu/BR27.3/bollier.html

—— (2002b) *Silent Theft: The Private Plunder of Our Common Wealth*, New York: Routledge.

Boyd-Barrett, O. (2003) in D. Schuler and P. Day, *Shaping the Network Society: The Role of Civil Society in Cyberspace*, Cambridge, MA: MIT Press

Brook, J. and Boal, I.A. (1995) *Resisting the Virtual Life*, San Francisco: City Lights

Bukatman, S. (1997) *Blade Runner*, London: British Film Institute

Burnham, V. (ed.) (2001) *Supercade: A Visual History of the Videogame Age 1971–1984* Cambridge, MA: MIT Press

Burrows, R. (1995) 'Cyberpunk as Social Theory: William Gibson and the Sociological Imagination', in S. Westwood and J. Williams (eds), *Imagining Cities: Scripts, Signs and Memories*, London: Routledge

Burrows, R. and Nettleton, S. (2000) 'Reflexive Modernisation and the Emergence of Wired Self-Help', in K. Renniger and W. Shumar (eds), *Building Virtual Communities: Learning and Change in Cyberspace*, New York: Cambridge University Press

Cartwright, L. (2000) 'The Visible Man: the male criminal subject as biomedical norm', in D. Bell and B. Kennedy (eds), *The Cybercultures Reader*, London: Routledge.

Castells, M. (1996) *The Rise of the Network Society: The Information Age: Economy, Society and Culture*, Cambridge, MA: Blackwell

—— (2001) *The Internet Galaxy: reflections on the Internet, business, and society*, Oxford: Oxford University Press

Cavallaro, D. (2000) *Cyberpunk and Cyberculture*, London: Athlone

Ceruzzi, P.E. (1998) *A History of Modern Computing*, Cambridge, MA: MIT Press

Cheung, C. (2000) 'At home on the web: presentations of self on personal homepages', in D. Gauntlett (ed.), *Web.Studies: rewiring media studies for the digital age*, London: Arnold

Chong-Moon, L. *et al.* (eds) (2000) *The Silicon Valley Edge: A Habitat for Innovation and Entrepreneurship*, Palo Alto, CA: Stanford University Press

Clegg, S. (1990) *Modern Organisations: Organizational Studies in the Post-Modern World*, Oxford: Blackwell

Cohen, S. and Wills, T. (1985) 'Stress, Social Support and the Buffering Hypothesis', *Psychological Bulletin*, 98: 310–57.

Coleman, S. (2000) *Elections in the Age of the Internet*, London: Hansard Society

—— (2001) *Cyber Space Odyssey*, London: Hansard Society

Coleman, S. and Gotze, J. (2001) *Bowling Together: online public engagement in policy deliberation*, London: Hansard Society

Cornford, J. and Pollock, N. (2003) *Putting the University Online*, Buckingham: Open University Press

Cringely, R.X. (1996) *Accidental Empires*, 2nd edn, Harmondsworth: Penguin

Cronberg, T. (1992) *Experiments into the Future*, Technical University of Denmark

Cronin, B. and Davenport, E. (2001). 'E-rogenous zones: positioning pornography in the digital economy', *The Information Society*, 17, 1: Jan.–March, 33–48

Cubitt, S. (1999) 'Le reel, c'est impossible: the sublime time of special effects', *Screen*, 40: 123–30

—— (2001) *Simulation and Social Theory*, London: Sage

Curtis, P. (1999) 'MUDding: social phenomena in text-based virtual realities', in P. Ludlow (ed.), *High Noon on the Electronic Frontier: conceptual issues in cyberspace*, Cambridge, MA: MIT Press

Danet, B., Ruedenberg, L. and Rosenbaum-Tamari, Y. (1998) ' "Hmmm ... Where's that Smoke Coming From?" Writing, Play and Performance on Internet Relay Chat', in F. Sudweeks, M. McLaughlin and R. Sheizaf (eds), *Network and Netplay: Virtual Groups on the Internet*, Cambridge, MA: MIT Press

Danziger, J. et al. (1982) *Computers and Politics: high technology in American local governments*, New York: Columbia University Press

Davies, M. (1992) *City of Quartz: Excavating the Future in Los Angeles*, New York: Vintage Books

Davies, S. (1996) *Big Brother: Britain's web of surveillance and the new technological order*, London: Pan Books

Davis, E. (1998) *TechGnosis: myth, magic and mysticism in the age of information*, London: Serpent's Tail

Day, P. and Schuler, D. (2004) *Community Practice in the Network Society: local action/ global interaction*, London: Routledge

DemocraticMedia: http://www.democraticmedia.org/issues/digitalcommons/ dotcommonstour.html

Denzin, N. (1998) 'In Search of the Inner Child: Co-Dependency and Gender in a Cyberspace Community', in G. Bendelow and S. Williams (eds), *Emotions in Social Life*, Routledge: London

Dery, M. (1996) *Escape Velocity: cyberculture at the end of the century*, London: Hodder & Stoughton

Diamond, D. (1999) 'The sleaze squeeze' *Business*, 2, February

Diani, M. (2000) 'Social Movement Networks Virtual and Real', *Information, Communication and Society*, 3, 3: 386–401

Dibbell, J. (1995) 'Viruses are good for you': http://www.levity.com/julian/ viruses.html

—— (1999) 'A rape in cyberspace; or how an evil clown, a Haitian trickster spirit, two wizards, and a cast of dozens turned a database into a society', in P. Ludlow (ed.), *High Noon on the Electronic Frontier: conceptual issues in cyberspace*, Cambridge, MA: MIT Press

Dick, P.K. (1968) *Do Androids Dream of Electric Sheep?*, New York: Ballatine

Dizzard, W.P. (1989) *The Coming Information Age: an overview of technology, economics, and politics*, 3rd edn, London: Longmans

Donk, W.v.d. et al. (eds) (2004) *Cyberprotest: New Media, Citizens and Social Movements*, London: Routledge

Douglas, K.M. and McGarty, C. (2001) 'Identifiability and self-presentation: computer-mediated communication and intergroup interaction', *British Journal Of Social Psychology*, 40: 399–416

Durkin, K. and Barber, B. (2002) 'Not so doomed: computer game play and positive adolescent development', *Journal of Applied Developmental Psychology*, 23 (4): 373–92.

Dutton, W.H. (1999) *Society on the Line: Information politics in the Digital Age*, Oxford: Oxford University Press.

Dutton, W.H. and Loader, B.D. (eds) (2002) *Digital Academe: The New Media and Institutions of Higher Education and Learning*, London: Routledge

Edge magazine: http://www.edge.com

Edwards, P. (1996) *The Closed World: computers and the politics of discourse in Cold War America*, Cambridge, MA: MIT Press

Featherstone, M. and Burrows, R. (1996) *Cyberspace/Cyberbodies/Cyberpunk: Culture of Technological Embodiment*, London: Sage

Federal Bureau of Investigation (2001) 'Carnivore'. There is a subsite devoted to Carnivore at http://www.fbi.gov/hq/lab/carnivore/carnivore.htm

Finn, C. (2001) *Artifacts: an archaeologist's year in Silicon Valley*, Cambridge, MA: MIT Press

Fountain, J.E. (2001) *Building the Virtual State: information technology and institutional change*, Washington, DC: Brookings Institutional Press

Funk, J.B. *et al.* (2002) 'Aggression and psychopathology in adolescents with a preference for violent electronic games', *Aggressive Behavior*, 28 (2): 134–44

Gibson, W. (1984) *Neuromancer*, London: Victor Gollancz

—— (1986) *Count Zero*, London: Grafton

—— (1988) *Mona Lisa Overdrive*, London: Grafton

—— (1993) *Virtual Light*, London: Viking

—— (1996) *Idoru*, London: Viking

—— (1999) *All Tomorrow's Parties*, London: Viking

Gillies, J. and Cailliau, R. (2000) *How the Web Was Born: The Story of the World Wide Web*, Oxford: Oxford Paperbacks

Gonzalez, J. (2000) 'Envisioning cyborg bodies: notes from current research', in D. Bell and B. Kennedy (eds), *The Cybercultures Reader*, London: Routledge

Goodwin, M. (ed.) (1996) *High Noon on the Electronic Frontier*, Cambridge, MA: MIT Press

GPPN Resource Group: http://www.gppnresearch.org/about/

Granovetter, M. (1973) 'The Strength of Weak Ties', *American Journal of Sociology*, 78: 1360–80

Gray, C. (ed.) (1995) *The Cyborg Handbook*, London: Routledge

—— (1997) *Postmodern War: the new politics of conflict*, London: Routledge

Greider, W. (1998) *One World, Ready or Not: The Manic Logic of Global Capitalism*, New York: Touchstone

Gurstein, M. (2000) *Community Informatics: enabling communities with information and communications technologies*, Hershey, PA: Idea Group

Habermas, J. (1989) *Structural Transformation of the Public Sphere*, Cambridge, MA: MIT Press

Hague, B. and Loader, B.D. (eds) (1999) *Digital Democracy: Discourse and Decision-making in the Information Age*, London and New York: Routledge

Haraway, D. (1995) 'Cyborgs and symbionts: living together in the New World Order', in C. Gray (ed.), *The Cyborg Handbook*, London: Routledge

—— (2000) 'A cyborg manifesto: science, techology and socialist-feminism in the late twentieth century', in D. Bell and B. Kennedy (eds), *The Cybercultures Reader*, London: Routledge

Harcourt, W. (ed.) (1999) *Women@Internet: creating new cultures in cyberspace*, London: Zed Books

Hardin, G. (1968) 'The Tragedy of the Commons', *Science*, 162: 1243–8

Harding, S. (1986) *The Science Question in Feminism*, Milton Keynes: Open University Press

Hauben, J.R. (1995) 'A Brief History of Cleveland Free-Net', *The Amateur Computerist*, 7, 1. Available online at: http://www.prometheusonline.de/heureka/kommunikationswissenschaft/monografien/hauben/brief.htm

Hauben, M. and Hauben, R. (1997): *Netizens: on the History and Impact of Usenet and the Internet*, Los Alamitos, CA: IEEE Computer Society

Hayles, N.K. (1999) *How We Became Posthuman: virtual bodies in cybernetics, literature, and informatics*, Chicago: University of Chicago Press

Haywood, T. (1995) *Info Rich, Info Poor: Access and Exchange in the Information Society*, New Providence, NJ: Bowker-Saur

Hebdige, D. (1979) *Subculture: the meaning of style*, London: Methuen

Heeks, R. (1999) *Reinventing Government in the Information Age*, London: Routledge

Hertz, N. (2001) *The Silent Takeover: global capitalism and the death of democracy*, London: Heinemann

Hess, D. (1995) 'On low-tech cyborgs', in C. Gray (ed.), *The Cyborg Handbook*, London: Routledge

Hill, K.A. and Hughes, J.E. (1998) *Cyberpolitics: Citizen Activism in the Age of the Internet*, Lanham: Rowman & Littlefield

Hutton, W. and Giddens, A. (2000) *On the Edge: Living with Global Capitalism*, London: Jonathan Cape

Indymedia: http://www.indymedia.org for umbrella site; individual nodes are identified, for example, as follows: http://seattle.indymedia.org

Ishida, T. and Isbister, K. (eds) (2000) *Digital Cities: Technologies, Experiences and Future Perspectives*, Berlin: Springer-Verlag

Jenkins, H. and Thorburn, D. (eds) (2003) *Democracy and New Media*, Cambridge, MA: MIT Press

Johnson, S. (1997) *Interface Culture: how new technology transforms the way we create and communicate*, New York: HarperCollins

Jordan, B. (1996) *A Theory of Poverty and Social Exclusion*, London: Polity Press

Kaloski, A. (1999) 'Bisexuals making out with cyborgs: politics, pleasure, con/fusion', in M. Storr (ed.), *Bisexuality: a critical reader*, London: Routledge

Keck, M. and Sikkink, K. (1988) *Activists Beyond Borders: Advocacy Networks in International Politics*, Ithaca, NY: Cornell University Press

Keeble, L. and Loader, B. (2001) *Community Informatics: Shaping Computer-Mediated Social Relations*, London: Routledge

Kellner, D. (1995) 'Mapping the Present from the Future: From Baudrillard to Cyberpunk', in A.D. Kellner (ed.), *Media Culture: cultural studies, identity and politics between the modern and the postmodern*, London: Routledge

Kember, S. (1999) 'NITs and NRTs: medical science and the Frankenstein factor', in Cutting Edge (eds), *Desire By Design: bodies, territories and new technologies*, London: I.B. Tauris

Kendall, L. (1996) 'MUDder? I hardly know 'er! Adventures of a feminist MUDder', in L. Cherney and E. Reba Weise (eds), *Wired Women: gender and new realities in cyberspace*, Seattle: Bay Press

Kennedy, T.L.M. (2000) 'An exploratory study of feminist experiences in cyberspace', *Cyberpsychology and Behavior*, 3 (5): 707–19

Kent, S.L. (2001) *The Ultimate History of Video Games*, Roseville, CA: Prima

Kernan, J. (ed.) (1991) *Retrofitting Blade Runner*, Bowling Green, OH: Bowling Green State University Popular Press

Kirkup, G. *et al.* (eds) (2000) *The Gendered Cyborg: a reader*, London: Routledge

Klein, N. (2000) *No Logo*, London: Flamingo

Kling, R. (1999) 'What is Social Informatics and Why does it Matter?', *D-Lib Magazine*, January: http://www.dlib.org/80/dlib/january/kling/01kling.html

Kneale, J. (2001) 'The virtual realities of technology and fiction: reading William Gibson's cyberspace', in M. Crang, P. Crang and J. May (eds), *Virtual Geographies: bodies, space and relations*, London: Routledge

Kubicek, H. and Wagner, R. (2002) 'Community Networks in a Generational Perspective: the change of electronic medium within three decades', *Information, Communication and Society*, 5, 3: 291–319

Landsberg, A. (2000) 'Prosthetic memory: *Total Recall* and *Blade Runner*', in D. Bell and B. Kennedy (eds), *The Cybercultures Reader*, London: Routledge

Lane, F. (2000) *Obscene Profits: the entrepreneurs of pornography in the cyber age*, London: Routledge

Lash, S. (2002) *Critique of Information*, London: Sage

Lawrence, S. and Giles, C. (1999) 'Accessibility of information on the web', *Nature*, 8, July: 107–9

Lee, J.Y. (1996) 'Charting the codes of cyberspace: a rhetoric of electronic mail', in L. Strate, R. Jacobson and S. Gibson (eds), *Communication and Cyberspace: social interaction in an electronic environment*, Cresskill, NJ: Hampton Press

Leebaert, D. (ed.) (1999) *The Future of the Electronic Marketplace*, London: MIT Press

Leuf, B. and Cunningham, W. (2001) *The Wiki Way: Collaboration and Sharing on the Internet*, Boston: Addison–Wesley

Levi, A. (1996) *Samurai from Outer Space: understanding Japanese animation*, Chicago: Open Court

Loader, B.D. (1997) *The Governance of Cyberspace: politics, technology and global restructuring*, London: Routledge

—— (ed.) (1998) *Cyberspace Divide: Equality, Agency and Policy in the Information Society*, London: Routledge

Lovink, G. and Riemens, P. (2003) 'The Rise and Fall of Amsterdam's Digital City', in D. Schuler and P. Day (eds), *Shaping the Network Society: The New Role of Civil Society in Cyberspace*, Cambridge, MA: MIT Press

Ludwig, M. (1996a) 'Introduction to *The Little Black Book of Computer Viruses*', in L.H. Leeson (ed.), *Clicking In: hot links to a digital culture*, Seattle: Bay Press

—— (1996b) 'Virtual catastrophe: will self-reproducing software rule the world?', in L.H. Leeson (ed.) *Clicking In: hot links to a digital culture*, Seattle: Bay Press

Lupton, D. (1994) 'Panic computing: the viral metaphor and computer technology', *Cultural Studies*, 8: 556–68.

—— (2000) 'The embodied computer/user', in D. Bell and B. Kennedy (eds), *The Cybercultures Reader*, London: Routledge

Lyon, D. (1994) *The Electronic Eye: the rise of surveillance society*, Cambridge: Polity Press

McCaffrey, L. (ed.) (1991) *Storming the Reality Studio: A Casebook of Cyberpunk and Postmodern Fiction*, London: Duke University Press

Machlup, F. (1962) *The Production and Distribution of Knowledge in the United States*, Princeton, NJ: Princeton University Press

MacKenzie, D. and Wajcman, J. (eds) (1999) *The Social Shaping of Technology*, 2nd edn, Milton Keynes: Open University Press

McLaughlin, M. and Sheizaf, R. (eds) (1998) *Network and Netplay: Virtual Groups on the Internet*, Cambridge, MA: MIT Press

McLaughlin, M., Osborne, K. and Smith, C. (1995) 'Standards of conduct on Usenet', in S. Jones (ed.), *Cybersociety: computer-mediated communication and community*, London: Sage

Margetts, H. (1999) *Information Technology in Government: Britain and America*, London and New York: Routledge

Marsden, C.T. (2000) *Regulating the Global Information Society*, London: Routledge

Martinez, D. (ed.) (1996) *The Worlds of Japanese Popular Culture*, Cambridge: Cambridge University Press

Miller, D. (2000) 'The fame of Trinis: websites as traps', *Journal of Material Culture*, 5: 5–24

Morais, R.C. (1999) 'Porn goes public', *Forbes*, 14, June: 214–20

Morris, D. (2003) 'Globalization and Media Democracy: The Case of the Indymedia', in D. Schuler and P. Day (eds), *Shaping the Network Society: The New Role of Civil Society in Cyberspace*, Cambridge, MA: MIT Press

Morse, M. (1994) 'What do cyborgs eat? Oral logic in an information society', in G. Bender and T. Druckrey (eds), *Culture on the Brink: ideologies of technology*, Seattle: Bay Press

Muncer, S. *et al.* (2000a) 'Births, deaths, sex and marriage ... but very few presents? A case study of social support in cyberspace', *Critical Public Health*, 10, 1: 1–18

—— (2000b) 'Form and structure of newsgroups giving social support: A network approach', *Cyberpsychology and Behavior*, 3 (6), 1017–29

Murphie, A. and Potts, J. (2003) *Culture and Technology*, Basingstoke: Palgrave

Nakamura, L. (2000) ' "Where do you want to go today?" Cybernetic tourism, the internet, and transnationality', in B. Kolko, L. Nakamura and G. Rodman (eds), *Race in Cyberspace*, London: Routledge

—— (2002) *Cybertypes: race, ethnicity, and identity on the internet*, London: Routledge

Negroponte, N. (1995) *Being Digital*, London: Hodder & Stoughton

Nielsen, J. (2000) *Designing Web Usability: The Practice of Simplicity*, Indianapolis: New Riders Publishing

NTIA (National Telecommunications and Information Administration) (1993) *The National Information Infrastructure: Agenda for Action,* September

—— (1999) *Falling Through the Net: Defining the Digital Divide*, Washington, DC: U.S. Department of Commerce: http://www.ntia.doc.gov/ntiahome/fttn99/contents.html

Oehlert, M. (2000) 'From Captain America to Wolverine: cyborgs in comic books: alternative images of cybernetic heroes and villains', in D. Bell and B. Kennedy (eds), *The Cybercultures Reader*, London: Routledge

Ostrom, E. (1991) *Governing the Commons: The Evolution of Institutions for Collective Action*, Cambridge: Cambridge University Press

Pierson, M. (1999) 'CGI in Hollywood science-fiction cinema 1989–95: the wonder years', *Screen*, 40: 158–76

Pilger, J. (2003) *The New Rulers of the World*, New York: Verso

Plant, S. (1997) *Zeros and Ones: digital women and the new technoculture*, London: Fourth Estate

—— (2000) 'On the matrix: cyberfeminist simulations', in D. Bell and B. Kennedy (eds), *The Cybercultures Reader*, London: Routledge

Pleace, N. *et al.* (2000) 'On-line with the Friends of Bill W: problem drinkers, the

Internet and self help', *Sociological Research On-Line*: www.socresonline.org.uk/5/2/pleace.html

—— (2001) 'A safety net? Some reflections on the emergence of virtual social support', in L. Keeble and B. Loader (eds), *Community Informatics: Computer Mediated Social Networks*, London: Routledge

Polikanov, D. and Abramova, I. (2003) 'Africa and ICTs: A chance for breakthrough', *Information, Communication and Society*, 6, 1: 42–56

Poole, S. (2000) *Trigger Happy*, London: Fourth Estate

Porat, M.U. (1977) *The Information Economy: Definition and Measurement*, Washington DC: U.S. Department of Commerce

Porter, D. (ed.) (1997) *Internet Culture*, London: Routledge

Poster, M. (1995) *The Second Media Age*, Cambridge: Polity Press

Purcell, D. and Kodras, J.E. (2001) 'Information Technologies and Representational Spaces at the Outposts of the Global Political Economy: Redrawing the Balkan image of Slovenia', *Information, Communication and Society*, 4, 3: 341–69

Putnam, R. (2000) *Bowling Alone: the collapse and revival of American community*, New York: Simon & Schuster

Qvortrup, L. (ed.) (1987) *Social Experiments with I.T. and the Challenges of Innovation*, Copenhagen: Kluwer

Raymond, E. (1999) *The Cathedral and the Bazaar*, Sebastopol, CA: O'Reilly – Doug

Reich, R. (1992) *The Work of Nations: Preparing ourselves for 21st century capitalism*, New York: Vintage.

Reid, E.M. (1996) 'Informed Consent in the Study of On-Line Communities: A Reflection on the Effects of Computer Mediated Social Research', *Information Society*, 12, 2: 169–74

Reinicke, W.H. (1999/2000) 'The Other World Wide Web: Global Public Policy Networks', *Foreign Policy*, Winter: 127–39

Rheingold, H. (1991) *Virtual Reality*, New York: Summit

—— (1993) *The Virtual Community: Homesteading on the Electronic Frontier*, available online at http://www.rheingold.com/book/

—— (1994) *The Virtual Community*, London: Secker and Warburg

Roberts, L. and Parks, M. (1999) 'The social geography of gender-switching in virtual environments and the internet', *Information, Communication and Society*, 2: 521–40

Robins, K. (1995) 'Cyberspace and the world we live in', *Body and Society*, 1, 3–4: 135–55

Robinson, S. (2003) 'Rethinking Telecenters: Microbanks and Remittance Flows – Reflections from Mexico', in D. Schuler and P. Day (eds), *Shaping the Network Society: The New Role of Civil Society in Cyberspace*, Cambridge, MA: MIT Press

Roe, K. and Muijs, D. (1998) 'Children and computer games – A profile of the heavy user', *European Journal Of Communication*, 13 (2): 181–200

Rony, E. and Rony, P. (1998) *The Domain Name Handbook: high stakes and strategies in cyberspace*, New York: R and D Books

Ross, A. (2000) 'Hacking away at the counterculture', in D. Bell and B. Kennedy (eds), *The Cybercultures Reader*, London: Routledge

Sammon, P. (1997) *Future Noir: The Making of Blade Runner*, London: Orion

Sandoval, C. (2000) 'New sciences: cyborg feminism and the methodology of the oppressed', in D. Bell and B. Kennedy (eds), *The Cybercultures Reader*, London: Routledge

Schiller, H. (1989) *Culture Inc.: The Corporate Takeover of Public Expression*, New York: Oxford University Press

Schuler, D. (1996) *New Community Networks: Wired for Change*, New York: ACM Press

Schuler, D. and Day, P. (eds) (2003) *Shaping the Network Society: The New Role of Civil Society in Cyberspace*, Cambridge, MA: MIT Press

Shortis, T. (2001) *The Language of ICT*, London: Routledge

Smith, M.A. and Kollock, P. (eds) (1999) *Communities in Cyberspace*, London: Routledge

Springer, C. (1999) 'Psycho-cybernetics in films of the 1990s', in A. Kuhn (ed.), *Alien Zone II*, London: Verso

Squires, J. (2000) 'Fabulous feminist futures and the lure of cyberculture', in D. Bell and B. Kennedy (eds), *The Cybercultures Reader*, London: Routledge

Stallabrass, J. (1999) 'The ideal city and the virtual hive: modernism and emergent order in computer culture', in J. Downey and J. McGuigan (eds), *Technocities: the culture and political economy of the digital revolution*, London: Sage

Stelarc (2000) 'From psycho-body to cyber-systems: images as post-human entities', in D. Bell and B. Kennedy (eds), *The Cybercultures Reader*, London: Routledge

Stephenson, N. (1992) *Snow Crash*, London: Roc

—— (1995) *The Diamond Age*, New York: Bantam

Sterling, B. (1994) *The Hacker Crackdown*, Harmondsworth: Penguin

Stone, A.R. (1995) *The War of Desire and Technology at the Close of the Mechanical Age*, Cambridge, MA: MIT Press

Stork, D. (ed.) (1998) *HAL's Legacy: 2001's Computer as Dream and Reality*, Cambridge, MA: MIT Press

Tanabe, M., van den Besselaar, P. and Ishida, T. (eds) (2002) *Digital Cities II: Computational and Sociological Approaches*, Berlin: Springer-Verlag

Taylor, P. (1999) *Hackers: crime in the digital sublime*, London: Routledge

Terranova, T. (2000) 'Post-human unbounded: artificial evolution and high-tech subcultures', in D. Bell and B. Kennedy (eds), *The Cybercultures Reader*, London: Routledge

Thomas, D. and Loader, B.D. (eds) (2000) *Cybercrime: law enforcement, security and surveillance in the information age*, London: Routledge

Tomas, D. (2000) 'The technophilic body: on technicity in William Gibson's cyborg culture', in D. Bell and B. Kennedy (eds), *The Cybercultures Reader*, London: Routledge

Turkle, S. (1997) *Life on the Screen: identity in the age of the internet*, London: Phoenix

—— (1999) 'What are we thinking about when we are thinking about computers?', in M. Biagiloi (ed.), *The Science Studies Reader*, London: Routledge

Van den Besselaar, P. (2001) 'E-community versus e-commerce: the rise and decline of Amsterdam Digital City', *AI and Society: the Journal of Human-cemtred Systems and Machine Intelligence*, 1: 280–8

Wajcman, J. (1991) *Feminism Confronts Technology*, Cambridge: Polity Press

Wakeford, N. (2000) 'Cyberqueer', in D. Bell and B. Kennedy (eds), *The Cybercultures Reader*, London: Routledge

Waldby, C. (2000) *The Visible Human Project: informatic bodies and posthuman science*, London: Routledge

Ward, K. (2000) 'A cyber-ethnographic analysis of the impact of the internet on community, feminism and gendered relations', unpublished PhD thesis, Staffordshire University

Wark, M. (1999) 'The Matrix: Keanu lost in Plato's Cave', *Cybersociety*: http://www.unn.ac.uk/cybersociety

Web Accessibility Initiative: http://www.w3c.org/WAI/

Webster, F. (ed.) (2001) *Culture and Politics in the Information Age: a new politics?*, London: Routledge

—— (2002) *Theories of the Information Society*, 2nd edn, London: Routledge

Webster, F. and Robins, K. (1998) 'The iron cage of the information society', *Information, Communication and Society*, 1: 1: 23–45

Weizenbaum, J. (1976) *Computer Power and Human Reason*, San Francisco, CA: W.H. Freeman

Wellman, B. and Gulia, M. (1999) 'Virtual communities as communities: Net surfers don't ride alone', in M.A. Smith and P. Kollock (eds), *Communities in Cyberspace*, London: Routledge

Wellman, B. *et al.* (2001) 'Does the internet increase, decrease, or supplement social capital? Social networks, participation, and community commitment', *American Behavioral Scientist*, 45, 3: 436–55

Whittle, S. (2001) 'The trans-cyberian mail way', in R. Holliday and J. Hassard (eds), *Contested Bodies*, London: Routledge

Williams, A. (2000) *Digital Libraries*, Cambridge, MA: MIT Press

Wilson, R. (1995) 'Cyber(body)parts: prosthetic consciousness', *Body and Society*, 1: 239–59

Wilson, S. (2003) *Information Arts: intersections of art, science, and technology*, Cambridge, MA: MIT Press

Winner, L. (1997) 'Cyberlibertarian myths and the prospects for community', *Computers and Society*, 27:3, September: 14–19.

Zizek, S. (1999) 'The Matrix, or, the two sides of perversion', *Cybersociety*: http://www.unn.ac.uk/cybersociety

INDEX